To. W.Bro. Roger Hollingrake
With best wishes
From the author

Roy A. Wells
12 Feb 1987

THE RISE AND DEVELOPMENT
OF
ORGANISED FREEMASONRY

At the Grand Lodge held at Merchant
Taylor's Hall Monday 24th June 1723

Present

His Grace the Duke of Wharton G: Master.
The Reverend J. T. Desaguliers LLD FRS D.G.M.
Joshua Timson . . . . }
The Reverend Mr. James Anderson } G: Wardens.

Ordered

That William Cowper Esqr. a Brother of the Horn Lodge at Westminster
be Secretary to the Grand Lodge _____

The order of the 17th Jan: 172¾ printed at the end of the Constitutions page 91.
for the publishing the said Constitutions was read, purporting That they had been before
approved in Manuscript by the Grand Lodge, and were then, viz. 17th January aforesaid
produced in Print and approved by the Society. _____

Then

The Question was moved, That the said General Regulations be confirmed,
So far as they are consistent with the Ancient Rules of Masonry

The previous Question was moved and put, whether the words [so far
as they are consistent with the Ancient Rules of Masonry] be part of the
Question _____

Resolved in the affirmative

But the main Question was not put

And the Question was moved.

That it is not in the Power of any person, or Body of men, to make
any Alteration, or Innovation in the Body of Masonry without the
Consent first obtained of the Annual Grand Lodge ―.

And the Question being put accordingly

Resolved ―

First entry in the First Minute Book *of the First Grand Lodge dated Monday 24th June 1723*

The
Rise and Development
of
Organised Freemasonry

Roy A. Wells

Volume Seventeen

of the publications of
The Masonic Book Club
Illinois, USA

LONDON

LEWIS MASONIC

© 1986
Roy A. Wells

First published in England 1986

Published by A LEWIS (Masonic Publishers) LTD
Terminal House, Shepperton TW17 8AS, England
who are members of the IAN ALLAN GROUP.

This book has been published for the MASONIC BOOK CLUB
which is a 'Not-for-Profit Corporation of Illinois' USA
and is number Seventeen in their series.

ISBN 0 8318 146 2

British Library Cataloguing in Publication Data
    Wells, Roy A.
    The Rise and Development of Organised Freemasonry.
    1. Freemasonry — England — History
    I. Title
    366' . 1'0942   HS596.A5

Printed in Great Britain by
Butler & Tanner Ltd, London and Frome

CONTENTS

APPENDICES

ILLUSTRATIONS

PREFACE

The Masonic Book Club has as its primary purpose the distribution of Masonic literature to provide useful historical insights to the Craft. In this pursuit the Club has offered reprints of rare manuscripts with suitable commentary and, as in this instance, original works by outstanding Masonic scholars.

A little over two years ago the directors of the Masonic Book Club approached Brother Roy A. Wells, who was known to them from inception, to ask him to write a book which would detail the Union of the two Grand Lodges in England in 1813. Brother Wells expanded this original concept to the more inclusive study of *The Rise and Development of Organised Freemasonry*.

Roy A. Wells is a well-known masonic researcher and author of exceptional merit. His first book, *Some Royal Arch Terms Examined*, was published in 1978 and that was quickly recognised as valuable and reliable reference material.

Brother Wells was born in South Woodford, Essex, England, in 1908 and details of his active life and involvement in Freemasonry are given in the following pages. He has lectured on Freemasonry for many years and in that capacity has travelled extensively. Through his many essays, lectures, and other publications he has sought to spread the light of Freemasonry throughout the world, and the Masonic Book Club is honoured that he decided to write the 1986 volume.

Louis L. Williams
Alphonse Cerza

ABOUT THE AUTHOR

W Bro Roy A. Wells was initiated in Five Orders Lodge No 3696 at the Holborn Restaurant on 26 January 1938, and became Master in 1952. He was exalted in Five Orders Chapter reaching the office of First Principal in 1957.

During active service with the Royal Navy from 1941 to 1945 he spent part of 1942/3 in Israel to his considerable advantage as a masonic student with biblical interest. Early associations with the Domatic Chapter of Instruction No 177 stimulated his thirst for knowledge in the Royal Arch and he was elected Scribe E, of that teaching authority in 1956 which office he still occupies. In that capacity he has provided terms of reference for a countless number of Companions both within and without this country. Among the many from whom questions were referred was the late Bro Harry Carr to whom, following his retirement in 1968 from business life with a leading Assurance office, he was invited to become Personal Assistant and after five years as such succeeded as Secretary/Editor of Quatuor Coronati Lodge No 2076, the premier Lodge of Masonic Research. He became Master of that distinguished lodge in 1973 but, on medical advice, handed over those clerical duties in December 1975.

His qualities as a masonic researcher, writer and personality have become widely known and appreciated. Numerous essays and articles from his pen have appeared in the world masonic press, Research Lodge publications both home and overseas, and he has two books to his credit: *Some Royal Arch Terms Examined*, a valuable book of reference, and *Freemasonry in London from 1875*, which has most interesting treatment of masonic history through the eyes and experiences of various personalities and authorities. He was appointed Prestonian Lecturer for 1977, his chosen subject being *The Tyler or Outer Guard* which proved immensely popular but, is now, unfortunately, out of print.

His masonic lectures commenced in 1960 and since then he has been in great demand in England, Wales, and the Channel Islands. His lecture travels include Norway, Trinidad, Guyana, Barbados, Jamaica, Nassau, and the USA. In 1980 he was awarded the James Royal Case Medal of Excellence 'for outstanding contributions in the field of masonic research' by the Masonic Lodge of Research of Connecticut. It is an annual award but Bro Wells was the ninth recipient and the second Englishman, the late Bro Harry Carr being the first. In 1985 the Grand Chapter of Massachusetts awarded the Benjamin Hurd Jr. Meritorious Service Medal, a high distinction. In appreciation many lodges and chapters, home and overseas, have elected him to Honorary Membership, and thus keep close association with him.

Bro Wells was honoured with London Grand Rank in 1965 and became President of the London Grand Rank Association in 1982. He was honoured with Active rank as a Grand Officer in Supreme Grand Chapter in 1966 and in the United Grand Lodge of England in 1971. Promotions in each have been conferred.

ACKNOWLEDGEMENTS

In the course of this exercise the author has perforce referred to the work of many colleagues, both past and present, and upon specific work of predecessors who also toiled in the quarries of authentic masonic history. The majority were full members of Quatuor Coronati Lodge No 2076 on the Register of the United Grand Lodge of England, the premier lodge of masonic research; most of those had been further honoured in appointment as Prestonian Lecturers for their particular year in that office by Grand Lodge. Authenticity is the keynote of all their work and, in association with them the author wishes to place on record due acknowledgement that such work is made available for the pursuit of masonic knowledge.

Grateful thanks are tendered to the lodge itself, and to the Management Council of Quatuor Coronati Correspondence Circle Ltd who now publish the Transactions—*Ars Quatuor Coronatorum*—for permission to quote from Papers and records.

A debt of gratitude is also due to the Board of General Purposes of Grand Lodge, and to the Committee of General Purposes of Supreme Grand Chapter, for their kind permission to quote from material in their archives, and the library at Freemasons' Hall, London as well as providing many of the illustrations. Thanks are also due to Ken Moreman FBIPP, who photographed several documents and portraits reproduced in the text. The opportunity is taken to express warm thanks to John Hamill, librarian and curator, to the assistant librarian Brian Page, and the assistant curator John Groves, for their ready and willing assistance whenever it has been requested to say nothing of the patience with which some requests have been met.

For convenience appropriate references have been included in the text for those who may wish to extend their research on a particular subject, or facet of the same. Lengthy references have been listed in the appendices. Nothing now remains but to allow the reader to join the author on the journey from the cradle of organised freemasonry through roughly 150 years on rocky roads, with personal conflicts, to produce a government of enviable quality which has set the standard for regular freemasonry throughout the world, and which continues into the present era.

Introduction

The inauguration of the premier Grand Lodge in London on St John's Day, 24 June 1717, may well be said to have been the commencement of organised freemasonry as it is understood today but, before examining the development from that date it would be helpful if earlier threads are drawn together and to take a look at pointers in that direction that are to be found prior to that date, and that event.

Following the Norman conquest of England in AD 1066 architectural styles began to change from the strong, sturdy and simple, to ornate structures. Designers, architects, sculptors, and artisans all gained considerably from the techniques that entered the country from other nations. Churches, cathedrals, and palaces were built on the grand scale and with added skills that were then necessary the time had arrived for a development of control, not only for protection of crafts and skills that were involved but for the maintenance of those higher standards. Trade Guilds arose in the cities and principal towns and the craftsmen met together there as well as on sites where the work went on; some projects were of such magnitude that decades were to pass and a lifetime was spent by some before they were completed. No artisan could pursue his skill without proper recognition from a controlling body and accredited evidence had to be forthcoming before any acknowledgement could be afforded in passing from one site to another. A system of tuition and control for apprentices and masters alike, as well as an elementary code of behaviour were devised and such details were drawn up for the mason craft on parchment rolls and read out on every convenient occasion for that purpose. As was to be expected in a Christian society when life in general was guided by scholars from the abbeys, monasteries, cathedrals and churches which represented the centrepiece for each community, large or small, each Guild had its patron Saint and attendance for Mass on that day was deemed an obligation and wages paid for attention to it.

The Regulations which came into being are known as the *Old Charges*, written by those who were literate for the benefit of those who were not, but constantly read over for the benefit of all. The earliest known survivor is the *Halliwell MS*, or *Regius Poem* as it is better known, having an attributed date of c 1390; it is in the care of the British Library housed in the British Museum, London. Other manuscripts have come to light since that time, some of which are originals but others are copies, or even copies of copies, each with some sort of variation; they have now been classified into families by certain students in that field of study. Their purpose was well served by being read over and communicated to the crafts-men and traders of their time in order that they should be made aware of their responsibilities. The most important occasion for that exercise was at the Annual Assembly which usually extended over several days at a Moot Fair when it was the usual custom for the Trade Fraternities to perform a religious or 'miracle' play that may have been individually allocated; it would have been an occasion for high spirits also, and temptation for apprentices generally.

William Preston, of whom more will be written later, in his *Illustrations of Masonry*, which was first published in 1772, writing of the period of Henry VI and of freemasons of that time, in his 2nd Edition of 1775 (p 228) quoted the following:

> The company of Masons, being otherwise termed Free-masons, of auntient staunding and good reckoninge, by means of affable and kind meetynge dy-verse tymes, and as a lovinge brotherhoode use to doe, did frequent this mutual assembly in the tyme of Henry VI, in the twelfth yeare of his most gracious reign, AD 1434. ... That the charges and laws of the Free-masons have been seen and perused by our late sovereign King Henry VI and by the lords of his most honourable council, who have allowed them, and declared, That they be right good, and reasonable to be holden, as they have been drawn out and collected from the records of auntient tymes. ...

Gatherings of operative masons were not only a known and a well established custom, they were no doubt a necessity as a means of communication. The architect, often the employer of the craftsmen and therefore master of the work, would meet the skilled workers in their huts, or 'lodges', to discuss the plans and problems common to all and a close affinity would become an automatic process; it would be no small step for all to eat together and continue with their discussion and that to take on an even wider scope beyond the limitations of the building and construction. Men of letters would have had much to contribute in such gatherings and an introduction to the liberal arts and sciences may well have been topics among their deliberations. The spread in social behaviour, always with a strong emphasis upon bible teachings, would have occupied leisure time, of which there would have been little enough in those days.

The earliest recorded admission in England of one among the operative masons who was not of their craft comes from an entry in the personal diary of the antiquary Elias Ashmole, founder of

Elias Ashmole (1617–1692), Founder of the Ashmolean Museum in Oxford. This was the first recorded admission in England of one among the operative masons who was not of their craft

the famous museum at Oxford which bears his name. There are earlier examples in Scotland and it is fairly obvious from the wording in Ashmole's entry that it was already then an established custom. His account reads thus:

> 1646. Oct: 16. 4^h 30′ p.m., I was made a Free Mason at Warrington in Lancashire, with Coll: Henry Mainwaring, of Karincham, in Cheshire. The names of those present that were then of the Lodge, Mr Rich Penket Warden, Mr James Collier, Mr Rich Ellam & Hugh Brewer. (folio 19)

A later entry in his diary described an event that was thirty-six years afterwards:

> 1682. 10 March. About 5^h p.m., I rec'd a summons to appe[ar] at a lodge to be held the next day, at Masons' Hall, London. 11 (March) Accordingly I went & about Noone were admitted into the Fellowship of Free Masons, Sr William Wilson Knight, Capt Rich: Borthwick, Mr Will: Woodman, Mr W. Grey, Mr Samuel Taylour & M. William Wise. I was the Senior Fellow among them (it being 35 yeares since I was admitted). There was present besides my selfe the Fellowes after named.
>
> Mr Tho. Wise M^r of the Masons Company this present yeare, Mr Thomas Shorthose, Mr Thomas Shadbolt,—Waindsford Esq., Mr Nich. Young, m^r John Shorthose, Mr William Hamon, Mr John Thompson, & Mr Will: Stanton.
>
> We all dyned at the halfe Monne Tavern in Cheapeside, at a Noble Dinner prepaired at the charge of the New-accepted Masons. (folio 69)

Commenting upon Ashmole's admission into Freemasonry, William Preston had this to contribute:

> The writer of Mr. Ashmole's life, who was not a Mason, before his *History of Berkshire* p 6, gives the following account of Masonry: 'He (Mr. Ashmole) was elected a brother of the company of Free-masons; a favour esteemed so singular by the members, that kings themselves have not disdained to enter themselves of the Society. From these are derived the adopted Masons, accepted Masons, or Free-masons; who are known to one another all over the

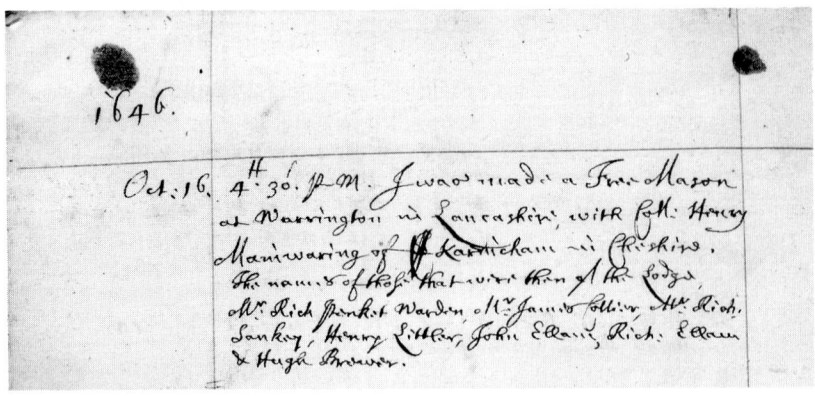

Entry from the personal diary of the antiquarian Elias Ashmole

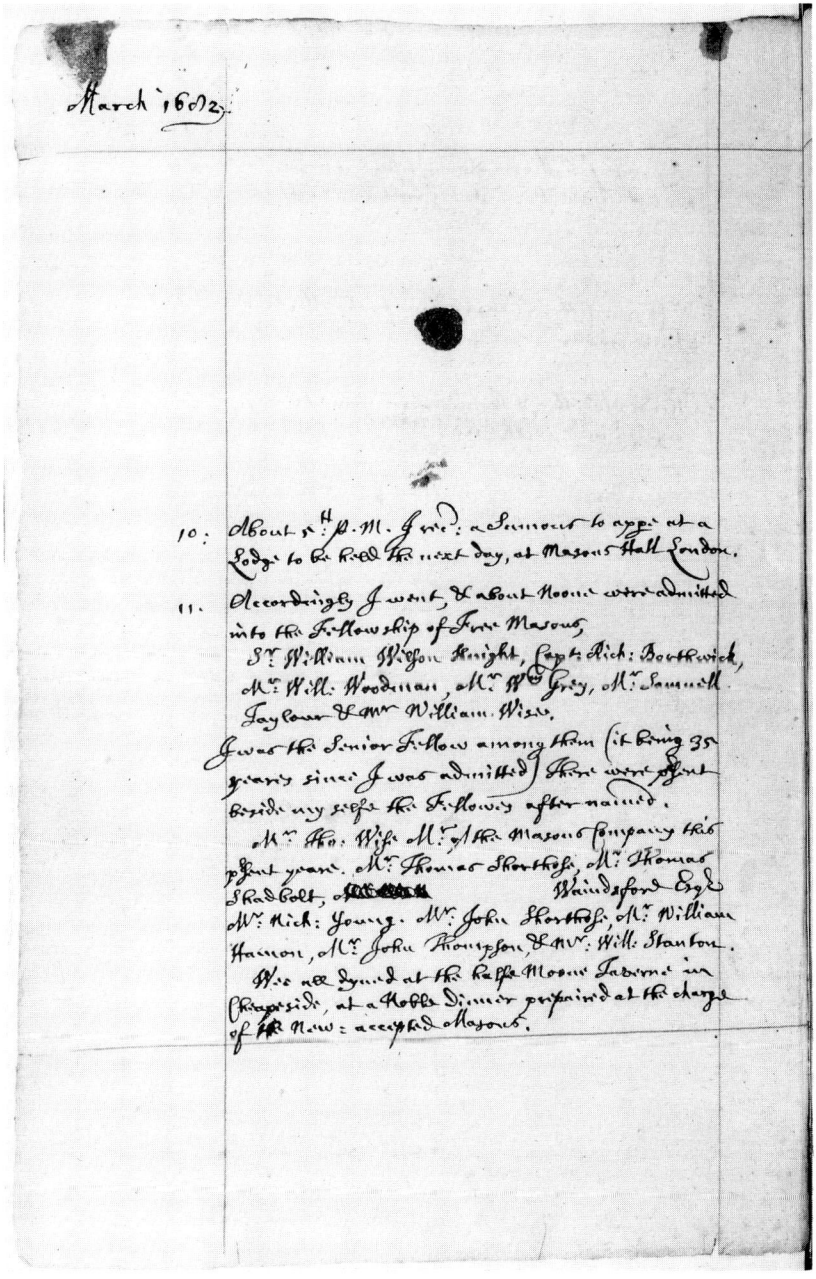

A further entry some thirty-six years later from the personal diary of Elias Ashmole

world by certain *signals* and *watchwords* known to them alone. They have several lodges in different countries for their reception; and when any of them fall into decay, the brotherhood is to relieve them. The manner of their adoption or admission is very formal and solemn, and with the administration of an oath of secrecy, which has had better fate than all other oaths, and has been most religiously observed; nor has the world been yet able, by the inadvertency, surprise, or folly of any of its members, to dive into this mystery, or make the least discovery.' ...

Dr Robert Plot, MD, who was appointed Keeper of the Ashmolean Museum by Elias Ashmole, in his book *The Natural History of Staffordshire* published in 1686, also contributed a useful comment on Freemasonry of the period. Although not a freemason himself he shows that the rather mixed-up traditional history that was being handed down and had become quite a controlling feature, was centred upon those *Old Charges* written on the 'Schrole or Parchment Volum':

85. To these add the *Customs* relating to the *County*, whereof they have one, of admitting Men into the Society of Free-masons, that in the Moorelands of this County seems to be of greater request, than any where else, though I find the *Custom* spread more or less all over the *Nation*: for here I found persons of the most eminent quality, that did not disdain to be of this *Fellowship*. Nor indeed need they, were it of that *Antiquity* and *Honor*, that it pretended in a large parchment volume they have amongst them, containing the *History* and *Rules* of the craft of *Masonry*. Which is there deduced not only for *sacred writ*, but *profane story*, particularly that it was brought into England by *Saint Amphibal*, and first communicated to Saint Alban, who set down the *Charges of masonry*, and was made paymaster and Governor of the *Kings works*, and gave them *charges and manners* as Saint Amphibal had taught him. Which were after confirmed by King *Athelstan*, whose youngest son *Edwyn* loved well masonry, took upon him the *charges* and learned the *manners*, and obtained for them of his Father, a *free-Charter*. Whereupon he caused them to assemble at *York*, and to bring all the old *Books* of their craft, and out of them ordained such *charges* and *manners*, as they then thought fit: which *charges* in the said *Schrole* or *Parchment* volum, are in part declared: and thus was the *craft* of *masonry* grounded and confirmed in *England*. It was also there declared that these *charges* and *manners* were after perused and approved by King Hen. 6. and his council, both as *Masters* and *Fellows* of this right Worshipfull *craft*.

86. Into which *Society* when any are admitted, they call a *meeting* or *lodg* as they term it in some places which must consist of at least 5 or 6 of the *Ancients* of the *Order*, whom the *Candidates* present with *gloves*, and so likewise to their wives, and entertain with a *collation* according to the custom of the place: This ended, they proceed to the *admission* of them, which chiefly consists in the communication of certain *Secret Signes*, whereby they are known to one another all over the *Nation*, by which means they have maintenance whither ever they travel: for if any man appear though altogether unknown that can shew any of these *signes* to a *Fellow* of the *Society*, whom they otherwise call an *accepted mason*, he is obliged presently to come to him, from what company or place soever he be in, nay tho' from the top of a *Steeple*, what hazard or inconvenience soever he run to know his pleasure, and assist him: viz, if he want *work* he is bound to find him some: or if he cannot doe that, to give him *money*, or

otherwise support him till *work* can be had: which is one of their *Articles*: and it is another that they advise the *Masters* they work for, according to the best of their *skill*, acquainting them with the goodness or badness of their *materials*: and if they be any way out in the contrivance of their *buildings* modestly to rectify them in it: that *masonry* be not dishonoured; and many such like are commonly known; but some others they have (to which they are *sworn* after their fashion) that none know but themselves, which I have reason to suspect are much worse than these, perhaps as bad as this *History* of the *craft* itself than which there is nothing I ever met with, more false or incoherent. ...

No evidence has ever been forthcoming that the mason craft, or Fraternity, included royalty in its membership in that era but the mix between operative stonemasons and those who were skilled in other areas in life became known and did expand as the years passed. Behaviour patterns common to the Guilds, to the church, in civic ceremonial, in military and naval customs were absorbed but the 'mysteries' that belonged to each were jealously guarded in all activity.

Following the Great Fire of London in 1666 which, according to Preston's record destroyed 13,000 houses, 89 parish churches, and many important civic buildings, it was decided that future buildings both in the city and its surrounding parishes should then be constructed of stone and/or brick; the former style of timber and plaster had served its time. Plans were drawn up and approved with Christopher Wren in the forefront of London activity, obviously in consultation with scholars with their common interest. Preston includes a list of fifty-four parish churches that were built in replacement, the Rev. James Anderson, in his 1738 Edition of the *Constitutions*, listed many grand houses also that were erected in the 17th century, and the expression 'full employment' when such a spate of building was current for so long is well justified; it attracted many immigrant craftsmen to the capital and other trades were to prosper as a result.

The following pages will provide a study of the rise and development of organised Freemasonry, the roots of which were nurtured from mediaeval times onward, sprouting into a Fraternity as time went on. The admission of gentlemen turned the craft into a symbolic representation of the old operative art which never lost sight of what is exhorted in the First Epistle of St Peter (ii, 17):

Honour all men. Love the brotherhood. Fear God. Honour the king.

Those principles enabled the brethren to open masonic doors for all men of goodwill, to those who would treasure such standards whereby freemasonry would become the 'centre of union between good men and true, and the means of conciliating friendship among those who must otherwise have remained at a perpetual distance'.

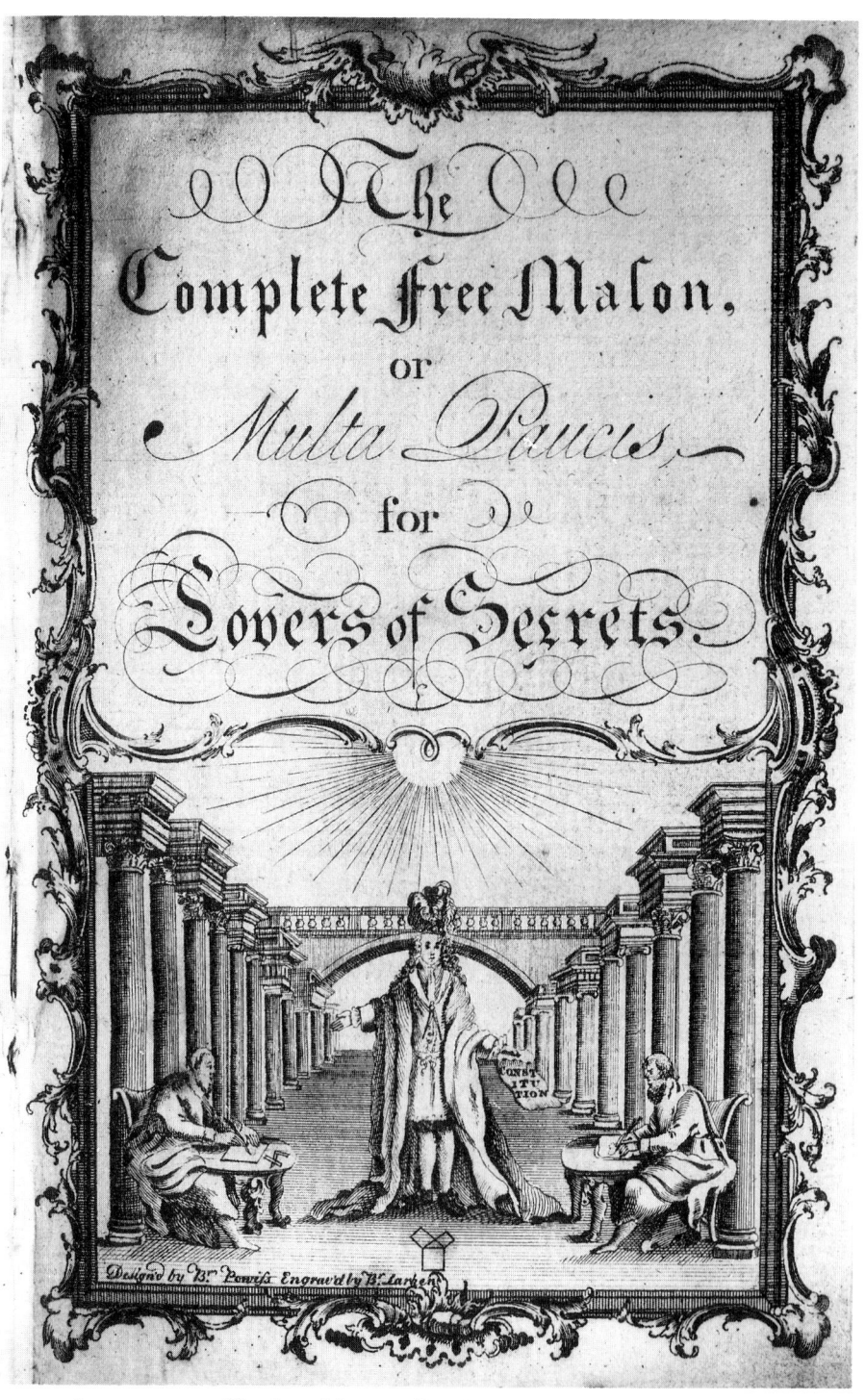

An anonymous publication with an attributed date of 1763–1764 forty seven years
after the inauguration of the premier Grand Lodge

Chapter 1

The Premier Grand Lodge

If any records of the Proceedings of the first Grand Lodge were taken prior to 24 June 1723, regrettably they have not survived as that is the date of the first entry in the first Minute Book; there is nothing that is official anywhere earlier than that date.

Two accounts of the inauguration of the premier Grand Lodge are on record, one of them is not accepted by masonic students but will nevertheless receive a modicum of attention here. It was contained in an anonymous publication entitled *The Complete Free Mason or Multa Paucis for Lovers of Secrets* and has an attributed date of 1763–1764, forty-seven years after the event. The relative extract from that is as follows:

> ... the Masters and Wardens of six Lodges assembled at the *Apple Tree* on *St John's Day*, 1716, and after the oldest Master Mason (who was also the Master of a lodge) had taken the Chair, they constituted themselves a GRAND LODGE '*pro tempore*', and revived their Quarterly Communications, and their Annual Feast. (p 83)

Rather a lot of embroidered material appeared in that book which, unfortunately, was copied in later years and with an increased circulation some imaginative points became grafted into masonic traditional history which remained until the Founders of Quatuor Coronati Lodge set a course for authenticity; they required supportive evidence whenever it was possible or the statement that any conclusion was speculative upon whatever circumstances could be summoned. There had been a strong tendency to create a 'history' for Freemasonry with royal patronage at a much earlier date than had actually happened and that book had a list of Kings of England from which few were excluded. R. F. Gould commented thus:

> ... the most noticeable [exclusions] being Richard I and James II. We are told that 'the King, with Grand Master Rivers, the architects, Nobility, Lord Mayor, Aldermen, and Bishops, levelled the Footstone of St Paul's Cathedral in due form, A.D. 1673' also, that 'in 1710, in the eighth year of the reign of Queen Anne, our Worthy Grand Master Wren, who had drawn the Design of St. Paul's, had the Honour to see it finished in a magnificent Taste, and to celebrate with the Fraternity, the Cape-Stone of so noble and large a Temple'

... but after the celebration of the cape-stone in 1710 'our good old Grand Master Wren, being struck with Age and Infirmities, did, from this time forward [1710] retire from all Manner of Business, and, on account of his Disability, could no more attend the Lodges in visiting and regulating their Meetings as usual. This occasioned the Number of regular Lodges to be greatly reduced; but they regularly assembled in Hopes of having again a noble Patron at their Head'. ...

(*The History of Freemasonry*, R. F. Gould 1884)

The framework for the *Multa Paucis* account had been provided by the Rev James Anderson whose record of it in the 2nd Edition of the *Constitutions*, published in 1738, derived from his contemporaries who were concerned in the inauguration. Anderson was appointed Junior Grand Warden by the Duke of Wharton on 17 January 1723 and in his time displayed ability as a collator, although he too was apt to be rather imaginative. However, he recorded useful evidence and guidance for those who were to piece together much of the pattern of events from that time. At the same meeting mentioned above he recorded:

G. Warden *Anderson* produc'd the *new* Book of *Constitutions* now in print, which was again approv'd, with the Addition of the *Antient Manner of Constituting a Lodge* ...

A second item stated:

GRAND LODGE in *ample* Form, 25 *April* 1723, at the *White-Lion Cornhill*, with former *Grand* Officers and those of 30 *Lodges* call'd over by G. Warden *Anderson*, for no Secretary was yet appointed.

Although only six years old the premier Grand Lodge had a Roll of thirty lodges but no Secretary up to that point. Their first Secretary was William Cowper (at first spelt as 'Cooper') who undertook that office later in that year; he was to become Deputy Grand Master in 1727.

Anderson's 2nd Edition (1738) bore the full title *The New Book Of CONSTITUTIONS of the Antient and Honourable Fraternity of FREE and Accepted MASONS* and in that he included a sequence of events and also supplied the only record to which we can refer in regard to the first six years of that first-ever Grand Lodge. Even Anderson deplored the scant records that were available and, after referring to the admission of Elias Ashmole and quoting that brother's entry in his *Diary*, then stated:

But many of the Fraternity's *Records* of this and former Reigns were lost in the next and at the *Revolution*; and many of 'em were too hastily burnt in our Time from a Fear of making Discoveries; So that we have not so ample an Account as could be wish'd of the Grand Lodge, ...

His description of events in the last decade of the 17th century supplies us with a clear picture of the state of affairs of freemasonry in London, for he wrote:

> Particular *Lodges* were not so frequent and mostly *occasional* in the *South*, except in or near Places where great Works were carried on. Thus Sir Robert *Clayton* got an *Occasional* Lodge of his Brother *Masters* to met at St *Thomas's Hospital* Southwark, A.D. 1693, and to advise the Governours about the best Design of rebuilding that Hospital as it now stands most beautiful; near which a *stated* Lodge continued long afterwards. Besides that and the *old* Lodge of St. *Paul's*, there was another in *Piccadilly* over against St. *James's* Church, one near *Westminster* Abbey, another near *Covent-Garden*, one in *Holborn*, one on *Tower-Hill*, and some more that assembled statedly.

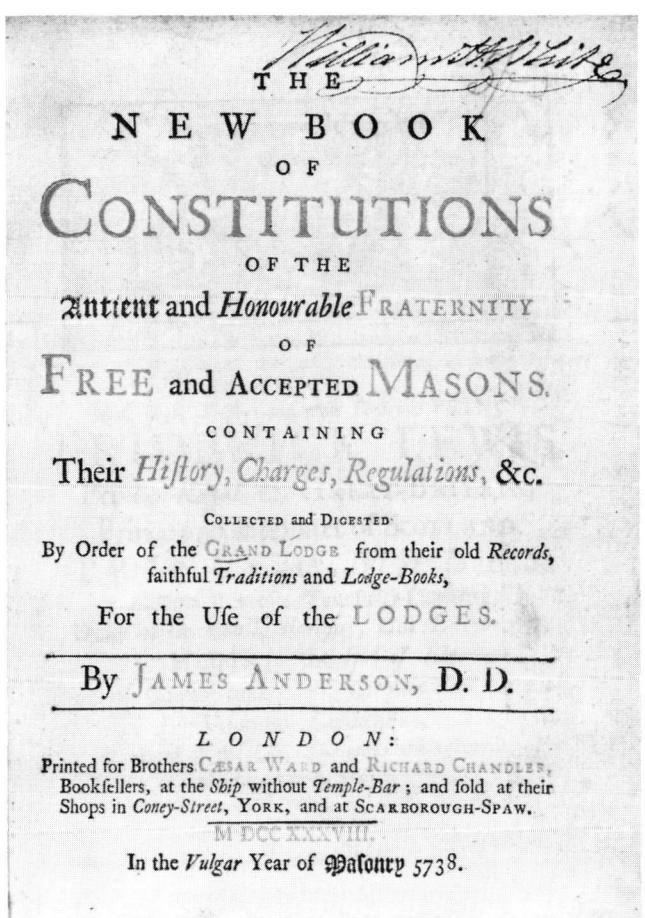

THE
NEW BOOK
OF
CONSTITUTIONS
OF THE
Antient and *Honourable* FRATERNITY
OF
FREE and ACCEPTED MASONS.

CONTAINING

Their *History, Charges, Regulations,* &c.

COLLECTED and DIGESTED

By Order of the GRAND LODGE from their old *Records,* faithful *Traditions* and *Lodge-Books,*

For the Use of the LODGES.

By JAMES ANDERSON, D. D.

LONDON:

Printed for Brothers CÆSAR WARD and RICHARD CHANDLER, Bookfellers, at the *Ship* without *Temple-Bar* ; and fold at their Shops in *Coney-Street*, YORK, and at SCARBOROUGH-SPAW.

M DCC XXXVIII.

In the *Vulgar* Year of Mafonry 5738.

Title page from the Rev James Anderson's 2nd edition of the Constitutions
published in 1738

Anderson made much of Sir Christopher Wren being a Freemason and Grand Master, although neglectful of 'the old Lodge near St Paul's' but it is an unproven subject; circumstantial evidence is forthcoming from the records of the Lodge of Antiquity (now No 2) one of the original four founding-lodges in 1717, the record of which is as follows:

> King George I. enter'd *London* most magnificently on 20 *Sept.* 1714. and after the Rebellion was over A.D. 1716, the few *Lodges* at *London* finding themselves neglected by Sir *Christopher Wren*, though fit to cement under a *Grand Master* as the Center of Union and Harmony, viz. the *Lodges* that met,
> 1. At the *Goose* and *Gridiron* Ale-House in St *Paul's Church-Yard*
> 2. At the *Crown* Ale-house in *Parker's-Lane* near *Drury-Lane*
> 3. At the *Apple-Tree* Tavern in *Charles-Street, Covent-Garden*
> 4. At the *Rummer* and *Grapes* Tavern in *Channel-Row, Westminster*
> They and some old Brothers met at the said *Apple-Tree*, and having put into the Chair the *oldest Master* Mason (now the *Master* of a *Lodge*) they constituted themselves a GRAND LODGE pro Tempore in *Due Form*, and forthwith revived the Quarterly *Communication* of the *Officers* of Lodges (call'd the GRAND LODGE) resolv'd to hold the *Annual* Assembly *and Feast*, and then to chuse a GRAND MASTER from among themselves, till they should have the Honour of a Noble Brother at their Head. Accordingly On St *John Baptist's* Day, in the 3d Year of King George 1. A.D. 1717, the ASSEMBLY and *FEAST* of the *Free and Accepted* Masons was held at the foresaid Goose and Gridiron Ale-house.
>
> (*Constitutions* 1738 Edn p 109)

Anderson's reference to Sir Christopher Wren, in association with Nicholas Strong, Inigo Jones, and Grinling Gibbons seems to have been based upon the probability that such persons would be in constant touch with those who carried out their plans and designs. In that sense they represented to him the speculative freemasons mixing with operative masons and setting up a governing class. It is worthy of recall here that the greatest tribute to Sir Christopher Wren is stated on his tomb in St Paul's Cathedral—*Si Monumentum requiris circumspice* [*If you seek his monument, look around*] The evidence of his skill surrounds one.

The Maul used by King Charles II to level 'in due form' the 'Footstone of New St Paul's' is now in possession of Lodge of Antiquity, the original No 1 listed above and classified as 'Time Immemorial'. It is ceremoniously presented to the Grand Master for use on celebratory events in which the Grand Lodge is now domestically concerned.

A mere paragraph was deemed sufficient by Anderson to deal with subsequent references to the annual 'Assembly and Feast' held on St John the Baptist's Festival—24 June. The expression 'reviv'd' would have some significance if there was any evidence to show that 'Officers of Lodges' had at any time previously had 'Quarterly Communications'; but it is well to remember that the mason craft were bound to attend an Annual Assembly if within a stated distance; it was an attraction to do so because of the opportunity thus presented of securing employment; of feasting; festivity; fairs; 'Miracle Plays'; recognition of work produced by an apprentice with a view to his becoming a Master able to teach others and undertake work on his own behalf. The 'Fellow of the Craft' was a later introduction. The well established craft custom became an established principle in speculative freemasonry in such a short time, for the transition from one to the other was automatic in an age when mode of life was so basic and minus distraction.

Chapter 2

Early Regulations

In 1871 Richard Spencer, a masonic publisher and supplier, of Holborn, London, produced a collection of old *Constitutions* under the title *Old Constitutions belonging to the Masons of England and Ireland*. The contents had dates ranging between 1722 and 1730, but in his Preface the author stated:

> ... The Constitutions of 1722 are reprinted from a copy which as far as I can ascertain, is unique. It came into my possession about a quarter of a century ago, bound up at the end of the scarce 1723 edition of the *Constitutions*: and from that time I have been searching for another unsuccessfully. On making enquiry I learn that the work is unknown at the British Museum, the Bodleian, and other public libraries ...

The 1722 pamphlet was originally published by J. Roberts in Warwick Lane in that year and its rediscovery of that, apparently sole remaining copy, justified giving it the distinction of being known from then on as '*The Roberts MS*'. Its title page bears the legend '*Taken from a manuscript wrote about Five Hundred Years since*'. At the end, after listing certain *Charges*, it has:

> *Additional Orders and Constitutions made and agreed upon at a General Assembly held at --------, on the Eighth Day of December, 1663.*
> 1. THAT no Person of what Degree soever, be accepted a *Free-Mason*, unless he shall have a Lodge of five *Free-Masons* at the least, whereof one to be a Master or Warden of that limit or Division where such a Lodge shall be kept, and another to be a Workman of the Trade of *Free-Masonry*.

How sad it is that the location of that General Assembly was not stated and dashes only printed; however, the date is quite important showing the mixing of speculative and operative brethren, with 'limits or divisions' mentioned to demonstrate that a control was then being exercised at an earlier date than the emergence of the premier Grand Lodge.

The Rev James Anderson's 1723 *Constitutions* bears the following dedication written by Dr J. T. Desaguliers, Deputy Grand Master, to His Grace the Duke of Montagu:

THE

Old Constitutions

Belonging to the

Ancient *and* Honourable

SOCIETY

OF

Free *and* Accepted

MASONS.

Taken from a Manuscript wrote above Five
Hundred Years since.

LONDON:

Printed, and Sold by J. ROBERTS, in
Warwick-Lane, MDCCXXII.

(*Price Six-Pence.*)

The Roberts MS *Its title page
bears the legend 'Taken from a
Manuscript wrote about Five
Hundred Years Since'*

(1)

THE

HISTORY

OF

Free Masons, &c.

HE Almighty Fa-
ther of Heaven,
with the Wisdom
of the Glorious
Son, thro' the
Goodness of the
Holy Ghost, Three
Persons in one
Godhead, be with our Beginning,
and

Part of the Roberts MS
shewing the illuminated text

My Lord,

By Order of his *Grace* the Duke of Wharton, the present Right Worshipful Grand-Master of the *Free-Masons*; and, as his *Deputy*, I humbly dedicate this Book of the *Constitutions* of our ancient *Fraternity* to your *Grace*, in Testimony of your Honourable, prudent, and vigilant Discharge of the Office of our Grand-Master last Year.

I need not tell your Grace what Pains our learned Author has taken in compiling and digesting this Book from the old *Records*, and how accurately he has compar'd and made every thing agreeable to *History* and *Chronology* so as to render these New Constitutions a just and exact Account of *Masonry* from the Beginning of the World to your *Grace's* Mastership, still preserving all that was truly ancient and authentick in the old ones: For every Brother will be pleased with the Performance, that knows it had your Grace's Perusal and Approbation, and that it is now printed for the Use of the *Lodges*, after it was approv'd by the GRAND-LODGE, when your GRACE was GRAND-MASTER. All the *Brotherhood* will ever remember the Honour your GRACE has done them and your Care for their Peace, Harmony, and lasting Friendship: Which none is more duly sensibly of than,

My LORD,

Your GRACE'S

Most oblig'd, and

Most obedient Servant,

And Faithful Brother,

J. T. Desaguliers

Deputy Grand-Master.

The Rev John Theophilus Desaguliers, Deputy Grand Master 1723

Anderson himself wrote 'Compiled first by Mr George Payne, Anno 1720 when he was GRAND-MASTER, and approv'd by the Grand Lodge on St. John Baptist Day Anno 1721, at Stationer's-Hall, London.' George Payne was Grand Master twice, first in 1718 and again in 1720. Writing of the year 1720 Anderson stated:

> This Year, at some private *Lodges*, several very valuable *Manuscripts* (for they had nothing yet in Print) concerning the Fraternity, their Lodges, Regulations, Charges, Secrets, and Usages (particularly one writ by Mr. *Nicholas Stone* the Warden of *Inigo Jones*) were too hastily burnt by some scrupulous Brothers; that those Papers might not fall into strange Hands. ... (1738 Edn p 111)

None of the brethren concerned in the formation of that premier Grand Lodge could possibly have visualised the widespread developments that were to take place. Growing pains, irritations, personal conflicts were to be expected and the human element did surface from time to time. As an example of that turn to the incident in which the Duke of Wharton tried to alleviate his frustration when Lord Montagu was prevailed upon to continue in office for a second year as Grand Master; here is what Anderson had to say:

> Ingenious Men of all Faculties and Stations being convinced that the *Cement* of the *Lodge* was Love and Friendship, earnestly requested to be made *Masons*, affected this amicable Fraternity more than other Societies then often disturbed by warm disputes.
>
> *Grand Master* Montagu's good Government inclin'd the better sort to continue him in the Chair another Year; and therefore they delay'd to prepare the *Feast*.
>
> But *Philip* Duke of *Wharton* lately made a Brother, tho' not the *Master* of a *Lodge*, being ambitious of the Chair, got a number of others to meet him at *Stationer's Hall* 24 June 1722 and having no *Grand* Officers, they put in the Chair the *oldest Master Mason* (who was not the *present* Master of a *Lodge*, also Irregular) and without the usual decent Ceremonials, the said *old Mason* proclaim'd aloud
>
> *Philip Wharton*, Duke of Wharton Grand Master of *Masons* and
>
> Mr. Joshua Timson Blacksmith ⎱ *Grand*
> Mr. William Hawkins Mason ⎰ *Wardens*
>
> but his Grace appointed no *Deputy*, nor was the *Lodge* opened and closed in due Form.
>
> Therefore the *noble* Brother and all those that would not Countenance Irregularities, disown'd Wharton's Authority, till Worthy Brother Montagu heal'd the Breach of Harmony by summoning the GRAND LODGE to meet 17 January 1723 at the *Kings-Arms* aforesaid, where the *Duke of Wharton* promising to be *True* and *Faithful*, *Deputy Grand Master Beal* proclaim'd aloud the most noble Prince and our Brother Philip Wharton, Duke of *Wharton* GRAND MASTER of *Masons* who appointed Dr DESAGULIERS the *Deputy Grand Master*,
>
> Joshua Timson ⎱ *Grand*
> James Anderson ⎰ *Wardens*
>
> for *Hawkins* demitted as always out of Town. When former *Grand* Officers, with those of 25 *Lodges* paid their Homage. (1738 Edn pp 114–115)

This was an age when landed gentry sent their sons on 'the Grand Tour' in Europe to study the liberal arts and architecture in particular; when they designed their own houses, palaces, and built extensions; when the ecclesiastics were similarly engaged in building churches and in cathedral enlargements. Following the Great Fire the demand for operative stonemasons and allied skilled trades was of the highest, and the changes in architectural styles were then giving cause for concern to some. Anderson gives a list of certain of the nobility and landed gentry and of ornate palaces, castles, and houses commissioned by them, the speculatives among the operatives with architecture as the main topic would have been at its highest. However, anchorage for the Grand Lodge was firmly fixed in Resolutions approved as the years unfolded. Four examples have been chosen here, quoting from the years 1723 to 1725 to show how the organisation and its control grew:

> (1) *Grand Lodge Minutes* 24 June 1723
> It was Resolved. THAT it is not in the power of any person, or BODY OF MEN to make any alteration, or innovation in the Body of Masonry without the Consent first obtained of the Annual Grand Lodge.

That Resolution made clear that the authority for any variation in the practice of freemasonry was vested in Grand Lodge.

> (2) *Grand Lodge Minutes* 19 February 1724
> THAT no Brother belonging to any Lodge within the Bills of Mortality be admitted to any Lodge as a Visitor unless personally known to some Brother of that Lodge where he visits, and that No Strange Brother however Skilled in Masonry be admitted without taking the Obligacion over againe, unless he be Introduced or vouched for by Some Brother known to, and approved of by the Majority of the Lodge. And whereas Some Masons have Mett and formed a Lodge without the Grand Mas^{rs} leave. Agreed That no such Person be admitted into Regular Lodges.
> (3) *Grand Lodge Minutes* 21 November 1724
> THAT if any Brethren shall meet Irregularly and make Masons at any place within ten miles of London the persons present at the making (the New Brethren Excepted) shall not be admitted even as Visitors into any Regular Lodge whatsoever unless they come and make Such Submission to the Grand Ma^r and Grand Lodge as they shall think fit to impose upon them.

Those Minutes confirmed the area of control which had by then extended beyond London and Westminster to include parishes within a radius of ten miles where Registers, or 'Bills of Mortality', were kept. They dubbed as 'Irregular' such brethren who held meetings unconstitutionally until they had been brought 'to heel' and their penance determined by Grand Lodge in demonstration of its authority. 'Regular' and 'Irregular' were now terms to be applied and measures decided in consequence.

Engrav'd by John Pine in Aldersgate Street London

Frontispiece to Anderson's Constitutions *1723. It is suggested that the personalities in the engraving are the two Grand Masters, with their respective Wardens and Deputy Grand Masters. On the left: John, 2nd Duke of Montagu (Grand Master 1721), Josiah Villeneau, Senior Grand Warden, Thomas Morris, Junior Grand Warden and Dr John Beal, Deputy Grand Master. On the right: Philip, Duke of Wharton (Grand Master 1722), Joshua Timson, Senior Grand Warden, Rev James Anderson, Junior Grand Warden and Dr John Theophilus Desaguliers, Deputy Grand Master.*

(4) *Grand Lodge Minutes* 27 November 1725
    THAT no B^r be recommended by a Lodge as an Object of this Charity but
    who was a Member of Some Regular Lodge which shall contribute to the
    Same Charity on or before the Twenty-first Day of Novr 1724 when the Genl
    Charity was first proposed in the Grand Lodge.

That Regulation was deemed necessary in order to protect the
money in the Charity Fund for their own needy brethren in Lodges
that had contributed and supported the Fund.

It was upon those Minutes that many of the future incidents
and problems were centred, mainly because of the ready access to
so-called ritual and ceremonial 'exposures' that seemed to be making freemasonry available to all and sundry, whether they were
seriously inclined, just dupes of the exploiters, or merely curious.

So much for the birth of organised freemasonry from that
stage, and in London, but seeing that Elias Ashmole is shewn to
have entered the Craft at Warrington in Lancashire in 1646, what
of the rest of England? Yet again, lack of records cannot support
any thought of co-ordination between lodges elsewhere as each
lodge, or each area, would have been its own authority for whatever time it remained in being. The common denominator was
possession of a copy of the *Old Charges* and representation at an
Annual Assembly if within travelling distance. Any admission as a
freemason would not have meant membership of the lodge even if
the lodge was established that far, but written evidence of the
'making' would have been provided; a crude form of certificate.
The existence of a lodge in a given city, or at a major building
project would have been common knowledge, known to the Guilds
of that area, and an invitation to the patron would have been an
obvious courtesy as well as a need in collaboration. 'Regularity'
and 'Irregularity' had not existed, skill and craftsmanship would
have been the only measure among the artisans and status and
interest combined for others. The obligation, doubtless common in
its basic form, with development of watch-words, and signs of whatever type, appeared as the years passed.

Chapter 3

Grand Lodge of All England 1725

It is timely now to turn our attention to the rise of another Grand Lodge, at York which, although meeting as a lodge prior to 1725 claimed as their title *The Grand Lodge of All England.* In a Paper on that subject read on 25 June 1889 (*AQC* Vol 2, pp 110–15) Bro T. B. Whytehead stated that whilst there is no proof of their meetings prior to 1725 it is unquestioned that tradition points to York as a great masonic centre for England, from which Masonry spread and to which freemasons in the earlier days looked upon as their *Alma Mater.* However, it is on record that a Minute Book of the 'Old Lodge at York' included a list of brethren who were 'Presidents' of it from 1705 to 1734, but that book was lost. The earliest Minute that has survived is dated 19 March 1712 and is worth quoting here as it gives a good illustration of the brevity of the period:

> March the 19th 1712. At a private lodge held at the house of James Borehams, situate in Stonegate in the City of York, Mr. Thomas Shipton, Mr. Caleb Greenbury, Mr. Jno. Morryson, Mr Jno Russell, Jno. Whitehead, and Francis Morryson were all of them severally sworn and admitted into the Honourable Society and Fraternity of Freemasons. Geo. Bowes Esq. Deputy President. Jno. Wilcock also admitted at the same lodge.

The admission was probably as simple in character as indeed as that entry. In that period, and for that lodge, the Minutes were written by various persons but on a long roll of parchment. They were kept until 1738 and then it would appear that the lodge was dormant until 1761 as there is no evidence of its activity between those dates, but in 1761 it was 'revived'. In that first period it is known to have constituted another lodge which, in an autonomous era was no difficulty. The record for that is of interest and is quoted from a Paper 'The Subordinate Lodges Constituted by the York Grand Lodge' compiled by Bro G. Y. Johnson, librarian of York Lodge No 236 (*AQC* Vol 52, pp 225–268):

After the Minutes of the York Grand Lodge Meeting held on 28 September 1778, there appears:

Copy of a letter sent to Mr Ben^e Bradley Worshipfull Jn^r Warden & Mr Willm Preston Worshipfull Past Master of the Lodge No 1 at ye Mitre Tavern Fleett Street London—at their request to Bro^r Bussey, to Sattisfie them &c of the Existance of the Antient Grand Lodge at York. Previous to the Year 1717.

In that letter Jacob Bussey, the Grand Secretary of this Grand Lodge stated that he 'inspected an Original Minute Book of this Grand Lodge, beginning in 1705 & ending in 1734'. Bro Johnson stated that the Minute Book has long since been lost, but that it existed is proved by the fact that it is mentioned in the York Grand Lodge Schedule of Regalia, Records, &c., dated 15 September 1779.

In giving particulars of 'a Grand Lodge at York', Bro Bussey stated:

... There is an Instance of its being holden once (in 1713) out of York viz. at Bradford in Yorkshire when 18 Gentlemen of the best families in that Neighbourhood were made Masons.

No further mention is made of that incident and there is no record of it in Grand Lodge at York Roll No 7 which seems to have served as the Register of Admissions from 1712 to 1730, nor of the meetings at which such admissions took place. From that Bro Whytehead draws inference that the gentlemen at Bradford were not considered members of the Old Lodge at York and suggests that the eighteen gentlemen were made masons with the idea of forming a lodge at Bradford which he deduces may have been formed about the year 1713 and perhaps constituted by members of the Old Lodge at York. It is more than likely that, because of Anderson's *Constitutions* reaching freemasons in York that they lost no time in declaring themselves a Grand Lodge under the 'Presidency' of Edward Bell; in 1725 the Minutes state 'the Society chose Charles Bathurst Esq as Grand Master'.

In his 2nd Edn of the *Constitutions* (p 196) Anderson acknowledges the independence of that Grand Lodge at York in the following manner:

But the *Old Lodge* at YORK CITY, and the *Lodges* of Scotland, IRELAND, FRANCE AND ITALY, affecting Independence, are under their own Grand Masters, tho' they have the same *Constitutions* Charges, Regulations, &c for substance, with their Brethren of England.

In the first period of the existence of the York Grand Lodge, in his Oration on 27 December 1726, Francis Drake MD, FRS, then Junior Grand Warden, used the legendary story of the connection of Prince Edwin with the craft of freemasonry; it was contained in various of the manuscript *Constitutions* and *Old Charges* much treasured by operatives and speculatives alike. He delivered his oft quoted *Speech* and included the following:

> *Edwin*, the first Christian King of the *Northumbers*, about the six Hundredth Year after *Christ*, and who laid the foundation of our Cathedral, sat as Grand Master. This is sufficient to make us dispute the Superiority with the Lodges at *London*: But as nought of that Kind ought to be amongst so amicable a *Fraternity*, we are content they enjoy the Title of Grand-Master of England; but the *Totius Angliae* we claim as an undoubted Right.

Thus was the title *Grand Lodge of All England* adopted. It would appear to have been a strange choice when compared with the ecclesiastical terminology for the Archbishops of Canterbury and of York, for the former is *Primate of All England* and the latter *Primate of England*, a reversal was selected by Francis Drake.

In his excellent *The York Legend in the Old Charges* (Lewis, 1978), Bro Alex Horne of San Francisco, a member of Quatuor Coronati Lodge, made clear the confusion that had been caused in the *Old Charges* and sundry copies, between King Edwin of Northumbria in the 7th cent and Prince Edwin of the 10th cent, the first purporting to have sat as Grand Master at York and the other who is said to have received a Charter and Commission from King Athelstan to hold an Annual Assembly of masons and thereby formed the Grand Lodge at York in AD 926.

In his Paper 'The Relics of the Grand Lodge at York' delivered to QC Lodge on 25 June 1900, Bro T. B. Whytehead stated that an artist member of the York Lodge:

> Offer'd some Drawings to the Grand Lodge which was approved of, the Grand Master with the unanimous consent of the Grand Lodge requested that he will make a painting agreeable to one of them, to be fix'd over the fire place in the Lodge room at the York Tavern. . . .

The entry for that was on 25 May 1778 (*AQC* Vol 13 p 104). Bro Whytehead went on to say that 'the Lodge Board, about 3 ft by 4 ft is now [1900] hanging on the staircase of the Masonic Hall in Duncombe Street, is painted in gold and colours and ... has the following legend in Old English text letters:

THE GRAND LODGE
of all England
founded by Prince Edwin
A.D. 926.'

In the same Paper Bro Whytehead gave an account of certain freemasons having been made in lodges under the premier Grand Lodge and had become known to one another whilst resident in York then petitioned London for a Warrant of Constitution. They were successful in that and their first meeting was held at the Punch Bowl, Stonegate, York on 2 February 1761 under the authority of the Warrant dated 12 January. They appeared in the current *List of Lodges* shewn at No 259.

That action revitalised those who had allowed the Old Lodge at York to fall into decline and they called a meeting the following month, which was also attended by brethren from the new lodge shewing that relationship was by no means strained between them. That renewed interest in the Old Lodge was such that No 259 fell by the wayside and the unpaid dues to the premier Grand Lodge became the subject of correspondence that was brought to the notice of the Grand Lodge at York which resulted in the following appearing in their Minutes:

> ... Several letters from the Grand Lodge in London having been received by the Grand Master, the same were at this Lodge considered, and the following answers there to agreed to be sent by the Secretary.
> Worshipful Brother,
>> At The Grand Lodge in York held 14th December 1767 Present the Right Worshipful Seth Agar G.M. of All England ...
>> Your account of the business done at the quarterly communication held at the Crown and Anchor in the Strand London addressed to the Right Worshipful Master of the Lodge at the Punch Bowl in Stonegate in this City having come to the hands of the Grand Master was produced and read and after due consideration thereof it was UNANIMOUSLY RESOLVED.
>> That the Grand Secretary do inform the Grand Lodge in London that the Lodge heretofore held under their Constitution No 259 at the Punch Bowl in Stonegate has been for some years discontinued, and that the most Antient Grand Lodge of all England held from time immemorial in this City, is now the only lodge held therein.
>> That this Lodge acknowledges no Superior, that it pays homage to none, that it exists in its own Right, that it grants Constitutions and Certificates in the same manner, as is done by the Grand Lodge in London, and as it has from time immemorial had a Right and used to do, and that it distributes its own Charity according to the true principles of Masons.
>
>   ...   .
>
>   (Signed) D. Lambert
>   Grand Secretary
>
> To
> Samuel Spencer Esq., Grand Secretary
> of the Grand Lodge of Free and
> Accepted Masons in London.

That letter was taken to London and handed over to Bro Spencer by Bro Joseph Atkinson, Senior Grand Warden of the York Grand Lodge and in consequence Lodge No 259 was erased from the Register in 1768 and of course disappeared from the *List of Lodges*.

The Grand Lodge of All England became moribund in the

latter part of the 18th century. The last surviving Minute Book has details of a meeting held on 23 August 1792 but three blank pages follow on. It is possible that another Minute Book was used after that but if so it has been lost. However, it is on record that the brethren who were members of it, when visiting other lodges, up to the time when the Moderns and the Antients joined to become the United Grand Lodge of England still retained their rank held in the York Grand Lodge and used it on all masonic occasions. That Grand Lodge had Constituted at least eleven subordinate lodges from which only two original Warrants have survived; it was also concerned with the erection of another 'Grand Lodge South of the River Trent' as it was called, details of which will arise in later pages.

The List of Lodges *for 1761 which shews No 259 meeting at the Punch Bowl, Stonegate, York on 27 Feb 1761*

Chapter 4

Anderson's Influence Elsewhere

The year 1723 had provided a milestone in the development of organisation in Freemasonry inasmuch as it saw the publication of Anderson's *Constitutions*, the first Minutes of the new Grand Lodge, and some new Regulations. It encouraged Ireland and Scotland to follow suit but it was Anderson's book that gave guidance.

About 1725 Ireland set up their own Grand Lodge, but the exact date of inauguration cannot be established. The earliest reference to it is in *The Dublin Weekly Journal* (No 13) dated 16 June 1725. It reports that a procession of hackney coaches made their way on St John's Day, 24 June, at 11 am to their venue the King's Inns, where the brethren elected 'the Rt. Hon. Earl of ROSS as Grand Master for the year ensuing'. The report states that after their masonic proceedings had ended 'they all went to the play, with their Aprons &c. ...' That is the date eventually adopted for all subsequent celebratory events for the Grand Lodge of Ireland. In parallel with that Grand Lodge was another at Munster but merged to make a national Grand Lodge in 1731. However, before that the Grand Lodge of Ireland issued a recommendation for each lodge to obtain a copy of the English *Constitutions* as guidance and, when their own were compiled by John Pennell and published in 1730 it was based largely upon Anderson's work.

Dr Desaguliers who wrote the Dedication in the 1723 book of *Constitutions* is reported to have paid a visit to a lodge at Dunblane in Scotland and there he presented a copy of the English *Constitutions*. Certain lodges in Scotland had enjoyed autonomy and so took longer to form a national Grand Lodge but it came in 1736.

The three Grand Lodges of England, Ireland, and Scotland provided a firm basis for mutual administration and a platform upon which Recognition was to be conferred; although difficulties were to arise between England and Ireland's jurisdiction in the latter half of that century.

It is fitting to bring to mind that Anderson's *Constitutions* was the first masonic book to be published in the Western Hemisphere when Benjamin Franklin reproduced it in facsimile print in 1734; it bore the legend '*Reprinted in Philadelphia, by special Order, for the Use of the Brethren in NORTH-AMERICA*'.

Chapter 5

Irregular Makings

At the end of the 17th century and at the commencement of the 18th many Societies sprang into existence, meeting in taverns and coffee houses. Some were of serious interchange with debate as the common interest, others, perhaps most, were based upon antics in which skits on freemasonry were not neglected and their jibes and mockery quite a feature. Serious reportage in newspapers of events in which the newly erected Grand Lodge were engaged, as well as the grand processions on the day of Installation of the Grand Master added zest for much counter activity, as well as counter articles in newspapers and journals. Charges came to be levelled against the Craft that, in the main, were centred upon masonic secrecy; the non-acceptance of females, bringing morals into question; departure from established forms of religion by bringing together men of other faiths. It was an age when charlatans abounded in all walks of life and attacks could be made on any club or group and freemasonry was no exception.

From the 1720s it became quite profitable to publish broadsheets against the Craft and its events, and it was almost a logical step for the compilation of so-called 'exposures' of ritual and procedure. It was an era in which Freemasonry itself was developing from a two-degree system into a three part exercise which eventually progressed into a fourth.

The first growth was for a Fellow-of-the-Craft to go forward to take what was termed 'the Master's Part'. We have no details as to what form it took, indeed such information would not have been placed on record, but it was made clear that in that period the progress was at the hands of specialised lodges some actually set up as 'Masters lodges'. But on that measure we find an interesting comment from an author's *NOTE* in a pamphlet *The Mystery of Free-Masonry* which was reprinted in the *Daily Journal* of 15 August 1730:

There is not one Mason in a Hundred that will be at the Expence to pass the Master's Part, except it be for interest.

That was not the case because from then on the three-degree system became well established, closely followed by a logical development from that to what was to become the Royal Arch.

The first progression can be seen to have occurred in the wording used in the first and second editions of Anderson's *Constitutions*. Whereas in the first edition it stated:

> No Brother can be a WARDEN until he has pass'd the part of a Fellow-Craft, ...

The 1738 edition had:

> The WARDENS are chosen from the Master-Masons, ...

It is generally accepted that the third part was being practised c 1725, but it was not a common feature, rather a specialist conferral. Admission into freemasonry did not imply membership of the lodge where that ceremony took place but it did entitle the new entrant to a certificate to show that he had been regularly admitted; often it was a crudely written statement but it served the purpose. We find evidence of that from quite an early period in the *Roberts MS* of 1663:

> 111. That no Person hereafter, which shall be accepted a *Free-Mason*, shall be admitted into any Lodge, or Assembly, until he hath brought a Certificate of the Time and Place of his Acception from the Lodge that accepted him, unto the Master of that Limit and Division, where such Lodge was kept, which said Master shall enroll the same on Parchment in a Roll to be kept for that Purpose, and give an Account of all such Acceptions, at every General Assembly.

The extent to which irregular masons were being made often gave cause for concern and there were occasions when Warranted lodges failed to act in accordance with accepted custom and procedure. One interesting case appears in the Minutes of Grand Lodge for 27 March 1729:

> Complaint being made that at the Lodge at the one Tun in Noble Street a person who was not a Mason was present at a Making, and that they made Masons upon a trifling Expence, only for the sake of a Small Reckoning, and that one Huddlestone of that Lodge brought one Templeman of the South sea house with him who was not a Mason and the obligation was not required. ORDERED That the Master and Wardens of the Lodge at the One Tun in Noble Street do attend at the next Quarterly Communication to answer the said Complaint, and in the mean time that they endeavour to make the said Templeman a regular Mason, and that a Copy of the Order be delivered to them.

It would appear that Huddlestone was treating the lodge meeting as just a convivial occasion to which he could invite a friend, even to witness a 'Making'; the house bill for the night, or 'small

Reckoning' as it was termed, leads one to think that the attendance was small. It seems also that if the non-mason had taken an obligation on the night his visit would then have been made 'regular'; the members were now instructed to initiate him and so balance the situation.

The year 1730 must be deemed to be a turning point in many ways, triggered by the appearance of a masonic exposure *The Mystery of Free-Masonry* which was reprinted in the *Daily Journal* No 2998 on 15 August. It caused the following to be Minuted on the 28th:

> D⁫ Desaguliers stood up and (taking Notice of a printed Paper lately published and dispersed about the Town, and since inserted in the News Papers, pretending to discover and reveal the misteries of the Craft of Masonry) recommended several things to the Consideration of the Grand Lodge, particularly the Resolution of the last Quarterly Communication for preventing any false Brethren being admited into regular Lodges such as call themselves Honorary Masons.
>
> The Deputy Grand Master seconded the Doctor and proposed several Rules to the Grand Lodge to be observed in their respective Lodges for their Security against all open and Secret Enemies to the Craft.

W. J. Songhurst, who transcribed the Minutes of Grand Lodge and on behalf of Quatuor Coronati Lodge published them in Vol 10 of the *Antigrapha* in 1913, commented in a footnote at that point 'No such resolution is recorded in the Minutes of the previous Meeting on 21 April 1730. Meetings of Honorary Freemasons were advertised in the Daily Papers at that time, and have been noted as late as 1739.'

Two months afterwards the comprehensive booklet *Masonry Dissected* was published by Samuel Prichard. He described its contents on the title page thus:

> As it is deliver'd in the Constituted Regular Lodges Both in City and Country, According to the Several Degrees of Admission. Giving an Impartial ACCOUNT of their Regular Proceeding in Initiating their New Members in the whole Three Degrees of MASONRY, Viz., I. Enter'd 'Prentice; II. Fellow Craft; III. Master. To which is added The Author's Vindication of himself, By Samuel Prichard, late Member of a CONSTITUTED LODGE. . . . (Price 6d).

That book caused the following to be Minuted on 15 December 1730:

> The Deputy Grand Master took notice of a Pamphlet lately published by one Prichard who pretends to have been made a regular Mason: In Violation of the Obligation of a Mason which he swears he has broke in order to do hurt to Masonry and expressing himself with the utmost Indignation against both him (stiling him an Imposter) and of his Book as a foolish thing not to be regarded. But in order to prevent the Lodges being imposed upon by false Brethren or Imposters: Proposed till otherwise Ordered by the Grand Lodge, that no person whatsoever should be admitted into Lodges unless some member

of the Lodge then present would vouch for such visiting Brothers being a regular Mason, and the Member's Name to be entered against the Visitor's Name in the Lodge Book, which Proposal was unanimously agreed to.

It is of some interest to note that at the same meeting Anthony Sayer, the first Grand Master (1717), was charged with having acted irregularly and in a clandestine manner but 'was acquitted of the charge against him and recommended to do nothing so irregular for the future'. Sayer was, at that period, Tyler for several lodges in London and the 'irregularity' may have had some

MASONRY

DISSECTED:

BEING

A Univerſal and Genuine

DESCRIPTION

OF

All its BRANCHES from the Original to this Preſent Time.

As it is deliver'd in the

Conſtituted Regular Lodges

Both in CITY and COUNTRY,

According to the

Several Degrees of ADMISSION.

Giving an Impartial ACCOUNT of their Regular Proceeding in Initiating their New Members in the whole Three Degrees of MASONRY.

VIZ.

I. ENTER'D 'PREN- ⎱⎰ II. FELLOW CRAFT.
   TICE,   ⎰⎱ III. MASTER.

To which is added,

The Author's VINDICATION of himſelf.

By SAMUEL PRICHARD, *late Member of a* CONSTITUTED LODGE.

LONDON:

Printed for J. WILFORD, at the *Three Flower-d. Luces* behind the *Chapter houſe* near St. Paul's. 1730.   (Price 6d)

Prichard's Masonry Dissected *contained the first printed account of the Hiramic legend in catechetical form* connection with those duties but we are denied the details. However, in his *Masonic Facts and Fictions* (pp 42–3) Henry Sadler comments rather whimsically—'This reads very much like a verdict of "Not Guilty—but don't do it again!"'

Prichard's *Masonry Dissected* has to be treated as a milestone in that it contained, in catechetical form, the first printed account of the Hiramic legend. His pamphlet appeared on 13 October 1730, price 6d, and was so much in demand that a second edition was produced the following week and a third ten days after that. It was reproduced in the newspaper *Read's Journal*, was translated into French and received special atention on the Continent, and was pirated by other publishers. It became the basis upon which various masonic ritual 'exposures' were mounted but not without further additions and embellishments; the communication of so-called masonic 'secrets' was ever a fascination as well as a profitable undertaking for many.

Whilst Prichard's book provided the details of the legend, its existence was hinted at four years earlier in a newspaper advertisement that was brought to notice by Henry Sadler, librarian at Freemasons' Hall, London, in his Inaugural Address as Master of Quatuor Coronati Lodge on 8 November 1910. The newspaper, unfortunately, has not since been traced and remains unspecified but was dated 23 June 1726; the subject is amusingly treated with Dr Desaguliers as one of the targets the full text of the advertisement is given below:

ANTEDILUVIAN MASONRY

This is to give Notice
To all Masons who have been made after the Antediluvian manner.

That there will be a Lodge held at the Ship Tavern in Bishopsgate Street tomorrow the 24th of this instant June, being the Feast of St. John the Baptist, the Forerunner of—who laid the first parallel Line—there not being Brethren enough assembled the last year to make a true and perfect Lodge.

There will be several Lectures on Ancient Masonry, particularly on the Signification of the Letter G. and how and after what Manner the Antediluvian Masons form'd their Lodges, shewing what Innovations have lately been introduced by the Doctor and some other of the Moderns, with their Tape, Jacks, Moveable Letters, Blazing Stars, &c., to the great Indignity of the Mop and Pail.

There will likewise by a Lecture giving a particular Description of the Temple of Solomon, shewing which way the Fellow Crafts got into the Middle Chamber to receive their Wages, and proving without lettering or giving the first or second, that the two Pillars of the Porch were not cast in the Vale of Jehosaphat but elsewhere; and that neither the Honorary, Apollonian, or Free and Accepted Masons know anything of the matter; with the whole History of the Widow's Son Killed by the Blow of a Beetle, afterwards found three Foot East, three foot West, and three Foot perpendicular, and the necessity there is for a Master to well understand the Rule of Three.

Lastly; there will be an Oration in the Henlean stile, on the Antiquity of Signs, Tokens, Points, Gripes, Knuckles, Wrists, Right-hands, bare-bended knees, naked left Breast, Bibles, Compasses, Squares, Yellow Jackets, Blue Breeches, Mosaic Pavements, dented Ashlars, broached Turnels, Jewels, movable and immovable, bow-bound Boxes, oblong-Squares, cassia, and mossy Graves, delivered neither sitting nor standing naked nor cloathed, but in due Form, concluding with a genuine Account of Penalties, Throats, Tongues, Hearts, Sands, Cables, Shoars, Tides, Bodies burnt, Ashes, Winds, solemn Obligations, &c.

N.B.—The Wax Chandler near Pall Mall will provide three Great Lights and a Gormogon to keep off the Cowin and Eves-droppers.

By Order of the Fraternity

Lewis Giblin, M.B.N.

The Eulogium on Masonry will not be deferred on any account.

It should not be construed that when the members of the 'Four Old Lodges' set up the premier Grand Lodge in 1717 that they automatically rendered 'irregular' other lodges, however few or scattered, then in existence. Speculative lodges were autonomous and self-centred and even when the Grand Lodge began to grant Warrants of Constitution and to compile *Lists of Lodges* under their jurisdiction it did not veto those who remained independent, and those lodges went unrecognized. Nothing was written into the *Regulations* against 'unrecognized' lodges, some of whom stayed in existence; others came into being, separate and apart from the Grand Lodge. Some applied for a Warrant in due course but the date and position on the *List* was determined by the date of issue of the Warrant.

Whilst the limits of control for the premier Grand Lodge were stated to be 'London and Westminster' they soon extended far beyond as Freemasonry was being taken by the military and by colonists to other lands, by Englishmen, Irishmen, and the Scots alike but with a common *modus operandi* of basic form.

Whatever measures to detect irregularly-made masons were put into operation, and quite when that happened is not recorded in the Minutes, it is generally accepted that changes did occur about the 1730's; one in particular, a special changeover of passwords went to the Continent and has remained ever since. The Grand Lodge in later years reversed to resume a *status quo*; that is a situation we will examine in later pages.

A Grand Lodge Minute of 29 January 1731 tends to show the state of affairs regarding unattached freemasons in London. Initiation in a particular lodge did not mean automatic membership of that lodge but a statement of admission enabled the brother to be acceptable when visiting another lodge.

Contact with such brethren was raised by the Senior Grand Warden as follows:

> Dr. Douglas observed that Several Brethren that are not of any regular Lodge, and Yet are good and faithful Brethren, can have no Notice (of the Grand Festival) without publick advertisement.
> Ordered, that this affair be left to the Direction of the Stewards.
> The Deputy Grand Master then ordered That all the Lodges do bring in Lists of their regular Members at the next Quarterly Communication in order that they may be entered in a Book prepared for that purpose.

The process of orderliness gradually extended to lodges themselves regarding consistency of their meetings, as the following Resolution was passed on 24 February 1735:

> THAT if any Lodge for the future within the Bills of Mortality shall not regularly meet for the space of one year, such Lodge shall be erased out of the Book of Lodges, and in case they shall afterwards be desirous of meeting again as a Lodge they shall lose their former Rank and submit themselves to a new Constitution.

It was a matter of a few months to show that the limitation to 'the Bills of Mortality', or in other words the Parish Registers, was exceeded as quite a number of Warrants had been granted for lodges overseas, as we see by the 1736 *List of Lodges*.

It was at that February 1735 meeting that a new edition of Anderson's *Constitutions* was mentioned:

> Br. Doctor Anderson formerly Grand Warden presented a Memorial Setting forth, that whereas the first Edition of the General Constitutions of Masonry, compiled by himself, was sold off, and a Second Edition very much wanted; And that he had spent some Thoughts upon Some Alterations and Additions that might fittly be made to the same, which was now ready to lay before the Grand Lodge for their approbation if they were pleased to receive them. . . .
> He further represented that one William Smith said to be a Mason, had without privity or Consent pyrated a considerable part of the Constitutions of Masonry aforesaid to the prejudice of the said Br Anderson it being his sole Property. It was therefore Resolved and Ordered That every Master and Warden present shall do all in their Power to discountenance so unfair a Practice, and prevent the said Smith's Books being bought by any Members of their respective Lodges.

William Smith's *The (Freemasons) Pocket Companion* was published in London in 1734 and Dublin in May 1735 then under the title *A Pocket Companion for Free-Masons*. It was the first of a series of similarly pirated works that were published in England, Ireland, Scotland, Germany and Holland during the 18th century and, as its title implies, was of more convenient size for a brother to have as ready reference. See Plates shewing the frontispiece of the London edition of 1735 and another dated 1754.

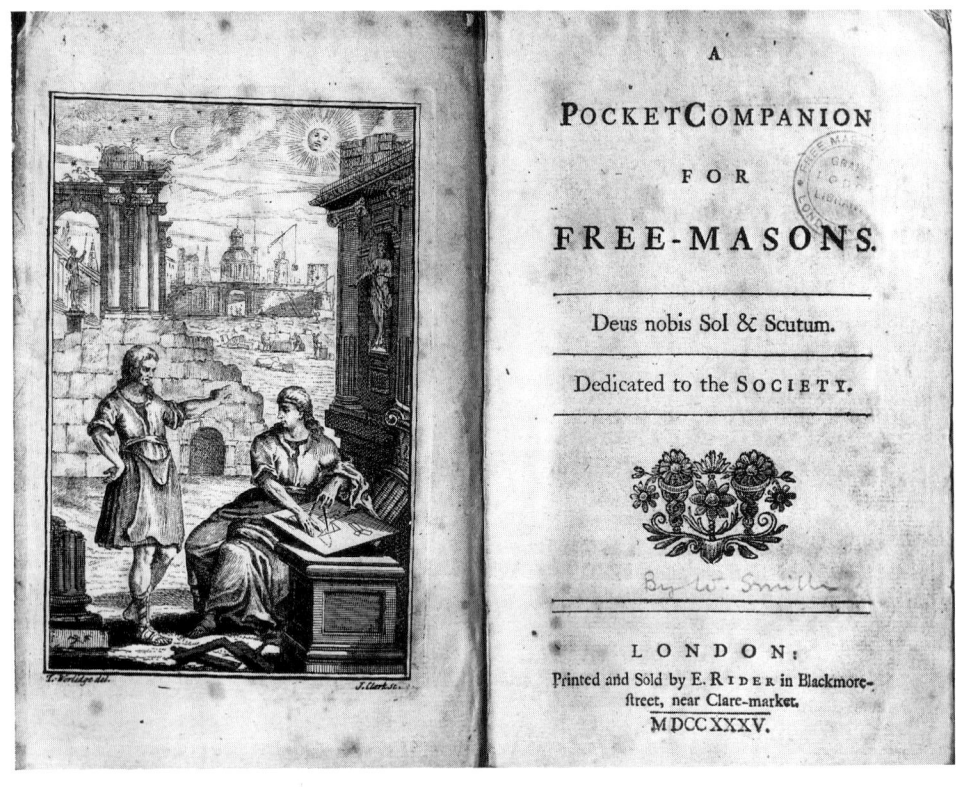

Frontispiece and title page of William Smith's Pocket Companion *(1735). It was the first of a series of printed works published in England during the 18th century and of a convenient size for a Brother to use as a ready reference*

THE
Pocket Companion
AND
HISTORY
OF
FREE-MASONS,
CONTAINING THEIR
Origine, Progress, and present State:
AN
ABSTRACT
OF
Their Laws, CONSTITUTIONS, CUSTOMS,
CHARGES, ORDERS and REGULATIONS,
FOR THE
Instruction and Conduct of the Brethren:
A
CONFUTATION
OF
Dr. *Plot's* False INSINUATIONS:
AN
APOLOGY,
Occasioned by their PERSECUTION in the Canton
of *Berne*, and in the POPE's Dominions:
And a select NUMBER of SONGS and other
PARTICULARS, for the USE of the SOCIETY.

Per bonam famam et infamiam.

LONDON:
Printed for J. SCOTT, at the *Black-Swan*, in *Duck Lane*, near
West-Smithfield; and Sold by R. BALDWIN, at the *Rose* in
Pater-Noster-Row.   M,DCC,LIV.

Frontispiece of a Companion printed for J. Scott in 1754

Anderson included a brief account of that meeting of February 1735 in his 2nd Edition (p 133) which was published in 1738. He had this to say:

> Brother *Anderson*, Author of the *Book* of *Constitutions*, representing that a *new Edition* was become necessary, and that he had prepared Materials for it, the GRAND MASTER and the Lodge order'd him to lay the same before the present and former *Grand Officers*; that they may report their Opinion to the G. Lodge. Also the Book call'd the *Free-Mason's Vade Mecum* was condemn'd by the G. Lodge as a pyratical and silly Thing, done without Leave, and the Brethren were warned not to use it, nor to encourage it to be sold.

It may have had small effect in London, but the book was quite successful and even William Smith's work was pirated in that it was published in Newcastle in 1736 under the title *The Book M or Masonry Triumphant*.

At the following Quarterly Communication held on 31 March 1735, with the Rt. Hon. The Earl of Crawford the Grand Master present, a significant Resolution was adopted to try to curb irregular practice:

> The Grand Master took notice (in a handsome Speech) of the Greivance of making extranious Masons in a private and clandestine manner, upon small and unworthy Considerations, and proposed that in Order to prevent that Practice for the future: No person thus admitted into the Craft nor any that can be proved to have assisted at such Makings shall be capable either of Acting as a grand Officer on Occasion or even as an Officer in a private Lodge, nor ought they to have any part in the General Charity which is much impaired by this Clandestine Practice.

Those Minutes end with two quite interesting paragraphs as they give an indication of the business being conducted under such *bonhomie:*

> His Lord^p was pleased to Order a large quantity of Rack that was made a present of from Bengal in the East Indies to the Grand Officers to be made into Punch and to be distributed among the Brethren.
>
> All Business being over the Grand Lodge was closed with an uncommon appearance of Harmony.

One can but speculate upon the meaning of the phrase 'uncommon appearance'!

The irregular 'Making' was ever a source of annoyance and it arose yet again in two meetings of the Grand Lodge in June and December 1739, the relative extracts being:

> The Complaint referred by the last Committee of Charity concerning the irregular making of Masons was taken into Consideration When the Sec^{ty} informed the Lodge that he had given Notice to the several persons complained of to attend & answer the same at this Q.C. And Bro. Stephenson one of the said persons attended & excused himself to the Satisfaction of the Lodge. But others of them not appearing & the S.G.W. who made one of the Complaints

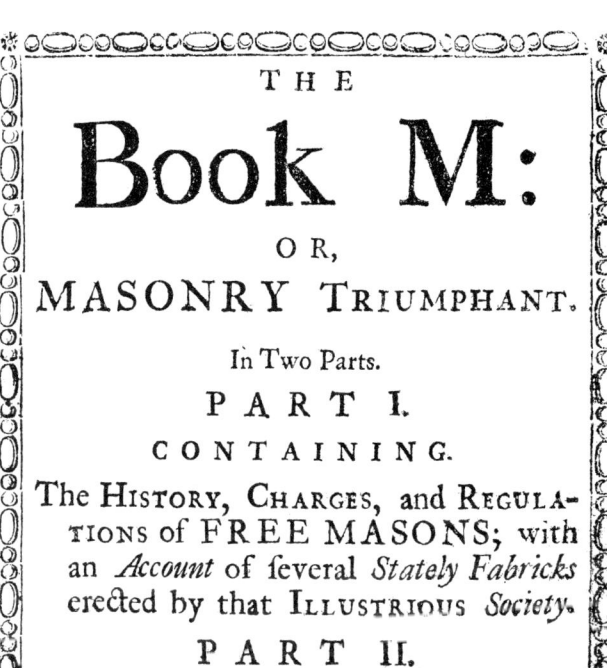

THE

Book M:

OR,

MASONRY TRIUMPHANT.

In Two Parts.

PART I.

CONTAINING.

The HISTORY, CHARGES, and REGULA-
TIONS of FREE MASONS; with
an *Account* of feveral *Stately Fabricks*
erected by that ILLUSTRIOUS *Society*.

PART II.

Containing,

The SONGS ufually fung in LODGES, PRO-
LOGUES and EPILOGUES fpoken at the *Theatres* in *LONDON* in Honour of the CRAFT;
with an Account of all the Places where REGU-
LAR LODGES are held.

Be wife as Serpents, yet innocent as Doves.

Newcaftle upon *Tyne*,
Printed by LEONARD UMFREVILLE
and COMPANY. M.DCC.XXXVI.

William Smith's work was pirated and published in 1736 under the title The
Book M or Masonry Triumphant

being absent in the Country.

Ordered that the farther Consideration thereof be deferred till some other Opportunity. (30 June)

Then the Lodge was moved to take into their farther Cons^n the Complaint concerning the irregular making of Masons.

Whereupon the G.M. took notice that altho some Brethren might have been guilty of an Offence tending so much to destroy the Cement of the Lodge & so utterly inconsistent with the Rules of the Society. Yet he could not bring himself to believe that it had been done otherwise than through Inadvertency and therefore proposed that if any such Brethren there were they might be forgiven for this Time Which was Ordered accordingly.

Ordered that the Laws be strictly put in Execution against all such Brethren as shall for the future countenance connive or assist at any such irregular makings. (12 December)

It will be of interest that neither of those meetings were held on the normal St John's Days (24 June and 27 December) a matter that was not accepted by the traditionalists.

Another matter that was to cause upset among freemasons who resided in certain countries outside Great Britain under the premier Grand Lodge was contained in the Minutes of the Quarterly Communication held 12 December 1739. A Petition was heard from Bro Thomas Crudelli, 'a prisoner in the Inquisition in Florence on Account of Masonry' and the sum of £20 was ordered to be applied towards his relief. It was the direct outcome of the Papal Bull—*In Eminenti*—issued on 28 April 1738 outlawing Freemasonry in all countries where such declarations were canon law. England was not subject to Papal direction but Italy, Spain, and Portugal where lodges were held under the premier Grand Lodge, and those lodges were not, became especially prominent for Inquisitorial Proceedings. John Coustos, a diamond cutter, who was initiated in what is now Britannic Lodge No 33, in London, went to Paris in 1735 and from there to Lisbon where he formed a lodge for the benefit of friends. He too was arrested and, in his case, tortured by the Inquisition but eventually released through influence in 1744.

We are left to conjecture as to what terms were imposed upon ritual, ceremonial, recognition terms or actions that were adopted to detect those initiated in 'irregular Makings'; what measures taken to prevent unqualified persons taking advantage of masonic charity. The 1730's saw those actions implemented probably in piecemeal fashion, but innovations they were and such was to be the later charge for their actions. Some brethren ignored the changes yet remained loyal to their Grand Lodge and have been classified as 'Traditioners'; they were the subject of an excellent and authoritative Paper by the late Heron Lepper (*AQC* Vol 56 pp 138-204). Their procedure and actions followed time-honoured

John Coustos, a diamond cutter who was Initiated into what is now the Britannic Lodge No 33. He was arrested and tortured by the Spanish Inquisition for his masonic activities, but was released in 1744

custom and they had affinity with brethren from Ireland and Scotland who were not affected by these imposed changes and with
those brethren who had remained unattached who condemned the
apparent neglect of certain traditions and new practices. Nevertheless the premier Grand Lodge was going along from strength to
strength and we have a clear indication of how high in the social
scale they had climbed when we read the list of those who attended
on April 7, 1735 for the Installation of the Rt Hon The Lord
Viscount Weymouth. The following were in the procession:

> Rt. Hon. The Earl of Crauford
> Sir Cecil Wray Bt.
> Sir Edward Mansell Bt.
> Duke of Richmond
> Duke of Athol
> Earl of Winchelsea
> Earl of Balcarrass
> Earl of Wymes
> Earl of Loudon
> Marquess of Bowman
> Lord Cathcart
> Lord Vere Bartee

and a vast appearance of former Grand Officers and Gen. (being Masons) all
clothed in White Aprons and Gloves ...

It was a far cry from the time when they hoped for 'a noble Brother
at their head' eighteen years earlier. That procession was almost a
House of Lords itself.

In the *Engraved List* published by John Pine for the year 1739
the premier Grand Lodge had 175 lodges. Anderson, in the 1738
Edition had a 'List of Lodges in and about London and Westminster' that totalled 106 up to May 1738. He had an interesting comment on one of the 'Four Old Lodges' which he placed as No 10 on
his List:

> 10. QUEEN'S HEAD in Knave's-Acre.
> This was one of the *four* Lodges mentioned in Page 109, viz the *Apple-Tree Tavern*
> in *Charles* Street, *Covent-Garden*, whose Constitution is immemorial: but after
> they removed to the *QUEEN'S* Head, upon some Difference the Members that
> met there came under a *new Constitution*, tho' they wanted it not, and it is
> therefore placed at this Number.
> N.B. The CROWN in *Parker's-Lane*, the other of the *four* old *Lodges* is now
> extinct.

Anderson noted that Lodge No 12 at 'Bury's *Coffee-house* in *Bridges
Street*, where there is also a *Masters-Lodge*' showed that the developed Hiramic legend was a specialised affair; a total of ten such
lodges were listed at the time. He also stated:

> Many Lodges have by accident broken up, or are partition'd or else
> removed to new Places for their conveniency, and so, if subsisting, they are

called and known by those new Places for their Signs. But the subsisting Lodges whose Officers have attended the Grand Lodge of Quarterly Communication and brought their benevolence to the General Charity within 12 months past, are here set down, as in the Grand Lodge Books and the Engraved List.

On the subject of removals and the frequency with which they took place, causing alterations for the printing Plate for the Lists, it occasioned the following to be Minuted in Grand Lodge on 13 April 1739:

> THAT every Lodge should they remove from one House to another should pay 2s. 6d. to the ENGRAVER appointed by the Society, and by every Lodge that should change the Times of their meetings 1s. for the trouble and Expense in Making the necessary Alteration in the Engraved List.

In his *Old Engraved Lists of Masonic Lodges* (Kenning, London 1920) A. F. Calvert commented: 'The 1739 Engraved List contains the signs of 109 London, 51 Country, and 11 Foreign Lodges—a total of 171 Lodges, of which the last is numbered 185.' But on the Plate illustrated by him four more were added in script, three for London and one for Spalding. Even in this atmosphere of prosperity however, the stage was being set for the emergence of a second Grand Lodge to be set up in London. It was to come from those brethren who had remained unattached, from members of lodges that had not applied for Warrants from the premier Grand Lodge, from brethren, particularly from Ireland, who had immigrated and had found employment in London, all of whom had something in common—unacceptance of the alterations that had been made by this governing authority; the charge of neglect of various but unspecified 'landmarks'; and following the adoption of the Hiramic legend the unrecognized Royal Arch legend that was its logical outcome. It not only confirmed their independence but drew them together and eventually it brought forth *The Grand Lodge of England According to the Old Institutions* which came into being from organised efforts in 1751. It was to last sixty-one years but its influence was to have tremendous effect world-wide as well as to produce Laurence Dermott whose steadying hand kept Freemasonry to a course more in keeping with tradition and practices that had stood the test of time.

Rules & Orders

to be Observed

By the Most Ancient and Hon.ble Society of

Free and Accepted Masons.

As agreed and Settled by a Committee appointed by a General Assembly held at the Turks Head in Greek Street Soho on Wednesday the 17th of July 1751. And in the Year of Masonry 5751.

By — { Phil.p McLoughlin. | James Shee } { Sam.l Quay. | Jos.h Kelly }

& Jno Morgan G.d Secret.y

Viz.t

for the Grand.

Morgan's Register *This contained a list of members followed by a code of Regulations and commenced with a meeting on 5 February 1752*

Chapter 6

The Antients' Grand Lodge from 1751

It has been shewn by various masonic scholars, in particular Henry Sadler (*Masonic Facts and Fictions*, London 1887) that the brethren who were responsible for the setting-up of the second Grand Lodge in London were not seceders, nor a breakaway group from the premier Grand Lodge of 1717. Murmurings about the changes and neglect of the premier Grand Lodge had become apparent over the years that was eventually to cause action to be taken. A group of brethren in London, mostly weavers and artisans, in the main from Ireland, met together and formed a Committee to do something about the situation. We have no record as to how long the preliminary period went on but their records commence with a meeting held on 5 February 1752 in which reference was then made to a previous meeting seven months earlier when positive action was taken to set up an independent organisation. That record was written into what was to become known as 'Morgan's Register' as it contained a list of members followed by a code of Regulations. It commenced with the following heading:

> RULES & ORDERS to be Observed By the Most Ancient and Honble Society of FREE and ACCEPTED MASONS.
> As agreed and Settled by a Committee appointed by a General Assembly held at the Turk's Head in Greek Street, Soho, on Wednesday the 17th of July 1751, ...

Thus was launched what was still a Committee which it seems was hesitant about calling itself a Grand Lodge at that stage, for like their earlier counterpart in 1717 hoped to attract 'a noble Brother at their head'. In fact it was expressed and recorded at the meeting held on 14 September 1752 in the following terms:

> WHEREAS it is highly expedient for the Universal Benefit of the Ancient Craft that a GRAND MASTER and Grand Lodge shou'd govern and direct the proceedings of the several Ancient Lodges held in and about the Cities of London and Westminster. And as the present low condition of the Ancient

Society of Free and Accepted Masons renders the hope of Obtaining the honour [of] a Noble Personage to preside over us at this time very precarious.

In Order to preserve the present remains of the true Ancient Craft &c. We the under Named being the present Masters and Wardens of the several Masonical meetings called Lodges of true Ancient Masonry aforesaid, do agree (pursuant to the powers vested in us by our Respective Brethren of the several lodges) to form a Grand Committee (we mean such a Committee) as may supply the deficiency of a Grand Master until an Opportunity offers for the Choice of a Noble Personage to govern our Ancient Fraternity: And that We will therein (by the Authority Aforesaid) make Statutes or Laws for the better government and well Ordering the said Fraternity Receive Petitions, hear Appeals, and Transact Business (that is to say such Business as ought to be peculiar to a Grand Lodge) with Equity and Impartiality—Dated in our Grand Committee Room on Thursday the fourteenth day of September New Stile 1752. And in the Year of Masonry 5752 In the presentce of [then were listed the names of the Masters and Wardens of lodges numbered 2, 4, 5, 6, 8, 11, 12 as well as two Past Masters of No. 4 and a PM of No 6]

(signed Lau. Dermott G.S.)

And whereas several of the lodges have congregated and made Masons without any Warrants: (not with a desire of Acting wrong but thro: the Necessity above mention'd) in order to Rectify such irregular proceedings (as far as in our power) It is hereby Order'd That the Grand Secretary shall write Warrants (on Parchment) for the Unwarranted Lodges, viz. The Lodges known by the title of No. 2, 3, 4, 5, 6, and that all the said Warrants shall bare date July the seventeenth One thousand seven hundred fifty and One being the day on which the said lodges met (at the Turk's Head Tavern in Greek Street Soho) to revive the Ancient Craft.

That the Secretary shall leave proper Spaces for the Grand Mast^r Deputy G.M. and Grand Wardens to sign all the said Warrants according to Ancient Custom.

That as soon as we shall arrive at the Great Happiness of installing proper Grand Officers the possessors of the Unsigned Warrants shall present them to the Grand Master for his Worship's Signature or Renewal, Until which time the said Warrants as well as those which have or may be (thro: necessity) granted in like manner shall be deem'd good and lawfull.

Lastly this our Regulation shall be Recorded in our Registry to show posterity how much we desire to revive the Ancient Craft upon true Masonical principles.

Signed by Order Lau. Dermott G.S.

Lau: Dermott G.S.

The signatory, Laurence Dermott, was to have the greatest impact upon Freemasonry from that time forward until his death in June 1791 at the age of 71 years. He was born in 1720 and initiated in Dublin under the Irish jurisdiction on 14 January 1740 whilst still.

under age 21. According to the Minutes of the Antients' Grand Lodge (having achieved that title by then) held on 2 March 1757. Dermott's regularity as a freemason was challenged by an aggrieved brother and that was dealt with in the following manner:

> Then arose Bro. Thomas Allen past Master of N.º 2 and proved that Brother Dermott had faithfully served all Offices in a very Respectable Lodge held in his House in the City of Dublin which servitude was prior to the said Dermott's coming to England: And further declared that he had never heard any crime (in or out of the Lodge) laid to his Charge.
>
> Brother Charles Byrne (Sen.) Master of N.º 2 proved that Bro. Lau: Dermott having faithfully served the Offices of Sen. and Jun. Deacon Jun. and Sen. Wardens and Secretary was by him Regularly Install'd Master of the good Lodge N. 26 in the Kingdom of Ireland upon the 24th day of June 1746 and all these Transactions were prior to M. Dermott's coming to England.
>
> Lastly Brother Dermott produced a Certificate (Signed Edwd Spratt G.S.) under the Seal of the Grand Lodge of Ireland of his good behaviour and servitude &c. &c. &c. which gave intire satisfaction. . . .

It is small wonder that the Antients had an affinity and close liason with the Grand Lodge of Ireland. In terms of administration that too was of Irish influence for, at the meeting of the Grand Committee held on 1 April 1752 when dealing with proposed Rules and Regulations we see the choice there recorded:

> The Copy of the Byelaws for private Lodges as Written by the late [former] G. Secretary J. Morgan, was read and compared with Brother Lau. Dermott's Copy of the Byelaws of his former Lodge N.º 26 in the City of Dublin, and the latter being deem'd the most correct. It was Unanimously Resolved that the most Correct Copy should be received & acknowledged as the only Byelaws for private lodges in future.

In effect we are back with James Anderson, for the Grand Lodge of Ireland accepted his 1st Edition book of *Constitutions* of 1723 as their authority and guidance for administration; they encouraged each lodge to obtain a copy and in their *General Regulations* at the meeting at Cork *'on St. John ye Evangelist day 1728'* re-stated the instruction:

> That the Master and Wardens of each Lodge take care that their Lodge be furnished with the Constitutions printed at London in ye year of masonry 5723 Anno Dom 1723 Intitled the Constitutions of Free Masons Containing the History, Charges, Regulations, &c. of that most Ancient and R.^t Worshipfull Fraternity.

When their own book of *Constitutions* was to be undertaken in 1729 by John Pennell it was advertised in the following manner:

> To be printed by Subscription.
> The *Constitutions* of the FREE-MASONS, containing the *History, Charges, Regulations,* &c., of that most Ancient and Right Worshipful *Fraternity:* Done

> from the *Constitutions*, printed at *London*, with new Additions, for the Use of the *Lodges*, and Brethren in the Kingdom of Ireland. . . .
>
> N.B. There will be but few printed, only those subscribed for.

Bro John Heron Lepper and Bro Philip Crossle placed a great store of detail on record for future students in their joint publication the *History of the Grand Lodge of Ireland* Vol 1 (Dublin Lodge of Research CC 1925).

We have already noted the proceedings of the Grand Committee at their meeting held on 14 September 1752 when it was agreed that Warrants for Lodges with numbers 2, 3, 4, 5, 6, should be prepared on parchment but with spaces left for the signatures of the Grand Master in the future, and his Deputy: but the indefatigable Dermott had already been at work in 'reviving the ancient forms' inasmuch that at a meeting held twelve days earlier on 2 September the Grand Committee Resolved:

> . . . that this Grand Committee shall be formed immediately into a Working Lodge of Master Masons in Order to hear a Lecture from the Grand Secretary Laurence Dermott.
>
> The Lodge was Opened in Ancient form of Grand Lodge and every part of Real freemasonry was traced and explained except the Royal Arch.

The 'noble personage at their head' was achieved when the Rt Hon Edward Vaughan became the second Grand Master 1754–1755 to be followed by Rt. Hon. William Stewart, Earl of Blessington, 1756–1759; although that installation was by proxy on St John's Day 27 December 1756.

The 'irregular Makings' in Freemasonry disturbed the Antients Grand Lodge, for we can now call them that, just as much as the premier Grand Lodge. Within a few months of the Installation (by proxy) we find reference to tightening the control upon 'all Masons whether members or visiters [*sic*] if found Makeing or Assisting to make in a Clandestine manner'. The following two items appeared in the Minutes for 2 March 1757:

> Order'd that a General meeting of Master Mason shall be held in this Room on the 13th Inst in Order to compare and Regulate several things (relative to the Antient Craft) which cannot be committed to writing.
>
> Order'd the Masters of the Royal Arch shall also be Summon'd to meet in Order to regulate things relative to that most valuable branch of the Craft.

Laurence Dermott was determined to justify the remark made by the brother who occupied the Chair on 5 August 1752 who in his address to the brethren urging the necessity of choosing a Grand Master ended by saying:

> Future ages will bless your memories, for preserving and reviving the Ancient Craft in England.

Later that year Dermott was engaged upon gathering whatever manuscripts could be traced and that story is worth our attention; it is taken from the Minutes of 6 December 1752:

> The Grand Secretary desired to know whether there was any other books or Manuscripts more ... To which several of the Brethren answer'd that they did not know of any. ... others said that they knew Mr Morgan had a Roll of parchment of prodigious length which contained some Historical matters Relative to the Ancient Craft, which parchment they did suppose he had taken abroad with him. It was further said that many Manuscripts were lost amongst the lodges lately Modernized where a vestige of the Ancient Craft was not suffered to be revived or practized: And it was for this Reason so many of them withdrew from lodges (under the Modern sanction) to support the true Ancient System. That they found the freemasons from Ireland and Scotland had been initiated in the very same manner as themselves which confirm'd their system & practice as right and just. Without which none could be deem'd legal, though possessed of all the books and papers on Earth. The Grand Secretary produced a very Old Manuscript written or copied by one Bramhall of Canterbury in the Reign of King Henry the Seventh which Manuscript was presented to Bro Dermott (in 1748) by one of the Descendants of the writer. On perusal it proved to contain the whole matter in the 'fore mention'd parchment, as well as other matters not in the parchment. The Grand Secretary expatiated much on the subject of this very old M.S. to the great satisfaction of the hearers. ...

In March 1754 an efficient move was made following the comment by Dermott that the proper business of the Grand Lodge (although then still a Committee) was continually being interrupted and retarded by the numerous petitions for Charity and he proposed that a Committee be instituted to deal with such matters. Thus was the Committee of Inspection formed which very soon became The Committee of Charity; it was the forerunner of the Stewards Lodge which in effect acted as a Board of General Purposes as we know it these days. It had its first mention in the Minutes dated 1 January 1755.

It was the custom for a Dispensation to be granted 'to form a lodge' and when that was established and after inspection and recommendation then to be Constituted and the Warrant granted. Here are a few examples of that system:

> Grand Committee 3 October 1753 Bells Tavern. ... Order'd a Dispensation for Bro^r Alex^r Dixon of N° 16 in order to Congregate and form a Lodge at the Rosemary Branch in Rosemary Lane.
> Heard a petition from John Browne McCoy Thomas Hancock and others praying to be Constituted &c. Accepted and Order'd to be Constituted on Wednesday the 12th Ins^t
> Heard a petition from some Brethren residing in the City of Bristol praying to be Warrented &c. Order'd that the Grand Secretary shall proceed according to the Antient Custom of the Court during the inter Magistrum.

Certificates of membership or good-standing, or for demit purposes

In 1810 the Royal Naval Lodge No 59 was still issuing its own certificates. This one is signed by the Rt Hon the Earl of Kingston as Right Worshipful Master and J.S. Duplessis as Secretary

were the normal custom for the Antients for we have seen how Dermott's Certificate from Ireland had been produced earlier in this account and Irish practice was obviously the basis for the revival of 'ancient masonry'. The premier Grand Lodge Minuted the following in their meeting held on 24 July 1755:

> Ordered, that every Certificate granted to a Brother of his being a mason, shall, for the future, be sealed with the seal of Masonry, and signed by the Grand Secretary, for which five shillings shall be paid to the General Fund of Charity.

It occasioned caustic comment from Dermott written at the end of his Minutes for 27 December 1755:

> Memorandum
> This Year 1755, the Modern Masons began to make use of Certificates: Though the Ancient Masons had granted Certificates time Immemorial.

Dermott's expression 'time Immemorial' was of course an exaggeration but his division of 'Modern Masons' and 'Ancient Masons' was quite the normal classification for the two Grand Lodges by that time.

To show the consolidation that had taken place in the Antients' Grand Lodge in such a short period here is an extract from a letter read at the meeting held on 6 December 1758; the Earl of Blesington, Grand Master, who had presided as Grand Master of the Grand Lodge of Ireland in 1738–1739 when he was Viscount Mountjoy, symbolised the affinity between Ireland and the Antients, and he was the subject of the letter:

> My Lord and R^t Worshipful Sire,
> We the Grand Lodge of Free and Accepted Masons of the Old Institution beg leave to return your Lordship our most sincere and hearty thanks for the great Honour your Lordship has been pleased to have done the Fraternity in condescending to be our Grand Master for two years last past And we hope your Lordship will excuse our non attendance in a public manner, which we should gladly have done ...
> The number of Warrants sign'd by your Worship is a convincing proof of the prosperity of the Craft under your L'dship's Sanction, and we have the pleasure to Assure your Worship that (notwithstanding the troublesome time of war and the bane of all good Society) we have not only been able to relieve a Great number of indigent Brethren but also bought An Hundred pounds stock in the 3 PC Annuities 1726, and still have money enough in the Grand Lodge Chest to answer all demands that are likely to made on us. ...

It was signed by William Holford, Deputy Grand Master.

The close liaison between the Grand Lodge of Ireland and the Antients' Grand Lodge had been firmly welded earlier when a letter from the Grand Secretary of Ireland was read to the Antients at their meeting on 1 March 1758 and so recorded in the Minutes:

Heard a letter from Mr. John Calder (G.S.) in Dublin wherein he assured the Grand Lodge of Antient Masons in London that the Grand Lodge of Ireland did mutually concur in a strict Union with the Antient Grand Lodge in London and promised to keep a Constant Correspondence with them.

Order'd that the Grand Secretary shall draw up an Answer in the most Respectful and Brotherly Terms wherein the General Thanks of this Grand Lodge shall be convey'd and assure them that we will to the utmost of our powers promote the welfare of the Craft in General.

Fitting sentiments, well expressed, and faithfully attended to by those brethren and their successors.

William Stewart, 3rd Viscount Mountjoy, later the 1st Earl of Blesington. Grand Master of the Grand Lodge of Ireland 1738–1739. Grand Master of the Antient Lodge of England 1756–1759

Chapter 7

Lodge Warrants

Because of the wording of *General Regulation VIII* in Anderson's 1723 *Constitutions* many brethren have been led to think that the premier Grand Lodge issued Warrants to their lodges from that period onwards, but such is not the case, a written statement of Constitution only was supplied.

In his *Masonic Records 1717–1894* John Lane states that the term 'Warrant' at that time was used purely in the sense of permission, without any implication of a formal document. The relevant extract from *Regulation VIII* is:

> ... If any Set or Number of *Masons* shall take upon themselves to form a *Lodge* without the *Grand-Master's* Warrant, the *regular Lodges* are not to countenance them, nor own them as fair *Brethren* and duly form'd not approve of their Acts and Deeds; but must treat them as *Rebels*, until they humble themselves, as the *Grand Master* shall in his Prudence direct, and until he approve of them by his Warrant, which must be signify'd to the *other Lodges*, as the Custom is when a *new Lodge* is to be register'd in the *List of Lodges*.

In a definitive Paper on this subject, 'English Grand Lodge Warrants' (*AQC* Vol 90 pp 92–141), John Hamill states that the earliest extant document which can be called a Grand Lodge Warrant under that jurisdiction is dated 14 January 1757. It was granted to Lodge No 218 which is now Palatine Lodge No 97 at Sunderland. Prior to that a written statement of the Constitution meeting was issued by the Grand Master, who usually did the Constitution, or his Deputy, in company with the Grand Wardens and Grand Secretary. Thus by the 1757 period the premier Grand Lodge was only beginning to conform to what had been common practice by the Antients from inception, and they had merely followed the procedure adopted in Ireland. On that subject we turn once again to Heron Lepper and Philip Crossle (*op cit* pp 94–5) to learn that via an advertisement, the lodges in Ireland were ordered to 'take out true and perfect Warrants and be enrolled in the Grand Lodge Book, or they will not be deem'd true and perfect Lodges'—and that happened in December 1731. But they too had their 'time Immemorial' lodges and they also had brethren who saw no reason to submit. However, nine years later the following appeared in *Faulkner's Dublin Journal* of 1 July 1740:

> Such Lodges as have not already taken out Warrants, are ordered to apply for them to John Baldwin Esq Secretary to the Grand Lodge, or they will be proceeded against as Rebel Masons.

It was perfectly natural for Dermott to bring to London those practices with which he was accustomed and to implement them from the start of his official activity. It was the cause of the premier Grand Lodge tidying up a little of their own neglected areas, Warrants and Certificates in particular.

In 1799, whilst forbidding clandestine Societies and the administering of oaths, etc the *Unlawful Societies Act* exempted masonic lodges then already in existence, but required them to be registered with the Clerk of the Peace and an annual Return to be made; that was repealed in this century. The wording of the Act was construed to bar any new lodges from coming into existence and that led to the practice of the reissue of dormant Warrants, or those handed back from lodges which ceased to function. That, however, was an additional use for the Antients as, from quite an early stage, it had been the custom for lodges to apply for possession of an available Warrant with a lower number than their own in order to gain status on the *List* in their jurisdiction. Such an instance is shewn by Lodge No 37 acquiring for the sum of £1.1.0. the Warrant No 6 which was one of the original Warrants held over until signed by the Rt Hon Edward Vaughan as Grand Master. The Warrant is held by Enoch Lodge No 11 whose seniority in consequence of that purchase dates from the Minute of Grand Lodge 2 October 1754:

> Brother William Cowen, Master of the Lodge No. 37 proposed paying one Guinea into the Grand Lodge Fund for No. 6 (now vacant) this proposal was accepted and the Brethren of No. 37 are to rank as No. 6 for ye future.

The payments were made by instalments which were not completed until the following year hence the dating of the reissued Warrant (see Appendix A).

The opening phrase used in the early Warrants issued by the Antients' Grand Lodge was: 'WE, the Grand Lodge in Ample form assembled ...' and ended with '... given under our hands and Seal of the Antient Grand Lodge, London ...' However, a marked alteration was made in 1759 when the commencement was expanded to read: 'WE, the Grand Lodge of Free and Accepted (York) Masons in ample form assembled ...' and the following year even more so:

> WE, the Grand Lodge of the Most Ancient and Honourable Fraternity of

Free and Accepted Masons according to the Old Constitutions granted by His
Royal Highness Prince Edwin at York Anno Domini 926 ...

Thus was perpetuated the legend, adopted as traditional history,
of Prince Edwin at York; it also showed the liaison that had been
formed between the Antients' Grand Lodge in London and the
Grand Lodge of All England at York which had so readily formed
itself into a Grand Lodge following the publication of Anderson's
Constitutions.

The expanded wording on the Warrants continued and used
on the engraved plate which followed within a few years for the
printed Warrants; appropriate spaces were left for details of person-
nel involved and for signatures of the Grand Officers concerned in
the issue. That was the format maintained until the Union of the
two Grand Lodges, the Moderns and the Antients' in 1813 who
had, by then, existed in parallel for over sixty years. For the sake
of comparison a Warrant of this period has been reproduced in
Appendix (B).

AHIMAN REZON:

OR,

A Help to a Brother;

Shewing the

EXCELLENCY of SECRECY,

And the firſt Cauſe, or Motive, of the Inſtitution of

FREE-MASONRY;

THE

PRINCIPLES of the CRAFT,

And the

Benefits ariſing from a ſtrict Obſervance thereof;
What Sort of MEN ought to be initiated into the MYSTERY,
And what Sort of MASONS are fit to govern LODGES,
With their Behaviour in and out of the Lodge.

Likewiſe the

Prayers uſed in the *Jewiſh* and *Chriſtian* Lodges,

The Ancient Manner of

Conſtituting new Lodges, with all the Charges, &c.

Alſo the

OLD and NEW REGULATIONS,

The Manner of Chuſing and Inſtalling *Grand-Maſter* and *Officers*,
and other uſeful Particulars too numerous here to mention.

To which is added,

The greateſt Collection of MASONS SONGS ever preſented to
public View, with many entertaining PROLOGUES and EPILOGUES;

Together with

SOLOMON'S TEMPLE an ORATORIO,

As it was performed for the Benefit of

FREE-MASONS.

By Brother LAURENCE DERMOTT, Sec.

LONDON:
Printed for the EDITOR, and ſold by Brother *James Bedford*, at the
Crown in St. *Paul's Church-Yard.*

MDCCLVI.

Laurence Dermott's Ahiman Rezon *of 1756. The title is of Hebrew origin and
Dermott's thinking is shown in the sub-title 'A Help to a Brother'*

Chapter 8

The Antients' Constitutions

Following the setting up of the Grand Committee then the attainment of status with 'a noble personage to govern the ancient Fraternity', the Grand Lodge of Free and Accepted Masons According to the Old Institutions reinforced the various *Rules and Orders* which had been adopted and went on to the next step to produce a book of *Constitutions*. The task fell to Laurence Dermott, one might even be tempted to say 'who else?' Under the title *Ahiman Rezon* the book was 'Printed for the Editor' in 1756 (see page 54) and was dedicated in these terms:

TO THE RIGHT HONOURABLE
WILLIAM
EARL OF BLESSINGTON

My Lord,

At the request of several Worthy Free-Masons, I undertook to publish the following sheets, wherein I have endeavoured to let the young Brethren know how they ought to conduct their Actions with Uprightness, Integrity, Morality, and Brotherly Love, still keeping the ancient Land-Marks in View.

On the perusal, Your Lordship will find that the Whole is designed not only for the Good of the Fraternity, but also to show the mistaken Part of the World, that the true Principles of Free-Masonry are to love Mercy, do Justice, and walk humbly before God.

My Lord, to speak of your Lordship's Zeal for the Craft, or to tell the Brethren that your Lordship has been as a Father to the Fraternity, &c would be making a Repetition of what is well known already.

Nor are the rest of Mankind less acquainted with your Lordship's Affability, Generosity, Benevolence, and Charity.

The Year 1740 has recorded so much of Your Lordship's Goodness and extensive Love to mankind, that there is no Room left to say more than that I know Nothing to recommend this Work so much as prefixing your Lordship's Name. . . .

Lau. Dermott.

The reference to the year 1740 was to the efforts made by Viscount Mountjoy, before he succeeded to the Earldom of Blesington, in distributing food and coal to the poor people of Dublin and his untiring dedication to alleviating the suffering they endured. Because of this self-imposed commitment he could not spare the time to attend the meetings of the Antients' Grand Lodge in London but willingly allowed himself to be elected as Grand Master (see page 50).

Dermott's approach to the work is contained in the Foreword:

> ... I was fully determined to publish a History of Masonry, whereby I did expect to give the World an uncommon Satisfaction; and in order to enable myself to execute this great Design, I purchased all or most of the Histories, Constitutions, Pocket-Companions, and other Pieces (on that subject) now extant in the *English* Tongue.
>
> My next step was to furnish myself with a sufficient quantity of Pens, Ink and Paper; this being done, I immediately fancied myself an Historian, and intended to trace Masonry not only to *Adam*, in his sylvan Lodge in Paradise, but to give some Account of the Craft even before the Creation: And (as a Foundation) I placed the following Works round about me, so as to be convenient to have Recourse to them as Occasion should require, viz. Doctor *Anderson*, Mr. *Spratt*, directly before me, Doctor *D'Assigny* and Mr. *Smith* on my *Right*-hand, Doctor *Desaguliers* and Mr. *Pennell* on my *Left*-hand, and Mr. *Scott* and Mr. *Lyon* behind me: ...

The *Constitutions* of 'Anderson' (1738 Edn) and 'Spratt' (Dublin 1751) are indicated; 'D'Assigny' implies his *Serious and Impartial Enquiry* ... (Dublin 1744) 'Smith' for his *Pocket Companion*, see pages 34–35 for title page (London 1734 and Dublin 1735); but 'Desaguliers'' numerous publications were mainly scientific and philosophical although, seeing that he was at the heart of Freemasonry in London and no mean influence, it is possible that pamphlets of his were to hand. Pennell compiled Ireland's first book of *Constitutions* (Dublin 1730) which was based entirely upon Anderson. We should now take note of what was written by Chetwode Crawley (*AQC* Vol 12 p 157):

> The Mr. Lyon here associated with Mr. Scott, the publisher, and probably the compiler of *The Pocket Companion* of 1754, is not known to students in the same way as the other authors mentioned. Can it be possible that he is Leon, with his name Anglicized?

The Rabbi Jacob Jehudah Leon (= Lyon) published a broadsheet which described King Solomon's Temple (AD 1641) and exhibited a model of it. Similarly, '*Mr Scott*' could well have meant Gerhard Schott (b 1641–d 1702) who also wrote *The Temple of Solomon* (London 1724) and constructed a model of the temple for exhibition.

Ahiman Rezon contained Laurence Dermott's dissertations on the principles of masonry, the character of those to be considered worthy of initiation, directions on general behaviour, in fact Anderson's influence had come through most of that work; Dermott included the *Old Charges*, and a prayer each for use in lodges which had brethren of the Jewish as well as Christian faiths; General Regulations, both Old and New, in comparative columns, followed by some new ones adopted by the Grand Lodge since inception; Regulations for governing the Grand Charity 'as practised in Ireland, and by York-Masons in England', also printed in comparative columns; ending with a collection of masons' songs which occupied the latter half of the book.

Much speculation has surrounded that unusual title but Dermott's thinking is really shewn by the sub-title '*A Help to a Brother*'. It was an exercise in Hebrew with a display of undue licence afforded to himself, but inspired in a dream which he describes in his Foreword. His whole approach was in accordance with his subtitle; there was no animosity whatsoever against brethren in the jurisdiction of the premier Grand Lodge, indeed, in that early period of the Antients there was just indifference on both sides. Provided that Moderns were prepared to take the appropriate obligation the Antients were quite prepared to accept them. Had he chosen to do so Dermott could have fastened upon a statement made at the Quarterly Communication of the Moderns' Grand Lodge held on 20 March 1755.

> The D:G:M: made a Complaint to the Grand Lodge of the Master & Wardens of the Lodge N.º 94 held at the Ben Johnson's Head in Pelham Street Spital Fields for forming & assembling with other Members of that Lodge under the denomination of a Lodge of Ancient Masons Who as such consider themselves as independent of this Society & not subject to our Laws or the Authority of our Grand Master. When he took Notice of the great Necessity there was to discourage such Meetings not only as the same were contrary to our Laws & particularly that made at the last Q: C. & were also a great Insult on the Grand Master & the whole Body of Free & Accepted Masons. But as they likewise tended to introduce into the Craft the Novelties & Conceits of opiniotative Persons & to create a Belief that there have been other Societies of Masons more Ancient than that of this Ancient & Honourable Society.

The brethren concerned in that incident stated that as they had all met together as private persons and not with the intention of making Masons or otherwise, claimed they had a right so to do; they acknowledged the charge of forming and assembling a lodge of masons. It caused the Deputy Grand Master to move:

> That the consideration of the irregular proceedings of the said Lodge at the Ben Johnson's Head might be postponed till next Q.C. hoping that a thorough Sense of their Misconduct & a Determination not to be Guilty of the like for the future will then appear & reconcile them to the Grand Lodge.

That was 'Ordered Accordingly' but the matter was revived on 24 July when the report included the following:

> The said Master & Wardens thereupon spoke what they thought proper for their Defence which they were ... indulged the Liberty of doing. ... that the Charge against them was unsupported by any Proof & attempted to induce

a Belief that their Meetings complained of were regular & in Consequence of their Constitution from this Society & that those Meetings & the Transactions therein were no Novelties but agreeable to those of this Society & free and open to every Brother. But the Contrary was made to appear by Bror.ˢ Jackson & Pollard who had been refused Admittance at those Meetings until they submitted to be made in their novel & particular Manner under the Denomination of Ancient Masons for which they paid the Expence of the Meeting ...

Those brethren asked that they might be permitted to meet at that venue and in that style but this was immediately defeated in Grand Lodge and they were then required to refrain from such irregularity and to reconcile themselves with the authorities, but that went without effect. The matter ended with Lodge No 94 being erased from the *List of Lodges* and the brethren who continued in those irregular meetings were banned from attending any lodge in that jurisdiction.

Frontispiece of the 2nd edition of Ahiman Rezon *published in 1764. The upper part shows the coat of Arms of the Antient Grand Lodge*

Chapter 9

The Antients and the Moderns

In order to appreciate how mild and amenable was Laurence Dermott in that period, reference must be made to *An Address to the Fraternity* that was included in the 1764 (2nd Edition) issue of *Ahiman Rezon* and all subsequent editions. Contrary to what has so frequently been stated by masonic writers, Laurence Dermott himself bore no animosity towards the Moderns, as such, it was bad feeling that built up between the brethren on each side as the years passed. Dermott spelt out the state of affairs in his *Address*:

> Several eminent Craftsmen residing in Scotland, Ireland and America, and other parts, both abroad and at home, have greatly importuned me to give them some account of what is called Modern Masonry, in London. I cannot be displeased with such importunities, because I had the like curiosity myself in 1748 when I was first introduced into that Society. However before I proceed any further concerning the difference between Antient and Modern, I think it my duty to declare solemnly what I have not the least antipathy to the gentlemen, members of the Modern Society; but, on the contrary, love and respect many of them, because I have found the generality to be worthy of receiving every blessing that good men can ask, or Heaven bestow. I hope that this declaration will acquit me of any design of giving offence, especially if the following queries and answers be rightly considered:
>
> *Quere 1st.* Whether Free-masonry, as practised in ancient Lodges is universal?
> *Answer.* Yes.
> *2d.* Whether what is called Modern Masonry is universal?
> *Ans.* No.
> *3d.* Whether there is any material difference between the Ancient and Modern?
> *Ans.* A great deal; because an Ancient Mason can not only make himself known to his brother, but in case of necessity can discover his very thoughts to him in the presence of a Modern, without being able to distinguish that either of them as Free-masons.
> *4th.* Whether a Modern Mason may, with safety, communicate all his secrets to an Ancient Mason?
> *Ans.* Yes.
> *5th.* Whether an Ancient may, with the like safety, communicate all his secrets to a Modern Mason, without farther ceremony?
> *Ans.* No: for, as a science comprehends an art, though an art cannot comprehend a science, even so Ancient Masonry contains every thing valuable

amongst the Moderns, as well as many other things that cannot be revealed without additional ceremonies.

6th. Whether a person made in a Modern manner, and not after the ancient custom of the Craft, has a right to be called free and accepted, according to the intent and meaning of the words?

Ans. His being unqualified to appear in a Master's Lodge, according to the universal system of Masonry, renders the appelation improper.

7th Whether it is possible to initiate or introduce a Modern Mason into the Royal Arch Lodge (the very essence of Masonry) without making him go through the Ancient ceremonies?

Ans. No.

8th. Whether the present members of Modern Lodges are blameable for deviating so much from the old land-marks?

Ans. No: because the innovation was made in the reign of King George the First, and this new form was delivered to them as orthodox to the present members.

9th. Therefore, as it is natural for each party to maintain the orthodoxy of their Masonic Preceptors, how shall we distinguish the original and most useful system?

Ans. The Number of Ancient Masons abroad, compared with the Moderns, prove the universality of the old Order, and the utility thereof appears, by the love and respect shown to the Brethren, in consequence of their superior abilities in conversing with, and distinguishing the Masons of all countries and denominations, a circumstance peculiar to Ancient Masons.

... Therefore, in order to satisfy the importunity of my good Brethren, particularly the Right Worshipful and very worthy Free-masons of America, who, for their charitable disposition, prudent choice of members, and good conduct in general, deserve the unanimous thanks and applause of the Masonic World., be it known, that the innovation already mentioned, originated on the defection of the Grand Master, Sir Christopher Wren, who, as Dr. Anderson says, neglected the Lodges. The Doctor's assertion is certainly true, and I will endeavour to do justice to the memory of Sir Christopher, ... Notwithstanding this state of inactivity in London, and at York, as well as those in Ireland, kept up their ancient formalities, customs, and usages, without altering, adding or diminishing, to this hour, from whence they may justly be called the Most Ancient, &c.

Dermott quoted an incident when a brother informed his lodge No 3 in London that eight persons were responsible for 'the invention of Modern Masonry' amongst whom was Dr Desaguliers and went on to say:

... From what has been said, it is evident that all unchartered Societies in England are upon equal footing in respect to legality of association.

In this we are to view the fraternities of Ancient and Modern Free-masons, who are now become the two greatest communities in the universe: the Ancients, under the name of Free and Accepted Masons, according to the old Institutions; the Moderns, under the name of Free-masons of England. And although a similarity of names, yet they differ exceedingly in makings, ceremonies, knowledge, Masonic language, and installations; so much, that they always have been, and still continue to be, two distinct societies, totally independent of each other. ...

I shall conclude this with saying, that I hope I shall live to see a general conformity, and universal unity, between the worthy Masons of all denominations. These are the earnest wishes, and ardent prayers, of, Gentlemen and Brethren,

Yours sincere friend, and most obedient
Servant and faithful brother,
LAURENCE DERMOTT.

Laurence Dermott, unfortunately did not live to see those difficulties resolved. In December 1787 he retired from his position as Deputy Grand Master, having been sorely afflicted with attacks of gout. Great tribute was paid to him by his successor who glowingly dwelt upon the forty-seven years of devoted service Dermott had given to the Craft. He died in June 1791 in the parish of St Dunstan in Stepney, but the exact date and the location of his grave are not known. Probate of his last Will and Testament was granted to his widow in London on 15 July 1791 and thus passed from the masonic scene one who had made what was probably the greatest impact of all on the Craft in his time, and for the future benefit of those who were to follow.

Dermott's mention of America was well justified in that Freemasonry had travelled there via the settlers and those brethren in military lodges who carried ambulatory Warrants granted by the various Grand Lodges of Ireland, Scotland, and the Antients in England; Warrants for such purposes were in the minority from the premier Grand Lodge (Moderns) but they did exist. It is now of interest to look at the report of the experience of brethren in Philadelphia, the details of which were placed on record in the *History of Freemasonry in Pennsylvania* by Bros Barratt and Sachse (quoted by John Heron Lepper in *AQC* Vol 56 pp 178–179) a precis of which follows:

> Bro John Blackwood, a former member of Lodge No 2 of the Antients and then a member of No 4 Philadelphia, sent a letter dated 10 January 1758 to the Secretary of No 2 in England and enclosed a petition signed by the Master and twelve members of No 4 Philadelphia, and reported the position which had arisen through their being Antient masons.
>
> 'We the under named having for years past Resided in the City of Philadelphia did form ourselves into a Body, being Antient masons. Descending from our Mother Lodges in England, Ireland and Scotland ... did propose and apply to William Allen Esquire Grand Master of Pennsylvania for a Warrant, which we readily obtained, but upon hearing we were Antients, we were call'd before the Grand Lodge and asked to change our ritual to which we answered that we neither could nor would and we are determined never to forsake the good old way. Whereupon our Warrant was confiscated. Brothers Blackwood and Jones recently arrived from England then suggested that we apply for an Antient Warrant from London.
>
> Enclosed was the Petition to the Earl of Blessington for a Warrant to be granted to them on the ground that the Warrant from the Provincial Grand

Lodge in Pennsylvania had been obtained by the Master who was from Lodge No 183 in Belfast, was an Arch Mason and registered in the books of the Grand Lodge of Ireland, but quite unaware that there were two Grand Lodges in England. They requested Lodge No 2 in London to kindly recommend the petition to Bro Dermott and the Grand Lodge of the Antients.

The petition was granted and Warrant No 69 issued on 7 June 1758; subsequently a Provincial Grand Master over the Antients was appointed for Pennsylvania and from that, eventually, was to develop the flourishing Grand Lodge of Pennsylvania. Grand Lodge Minutes of 2 December 1772 record:

> D.G. Master Dermott laid before this Lodge a certain manuscript attested by B.ᵣ John Wood, G.S. in Philadelphia as the Transactions of the Provincial Grand Lodge of Pennsylvania, commencing on the 30th day of December, 1763, and continued to the 30th April, 1772. Unanimously Agreed and Ordered that a Committee consisting of Grand Officers should take the said Transactions, &c into their serious consideration, and that their judgment upon the whole should be Decisive and final.
>
> *Grand Lodge Minutes* 15 December 1773:
>
> Heard the Answer sent to the Provincial Grand Lodge of Pennsylvania to their Transactions, which was unanimously approved.

Freemasonry in Pennsylvania was in evidence from 1730 as recorded in Benjamin Franklin's *Pennsylvania Gazette* in December of that year:

> As there are several Lodges of Free Masons erected in this Province and people have lately been much amus'd with Conjectures concerning them; we think that the following account of Free Masonry from London will not be inacceptable to our readers.

It must be recorded that Benjamin Franklin produced a facsimile reprint in 1734 of Anderson's first book of *Constitutions*. As brethren under the Moderns' jurisdiction faded somewhat, and the Antients went from strength to strength, it was a natural follow-on that in 1783 came *Ahiman Rezon Abridged and Digested: as a Help to all that are, or would be Free and Accepted Masons, and compiled by Wm. Smith D.D.* This was a revision of the Pennsylvanian *Constitutions* and was based upon Laurence Dermott's *Ahiman Rezon* of 1756.

Chapter 10

Arms of the Grand Lodges

In the 14th century a body of operative stonemasons became known as the Fellowship of Masons and were of such vigour that they appeared before the Mayor and Alderman of London at the Guildhall to settle what might well be termed today 'an industrial dispute'. That body eventually gave rise to the London Masons Company which received a Grant of Arms in 1472, the main motifs of which were:

> a field of Sable, a Chevron of Silver, grailed, three Castles of the same, garnished with doors and windows of the field,
> In the Chevron, a Compass of Black.

The early form did not have a motto or legend, their faith, as indeed was that of all Corporate bodies, Livery Companies and the like, was firmly anchored to the church and plainly expressed in the coat of Arms. By the 17th century the declaration 'In The Lord Is All Our Trust' had been added.

The coat of Arms of the London Masons Company which received a Grant of Arms in 1472

The early form did not have a motto or legend but in the 17th century the dedication 'In the Lord is All Our Trust' had been added

Soon after its formation in 1717 the premier Grand Lodge adopted the Arms of the Masons Company, and the three castles with chevron and compass were soon brought into use in their Seal. There is no record of their entitlement to use those devices but it became time-honoured.

Laurence Dermott is responsible for the adoption of the coat of Arms for the Antients Grand Lodge. It formed the upper part of the frontispiece of the 2nd Edn. of *Ahiman Rezon* published in 1764 (see page 58). In 1775, under the Grand Mastership of the 4th Duke of Atholl, the Arms were approved and then ordered to be used as their Seal. Dermott gave a full account of how it happened:

The free masons arms in the upper part of the frontispiece of this book, was found in the collection of the famous and learned hebrewist, architect and brother, Rabi, Jacob Jehudah Leon. This gentleman at the request of the states of Holland, built a model of Solomon's temple. The design of this undertaking was to build a temple in Holland, but upon surveying the model it was adjudged that the united provinces were not rich enough to pay for it; whereupon the States generously bestowed the model upon the builder, notwithstanding they had already paid his demand, which was very great. This model was exhibited to public view (by authority) at Paris and Vienna, and afterwards in London, by a patent under the great seal of England, and signed Killigrew in the reign of King Charles the Second. At the same time, Jacob Judah Leon published a description of the tabernacle and the temple, and dedicated it to his Majesty, and in the years 1759 and 1760 I had the pleasure of perusing and examining both these curiosities. The arms are emblazoned thus, quarterly per squares, countercharged Vert. In the first quarter Azure a lyon rampant Or, in the second quarter Or, an ox passant sable; in the third quarter Or, a man with hands erect, proper robed, crimson and ermin; in the fourth quarter Azure, an eagle displayed, Or. Crest, the holy ark of the Covenant, proper, supported by Cherubims. Motto, Kodes la Adonai, i.e., Holiness to the Lord. To this I beg leave to add what I have read concerning these arms.

'The learned Spencer says, the Cherubims had the face of a man, the wings of an eagle, the back and mane of a lion, and the feet of a calf. *De Legib. Hebr, lib* 3. *diss:* 5 *ch.* 2.'

'The prophet Ezekiel says, they had four forms, a man, a lion, an ox, and an eagle.'

'When the Israelites were in the wilderness, and encamped in four cohorts, the standard of the tribe of Judah carried a lion, the tribe of Ephraim an ox, the tribe of Ruben a man, and the tribe of Dan an eagle; those four standards composed a Cherubim; therefore God chose to sit upon Cherubims bearing the forms of those animals, to signify that he was the leader and king of the cohorts of the Israelites. *Trad of the Heb.*'

'Bochart says, that they represented the nature and ministry of angels, by the lion's form is signified their strength, generosity and majesty, by that of the ox their constancy and assiduity in executing the commands of God; by their human shape their humanity and kindness, and by that of the eagle, their agility and speed. *Bochart de animal sacr. P. 1*'

'As these were the arms of the masons that built the tabernacle and the temple, there is not the least doubt of their fraternity of free and accepted masons, and the continued practice, formalities and tradition, in all regular lodges, from the lowest degree to the most high, i.e., The Holy Royal Arch, confirms the truth hereof.' (pp. xxxiv–xxxvi).

In a definitive Paper on the Rabbi Leon and his works (*AQC* Vol 12 pp 150–163) Chetwode Crawley stated:

> Few learned men have enjoyed such a complicated variety of aliases as Rabbi Jehudah Leon, or Arje, or Arye, or Leonitius, or Templo, or Hispanus. His Hebrew cognomen, variously rendered on the Continent as Leo, Leon and Leonitius, and in England as Lion or Lyon ...

and in a comment supporting that Paper Bro. Hughan stated that he had been fortunate to trace a thin octavo pamphlet, published in 1778, with the title *An Accurate Desctription of the GRAND and GLORIOUS TEMPLE of SOLOMON ... by that celebrated Architect, Jacob Juda Lyon in the year MDCXLIII. Translated by M.P. Decastro (Proprietor of the said Model and a near relation to the Author)*. The work was introduced as follows:

> The following Treatise ... translated into English from the original, composed by that very learned and great Architect, J. Juda Lyon, (Hebrew) printed in the years 1642, 1643 and 1669, the Inventor and Maker of the model of the said Temple ... which may be seen at No. 1 Gun Square, Houndsditch. The model of which I have in my Possession, made all of wood, with its appendages, being three feet and a half long, from East to West, seven feet wide from North to South, and one foot and a half high.

Dr Crawley's surmise that 'Mr. Lyon' was the Rabbi Leon was happily established, the link of 'Scott' with Schott cannot be so well defined; but his model of the temple being on display in the years 1729 and 1730, and his treatise printed in London in 1724, is a parallel that cannot be dismissed.

The vision of Ezekiel had perhaps inspired Rabbi Leon in the construction of the coat of Arms and a painted board came into the possession of W. H. Rylands about the year 1882 which has been attributed to that period. The addition of the Hebrew characters and the legend 'Holiness to the Lord' was presumably the responsibility of Dermott who allowed himself full indulgence with Hebrew, not always with the accuracy necessary to his wishes; one can only say that his spirit was willing! He was, of course, stretching our credulity to state they were 'the arms of the masons who built the tabernacle and the temple' – but life in that period was founded upon legend, tradition, and fanciful notions.

When the two Grand Lodges joined together in 1813 under the *Articles of Union* and thus became The United Grand Lodge of England, the coat of Arms adopted was a combination from the two sides. The Grant of Arms in the new form was formally approved a century later (in 1919) that matter having been rather neglected until then; the eight lions were added to the border of the shield in 1933 their purpose being to commemorate the completion and dedication of Freemasons' Hall, London, as the Masonic Peace Memorial to those freemasons who gave their lives during the Great War 1914–1918.

When the two Grand Lodges were united in 1813 the coat of Arms was a combination from the two sides. The eight lions were added to the border in 1933 to commemorate the completion and dedication of Freemasons' Hall, London

Chapter 11

An Unrecorded Grand Lodge

On 5 May 1905 Bro Henry Sadler gave a Paper entitled 'An Un-recorded Grand Lodge' to Quatuor Coronati Lodge and brought to notice for the first time particulars of a Grand Lodge which arose in London in 1770.

The sparse details available were published in *AQC* Vol 18 part 2, pp 69-90 and Bro Sadler was highly praised for that dis-covery and his further contribution to masonic history. Although this Grand Lodge had no great effect on the course of the future of organised Freemasonry, a few extracts from this Paper will be of interest. Apparently the seeds of dissension were sown as early as 1759 in the Antients Grand Lodge as shewn by the Minutes of December 5:

> M[r] William Dickey, Sen[r] and M[r] Charles Stuart of N[o] 9 were nominated for the Jun[r] Warden's Chair, when the Poll appeared thus, For M[r] William Dickey 30, For Cha[s] Stuart 18. Many disagreeable altercations arose from B[r] Cha[s] Stuart and friends on account of his not being chosen G. Warden, and some of the disputants declar'd that the members of N[o] 9 shou'd never pay another shilling into the Grand Charity.

The Warrant for Lodge No 9 had been purchased by members of No 59 the majority of whom appear to have been Scots. Dues to Grand Lodge were paid up to March 1761 after which date no returns were made and it was erased. However, the lodge did not cease working for many brethren are shewn as 'visitor from No 9' in the records of Lodge No 12 which also had many Scottish names in the membership. On 13 June 1770 Lodge No 12 received a letter from No 59 inviting them to dine on St John's Day. Also, their Minutes state that on the 8 August the lodge 'had the honour of a visit from the Worshipful Master of No 9 and the Worshipful Mas-ter of No 59'. The Minutes for the remaining part of 1770 and up to August 1771 were available and were duly published by Bro Sadler from which the following extracts are of interest here:

Sep.^{t} 12th 1770, Being Regular Lodge night, the Master present, Wardens absent. Bro.^{r} Cowie Passed and raised, rec'd a visit from ye Worshipful Masters of No. 9 & 59, Bro.^{r} Grieg of No. 9 and B^{ro}. Gibson of No. 59. Open'd at Seven, closed in harmony. At ye same time rec'd Proposals from No. 9 for forming a Grand Lodge which was agree'd to by ye members present.

Feb.^{t} 20th 1771 ... Received a visit from the Grand Lodge. At the same time the Lodge was honoured with a Constitution from the Supreme Grand Lodge under the Name of St. David's, London.

June 24th, 1771, Being St. John's day, Master and Wardens and other Brethren of this Lodge went and dined at Chelsea with the Supreme Grand Lodge and the Lodges under their Constitution, Where the officers of this Lodge were Install'd.

It is worthy of note that on the 24 June 1771 the Antients Grand Lodge dined at the Half Moon in Cheapside to commemorate the Festival of St. John which shows that the breakaway was complete.

Among the comments on Bro Sadler's Paper the point was made by Bro W. J. Hughan that the terms 'Grand Lodge' and 'Grand Master' were often loosely applied when reference was being made to what was no more than a private lodge and its Master, but, this actually was a Grand Lodge formed on 12 September 1770 by:

> ... three or more ancient or Atholl Lodges, in the Lodge of No. 12, at the suggestion of No. 9 with No. 59 also participating. Warrants were issued to the subordinate Lodges early in the following year, as No. 12 received its Charter in February 1771, and selected the name of St. David. St. John's Festival *in Winter*, 1770, was celebrated by the Grand Lodge visiting No. 12 aforesaid, and St. John's *in Summer*, 1771, was observed at Chelsea by this Organisation with 'the Lodges under its Constitution'. The Grand Lodge did not last long for in 1775 its members apparently gave up the struggle, the St David's (old No 12) joining the Antients once more as No 193 (being now St Thomas's No 142) three others falling into line as Nos 194, 195, and 198 (being now respectively Middlesex No 143, Lodge of Prudent Brethren No 145, and Lodge of Justice No 147 who hold the second issue of that Warrant).

It was not unusual for brethren to change sides and an Antient lodge would sometimes petition for a Moderns' Warrant and *vice versa*, here we have details of a petition from brethren who may have had their feet in two or even three camps. The petition was addressed to Lord Petre Grand Master of the Moderns 1772–1776, the Deputy GM Rowland Holt (1775–1786), Grand Wardens and the rest of the Grand Officers, and was worded:

> That your Petitioners are Desireous of Becoming under your patronage as Brethren of your Honble. Society willing to contribute towards your fund of Charity and to answer all dues and demands whatsoever from your Grand Lodge whenever & at all Times demanded of us. We do therefore hope you will be pleased to grant us your Warrant for the same, we have several worthy Brethren Under your authority who have joined us, to wit B^{r} Willm Shepperd of Oxford Street as Master, B^{r} Ja^{s} Hamilton as Sr Warden and B^{r} James

Wilson, J^r Warden, who will take upon themselves in behalf of us to act according to your forms and ceremonies as becoming Men and Masons the granting of which your Petitioners for ever wishing of you health and felicity and Brotherly Love as in duty bound will ever pray.'

St. Andrews Lodge, Feb. 14, 1776

Intend meeting First Friday in every month.

Signed by the Master, Senior and Junior Wardens Elect,

Willm Shepperd, Master Elected

Br^o James Hamilton, Senr Warden elected

James Wilson, Junr Warden elected.

as petitioners *already under your authority* [author's italics]

We the under subscribing petitioners and late members of the Lodge have renounc'd the authority of and never intend to have any further connexion with the former Grand Lodge as witness our hands. [then follows eleven signatures]

The St. Andrew's Lodge is held at Br. Andrew Wilson's the Coach and Horses in Little Queen Anne Street East, the corner of Edward Street Portland Chaple St. Marylebone in the County of Middlesex. Br^o Andrew Wilson is a member and was made a Mason at ye Lodge of Relief with Truth held at ye Coach and Horses High Holborn many years ago.

We the undermentioned Masters of ye several Lodges, Near our B^r Wilson, have signed our Names, being desireous and willing to extend our Society well knowing the same will not affect our respective Lodges.

D. Taylor, Master of the Tyrian Lodge No. 5

Wm Adams, Master of the Cumberland Lodge

Willm Shepperd, P. Master Tyrian Lodge

Thos. Tiffin, a Brother of the Lodge of Truth at The Cock, Margaret Street.

F. I'Anson, of ditto

And^w Wilson, member of ye Coach & Horses Holborn

Jno Moore, member of ye Tyrian Lodge No. 5

So ended a previously unrecorded 'Supreme Grand Lodge' the details of which came to light through the diligent research of Henry Sadler, a Master of Quatuor Coronati Lodge, a librarian at Freemasons' Hall, a Grand Tyler, a Grand Janitor, and noted masonic historian.

Chapter 12

'Re-making' From One to Another

So far as brethren under either Antients or Moderns jurisdiction were concerned, in the early period, there was little evidence of partisanship, and friendship proved to be the stronger element which often occasioned a brother to change sides, as it were. Certificates might well be held by a brother from both Grand Lodges thus supplying the respectability that would be called for on visiting in an unknown locality. The official attitude, however, came to a head in 1777 when the premier Grand Lodge at a Quarterly Communication held on April 18 resolved:

> THAT the Persons who assemble in London and Elsewhere in the character of Masons, calling themselves 'Ancient Masons' by virtue of an Authority from a Pretended Grand Lodge in England, and at present said to be Under the Patronage of the Duke of Athol, are not to be countenanced or Acknowledged as Masons by any Regular Lodge or Masons under the Constitution of England; nor shall any Regular Mason be present at any of their Conventions to give Sanction to their Proceedings, under the Penalty of forfeiting the Privileges of this Society, neither shall any Person Initiated at these Irregular Meetings be admitted into any Lodge without being re-Made and paying the usual Making Fees. Resolved THAT this Censure shall not extend to any Lodge or Mason Made in Scotland or Ireland under the Constitution of either of these Kingdoms, or to any Lodge or Mason Made abroad Under the Patronage of any Foreign Grand Lodge in Alliance with the Grand Lodge of England, but that such Lodges and Masons shall be deemed Regular and Constitutional.

The premier Grand Lodge had thus declared that Regularity and Recognition were synonymous as indeed were Irregularity and Non-Recognition whether in or out of England. The cleavage was practised by extremists on both sides but honour was quite easily satisfied in the re-making process that was also practised everywhere on both sides; the following instances are but examples of that common practice:

Grenadiers Lodge (Moderns) now No 66 11 June 1766
> Br. Cann proposed Mr. Will. Graham to be Re-made a Mason from ye Ancient to ye Moderns in this Lodge which was agreed to nem con.

In 1764 that lodge had approved a by-law stating:

> If any gentleman who is an Antient Mason and desires to be remaid and rais'd a modern MASON in this LODGE must pay for the same ten shillings and Sixpence.

Lodge of Antiquity (Time Imemorial) now No 2 11 March 1767:

> It was proposed by the R.W.M. that Gentlemen who have been duly made Irish or York Masons may be made Masons under the English Constitution in all the three Degrees in this Lodge at the Expense of One Guinea only, which was the Unanimous opinion of the Brethren present.

Earlier, on 12 February 1754 the members had adopted:

> A Motion was made not to admit any Brother that is not a Member of a Regular Constituted Lodge without paying Two Shillings for his Visit, and a by law agreed upon to be Made accordingly.

The general behaviour of that lodge, however, may well be classified as 'Traditioner' for it paid dues and 'supported' the premier Grand Lodge but did not practise all of the forms that had been adopted, innovated, or neglected by their governing body. It should be noted that the term 'Irish Masons' used above was often applied to the Antients. Their affinity with the Old Lodge at York and its subordinates is an example of coming events casting shadows beforehand as we will see in due course.

From a countless number of instances of the re-making from Modern to Antient here are two:

Neptune Lodge (Antient) now No 22   24 June 1754

> Lodge open'd at two—at Noon being at the Festival of St. John. Call'd off to Refreshment at three. Call'd on in order to make Bro.: Robert Whitehall an Antient Mason, he being a Modern Mason before. Made him in all parts. Master enstall'd & Wardens. Call'd of the Second time to Refreshment. Call'd on to work. Clos'd at 10 with good harmony.

Enoch Lodge (Antients) now No 11   11 March 1771

> Mr. Moses Meyers sent a Forring [sic] Certificate and was proposed by Bro. Chas. Bearblock, if he was Modern, to become an Antient Mason—after Examination he being found a Modern was by consent of the Lodge made an Antient, the Lodge being first moved accordingly, and paid 10s. 6d. for his dues.

Whilst the re-making process did not qualify for membership of the lodge involved in that task, it did enable the brother to become registered with the Grand Lodge and to receive the appropriate Certificate on payment; many lodges supplied a statement in certificate form as evidence. Having a foot in each camp did not remain with brethren, for some lodges even held a Warrant from each Grand Lodge. The classic example of all, one might even class it as a switch in mid-stream, is provided in a letter from Thomas Dunckerley, Provincial Grand Master of Hampshire (among others) to the Grand Secretary William White on 8 August 1792 here is the relevant extract:

> ... At the request of the Corporation of Southampton I laid the first Stone of All Saint's Church in that Town last Friday, for which purpose I had summoned the Lodges of the County to attend. I have the pleasure to acquaint you that a Lodge of *Antient* Masons of Southampton, near 60 in number, requested to join ye Procession which I refused, unless they would come under the authority of our Grand Lodge. In two hours time I received their Petition for a Constitution, and immediately granted them a dispensation ...

We are indebted to Henry Sadler for his research on that incident. He commented that the capture of that lodge was highly gratifying to Dunckerley who had for some years tried to wean it from its allegiance. It is possible that Dunckerley's report on the subject may have been magnified because the Minutes of that Lodge for their meeting on 2 August 1792 contain:

> ... To consider the propriety of accepting an offer from Bro. Dunckerley of giving us a dispensation to hold a lodge under the disration [sic] of his Royal Highness the Prince of Wales, and on ballotting for the purpose, there appeared for it eleven; against it four.

At a subsequent meeting attended by twelve brethren it was agreed to 'Petition Br. Dunckerley for a Warrant of Constitution, which request he was pleased to comply with, and the sum of £5. 15s was paid into his hands for that purpose.' On the 17th September it was recorded: 'Br. Thos. Dunckerley then read the Warrant of Constitution & the Lodge was accordingly constituted under the name of the Royal Gloucester Lodge under the sanction of H.R.H. the Prince of Wales. After which the necessary Charges and regulations were read by order of the Prov. G.M. from the book of Constitutions. ... Br. Dunckerley then proposed himself & Br. Grierson to become members of this lodge ...'

It is of some interest to note that when Laurence Dermott was appointed Deputy Grand Master his successor as Grand Secretary in 1771 was William Dickey who had been initiated in the Antients Lodge No 14 in June 1765. But, in the records of Lebeck's Head Lodge No 246 on the Moderns' Register we find the following entry on 21 March 1766:

> Br. Lownie proposed Mr. Wm. Dickey Junr. and Mr. James Burn to be made modern masons of in this lodge which was Firsted and seconded, and they went through the three Regular degrees.

The expressions used for re-making varied from 'apostatised', 'translated', 'healed' or 'from the other Grand Lodge'.

A directive on the amount to be charged was issued by the Antients Grand Lodge on 29 September 1785:

> The proper Sum for Making Modern Masons Antient was carried in the

Majority to be one pound one shilling and a fine lay'd on each Warrant if not strictly observed the sum of one pound one shilling.

It is on record that some lodges charged up to double that amount.

We should now take notice of the arrival in London of William Preston, who joined a lodge under the Antients jurisdiction, switched to the Moderns, and became a joining member of Lodge of Antiquity which has been classified as Traditioner; with such a wide coverage even that was not enough because, due to a personality clash and a petty incident that was blown up out of all proportion, Preston and his supporters from that Time Immemorial lodge set up yet another Grand Lodge that was to last for ten years approximately before the breach could be healed.

Chapter 13

William Preston

William Preston was responsible for yet another Grand Lodge to come into existence in London, but before dealing with that it is proper that we learn something of the man who set such a mark upon the pattern of Freemasonry.

Preston was born on 20 July 1742 in Edinburgh where his father, a Greek and Latin scholar, was in practice as 'Writer to the Signet' [=lawyer]. William's education followed in similar manner but his father suffered a financial set-back and ill-health followed. When his father died Preston's tutor became his guardian. In due course he was apprenticed to a printing firm in Edinburgh where his talent was given ample scope with the advantage of further education with his patron and family.

In 1760 he travelled to London equipped with letters of recommendation and introduction and was given employment with the firm of William Strahan, 'The King's Printer', with whom he maintained a connection for the rest of his life. Another employee there was John Noorthouck, the son of a well-known London bookseller of Dutch origin, who some years later was to edit the fifth book of *Constitutions* for the premier Grand Lodge, but quarrelled with Preston causing an incident to grow out of all proportion from which the next Grand Lodge was to arise.

Soon after his arrival in London Preston met a number of fellow-Scots who were anxious to form a masonic lodge and had applied for a Warrant from the Grand Lodge of Scotland. They pointed out that such a grant would be an infringement upon territorial boundaries but referred them to the Grand Lodge of the Antients, showing that the liaison between them was stronger in character than with the Moderns. A Dispensation to meet as a lodge was granted and they met at the White Hart in the Strand and although the records are obscure it is usually accepted that Preston was their second Initiate, on 20 April 1763, and then the lodge was formally Constituted by Grand Officers and given No 111 on the Register of the Antients. Shortly afterwards Preston and some of the members joined a lodge meeting at the Talbot Inn nearby in the Strand which was under the Moderns jurisdiction. It resulted in dissatisfaction with the status of the Antients Grand Lodge and they persuaded the other members of No 111 to transfer from the Antients to the Moderns with the result that the lodge was Constituted for a second time and to take the name of The Caledonian Lodge with Warrant No 325 on the Register of the premier Grand Lodge; it still exists today under that name but as No 134 on the Register of the United Grand Lodge of England.

William Preston Past Master of the Lodge of Antiquity and author of
Illustrations of Masonry

Preston became absorbed in the collection of masonic lecture material which was scattered and disconnected, or perhaps one might even say unconnected, for he did considerable work in collecting and collating. He was an undoubted master of that subject, because of his natural talent and retentive memory, and constructed versions which were imparted at his sessions of instruction.

ILLUSTRATIONS

OF

MASONRY.

By WILLIAM PRESTON,

PAST MASTER OF THE LODGE OF ANTIQUITY,

ACTING BY IMMEMORIAL CONSTITUTION.

> The man, whofe mind on virtue bent,
> Purfues fome greatly good intent
>   With undiverted aim ;
> Serene, beholds the angry crowd,
> Nor can their clamours, fierce and loud,
>   His ftubborn honour tame.   BLACKLOCK.

THE TWELFTH EDITION,

WITH CONSIDERABLE ADDITIONS.

LONDON:

PRINTED FOR G. WILKIE, N° 57, PATERNOSTER-ROW.

1812.

Preston first published his Illustrations of Masonry *in 1772. It was commended by Sanction of the Grand Master, his Deputy, the Wardens and Grand Secretary*

On 21 May 1772 he held a Gala meeting which attracted the approval of eminent leaders in the craft and in that year published his *Illustrations of Masonry* which carried the sanction of Lord Petre, the Grand Master, his Deputy, the Wardens, and Grand Secretary stating, '... we having perused the said book, and finding it to correspond with the ancient practices of this Society, do recommend the same'. By 1775 he had instituted a system of lectures and tuition and in presenting his prospectus with the 2nd Edition he stated:

> No Society ever subsisted which [was] raised on a better principle or more solid foundation than Free-Masonry ... It is indeed true, that in some Lodges the Work of Masonry is much neglected, and little or no regard shown to the fundamental principles of the Society; arising partly from inexperience and partly from the inability of those Brethren who have the honour to preside over them ... Thus men of letters have been discouraged from pursuing a study which might otherwise have proved of public utility; by giving sanction to the Society, and employing their genius in the elucidation of Mysteries, the greatest Monarchs have not been ashamed to countenance. As the neglect is owing, in a great measure to a want of method, which a little application might easily remedy Brother Preston is induced to offer his assistance to all regular masons desirous of making progress in the Art ... If Brother Preston succeeds in his expectations of giving his Brethren a just idea of Masonry, or promoting a uniformity in the Lodges under the English Constitution, he will be perfectly happy in the attempt he has made ...

Many brethren were attracted to his Courses which were given three times per week, but it courted opposition grounded in jealousy on the one hand but charged with 'innovation' on the other. Nevertheless his work brought scattered material together and was thus made available to all. During his lifetime the book reached twelve editions, but printing continued afterwards under the editorship of Stephen Jones (his nephew by marriage) and later on by Rev George Oliver to the seventeenth edition. It was reissued in other countries and achieved such status that it was presented to Initiates and, at that time, took its place alongside the book of *Constitutions*.

Preston was engaged by James Heseltine, Grand Secretary, to assist in re-arranging the General Regulations of the Craft and in revising foreign and country correspondence. That task led to his appointment as Assistant to the Grand Secretary in 1769 at an annual salary of £20. He rendered invaluable service in that position but resigned at the end of 1777. During that period he also prospered in the business of the printing firm of William Strahan—'The King's Printer'—upon whose death he received an Annuity of £30 for life. He then took up position of chief reader and superintendent for the son Andrew Strahan who succeeded to the business.

Preston joined several lodges and filled the Chair to the credit of each one and Noorthouck, who had received an Annuity of £20 a year on the death of William Strahan, introduced him to the Time Immemorial Lodge of Antiquity to rescue it from its flagging state. He joined on 1 June 1774 and at the next meeting two weeks later was elected Master in succession to James Bottomley. Under Preston's mastership the prosperity of the lodge was soon restored as he was so well supported through his system of instruction. Later that caused Noorthouck to complain to Grand Lodge in the following terms:

> Brother Preston after being not only admitted but honour'd with the Master's Chair, crowded in such a succession of young masons, as totally transferred all the power of the Lodge to him and his new acquaintances and enabled him to keep possession of the Master's Chair for three years and a half ... During this time Bro. Preston kept up private weekly meetings of these young Brethren, under the name of a Lodge of Instruction, in which meetings, he occasionally as your memorialists have been informed propagated matters of peculiar original powers residing in their Lodge, exempt from the authority of the Grand Lodge, pretensions of which your Memorialists and the other Old Members of the Lodge before entertain'd any idea. . . .

In his study of William Preston (*AQC* 41 pp 163–184) Gordon Hills remarked:

> It strikes one as less than generous that Brother Preston would be blamed for holding the Mastership during a period of three and a half happy and prosperous years when his predecessor, Brother Bottomley, had occupied the Chair for an exactly similar period under the depressed circumstances then prevailing in the Lodge.

and that seems to say it all!

Thus was built up within that lodge the strong support for Preston and the two or three senior members perhaps activated through jealousy. His talent, his powers of memory for ritual, his tuition at his lodges of Instruction, his construction and the Working of his Lectures, brought about two factions the one in wholehearted support and the other opposed to his methods. It came to a head by the end of 1777 and the partition resulted in two lodges of Antiquity, a completely untenable circumstance which brought the expulsion of Preston and his supporters from the premier Grand Lodge on 29 January 1779. It was to last ten years which was the duration of the next Grand Lodge which they formed under the patronage of the Old Lodge at York, the Grand Lodge of All England, and chose to call themselves The Grand Lodge of England South of the River Trent. The choice of title may have been influenced by the division instituted by the College of Arms as a convenient boundary for their administration. Let us now see how that came into existence.

Thomas Dunckerley (1724–1795) Past Grand Warden

Chapter 14

The Grand Lodge
South of the River Trent

On 27 December 1777 Preston in company with some of the brethren of Antiquity attended a St John's Day service at St Dunstan's
Church in Fleet Street to hear the sermon by their Chaplain. They
put on their masonic clothing in the vestry and sat together in the
church. At the end of the service they were due to return to the
Mitre Tavern where the lodge was held their short journey across
the road was recorded in Preston's words:

> ... We accordingly returned to the Tavern in jewels and clothing as
> representatives of the Lodge, preceded by the Beadles but without any formal
> procession as Masons.

Noorthouck and Bottomley were not present but together with two
of their supporters they submitted a Memorial to Grand Lodge
regarding this 'flagrant outrage against the Laws and Constitution
of Masonry' and stated that:

> Bro. Preston contrary to his duty as a Mason, justified public processions
> in a long confused harangue; claiming an inherent power in the Lodge, to act
> in such affairs independent of the regulations made by Grand Lodge, and
> asking why we should go to the Grand Lodge for a power we had in our-
> selves ...

At the next meeting of Antiquity on 7 January 1778 a letter was
read from Bro Noorthouck charging Preston with those 'recent
unwarrantable Proceedings' stating that 'it was a rash and gross
violation of the Constitutions' and further described Preston as
having an 'eager fondness for the Trappings and parade of Masonry is but too apt to get the better of his knowledge'. It was a
personal attack with the walk across Fleet Street in regalia as the
excuse. Preston replied that such abuse was unexpected and he
hoped undeserved and justified his action by claiming that an inherent right was vested in the lodge by virtue of it being 'Time
Immemorial' and it was not in the power of Grand Lodge to
deprive them of that right. He sent a counter-letter of circumstance

to Grand Lodge which caused them to have to consider the problem through the Committee of Charity, the forerunner of what
eventually became the Board of General Purposes. Preston was
asked to make a public withdrawal of his claim and because he
refused to do so was warned that expulsion was inevitable. Within
a week, at the next Quarterly Communication of Grand Lodge
Preston produced a written statement 'confessing his error' affirm-
ing that he had 'no sinister intention in view'. After a lengthy
discussion Preston was required to sign an apology withdrawing
the 'inherent right' assertion. All this and subsequent controversial
incidents connected with it had but one effect; the lodge was div-
ided but each claiming itself to be Antiquity Lodge.

Noorthouck named Preston and his supporters as 'formentors
of disturbance in the Lodge' and at the next meeting Preston and
his colleagues voted to expel Noorthouck and two of his associates
from the lodge. They immediately appealed to Grand Lodge who
ordered their re-instatement which caused Preston and his supporters to pass the following Resolution on 4 November 1778:

> That the Officers of the Lodge of Antiquity do not any more attend the
> meetings of the Grand Lodge and do withdraw themselves from the said
> Society.

Four days later both sections of the lodge met at the Mitre Tavern,
but in separate rooms. Preston's group had the furniture, jewels
and equipment and they decided to move to the Queen's Arms
Tavern in St Paul's Church Yard and to transfer the furniture
forthwith. That removal is described in the Minutes that were
taken by Noorthouck's section of the Lodge and recorded thus:

> This juncto of apostates, waiting for the deadliest hour of the night, as the
> season best suited to acts of perfidy and rapine; with the assistance of some
> desperados from a press gang, most outrageously carried off all the furniture,
> the joint property of the whole lodge, in three or four coaches.

Bro G. Y. Johnson in his Prestonian Lecture for 1947 commented:
'There was more truth in this florid language than one might sup-
pose, as two members of Preston's lodge were Officers in the Press
Gang.'

During the past few months Preston had been in communication with the Grand Secretary of the York Grand Lodge and had
printed his full account of the affair under the title *State of Facts*
(Being a Narrative of some late Proceedings in the Society of Freemasons Respecting William Preston) an 88 page pamphlet, and
issued a lengthy *MANIFESTO* (see Appendix C). The following
sequence of extracts from Minutes of *Old Dundee Lodge* (Moderns)
make interesting reading in that connection:

1779, Jan. 4. The R.W.M. presented the Manifesto of the Lodge of Antiquity to be Read which was put up and seconded and thirded To be postponed till the next Lodge Night.

Jan. 28. Br. Nath. Allen proposed That the Memorial from the Lodge of Antiquity be *Not Read* by the Master but lye [sic] on the Table for the perusal of any Brother that Chuses [sic] which was 2nd and 3rd and carried.

1779, March 11. At a Meeting of the Quarterly Communication held at Free Masons Hall 29th Jany. 1779, It was Resolved Unanimously That John Wilson of Furnivals Inn [Attorney at Law], Samuel Bass [Doorkeeper at ye Opera House], Benjn. Bradley of Clements Inn [Merchant], James Donaldson [Linen Draper], John Sealy of Austin Friars [Attorney's Clerk], Thomas Shipton of St. Thomas, Southwark [Fellmonger], Daniel Nantes of Fenchurch Street [Merchant's Clerk], Gilbert Buchanan [Merchant's Clerk], Samuel Goddard and—Lloyd [in the Impress Service on board the Nightingale Tender, Tower Wharf], and William Preston [Journeyman Printer]; the above-named Persons be expelled the Grand Lodge; Bro. Joshua Kitson [W.M. 1776] proposed That their Names be written on a Paper and pasted on a Board and hung on the Door on a Lodge Night, 2nd and 3rd, and carried. Business being over the Lodge was closed in due Form.

It would appear that the first approach to York Grand Lodge was through a visit to Antiquity by Jacob Bussey the Grand Secretary and in the discussion a request to be satisfied regarding the York Grand Lodge claim to have existed previous to the formation of the premier Grand Lodge in London in 1717. It produced the letter, regarding the list of Grand Masters shown in their Minute Book commencing in 1705 and ending in 1734, and the letter ended:

> ... I have intimated to this Lodge what passed between us of your intention to apply for a Constitution under it and have the satisfaction to inform you that it met with universal approbation. You will therefore be pleased to furnish me with a petition to be presented for the purpose specifying the Names of the Brethren to be appointed to the several Offices, and I make no doubt that the matter will be speedily accomplished. ... Jacob Bussey, G.S. (29 Sept. 1778)

It drew from Bradley the following:

> ... the information it gives is very satisfactory to me and all the other friends of York Grand Lodge ... As to a petition for a Constitution for a private Lodge here we cannot think of it as we are all at present Members of a Lodge whose Constitution is universally allow'd to be IMMEMORIAL and which nothing can invalidate but a violation of the principles of Masonry and the rules of the Institution, which I hope will never happen. ... A Warrant or Deputation from York to a few Members of the R.W. Lodge of Antiquity to Act as a Grand Lodge for that part of England South of the Trent with a power of constituting Lodges in that Division when properly applied for ... The following are the names of the Brethren I could wish to have specified in the Warrant or Deputation should the Grand Lodge think proper to grant one, viz:

John Wilson Esq (present Rt. W. Master of the Lodge of Antiquity as R.W. Grand Master)

William Preston (Present Rt. W. Past Master ditto as W. Dep. Grand Master)

Benjamin Bradley (present Rt. W. Junr. Warden of ditto as W. Senior Grand Warden)

Gilbert Buchanan (present Secretary to ditto as W. Junior Grand Warden)

John Sealy (present Steward of ditto as Grand Secretary) and two other Brethren whom we may appoint here after, out of the said Lodge.

On the 19 October 1778 the unanimous consent for a deputed authority to act as a Grand Lodge in London and for that part of England South of the River Trent was sent, but with the following conditions:

1st. That the Grand Lodge at York receive an annual acknowledgement for this deputed authority.

2nd. That every Constitution to be granted under this sanction be registered in the Books of the Grand Lodge at York, for which some consideration will also be expected.

We are happy to repose this trust in men whose abilities we admire ... We act upon the same plan, we treat with you in a Confidential Manner as Brethren, and to convince you we have no sinister mercenary views, we leave it to yourselves to fix the sums to be paid to the Mother Lodge as well for the annual acknowledgements as for each Constitution. ...

Those conditions were not acceptable and upon receipt of the objection were readily withdrawn. On 3 April 1779 Jacob Bussey was authorised to go to London with The Constitution for the Grand Lodge of Free and Accepted Masons of England South of the River Trent and hand it over to the Lodge of Antiquity. It gave due recognition in the words:

... We do give and grant unto them (Independent of the Power and Authority which they already possess as a private Lodge of Masons acting by an Immemorial Constitution) full power and authority at all times here after to assemble as a Grand Lodge of free and accepted Masons. ... (See Appendix D)

The first meeting of the new Grand Lodge was advertised in the *Morning Post* for 21 June 1779 which stated that the Installations would take place on St John's Day at the Queen's Arms Taverns. Thirty-four brethren were present and John Wilson Master of Antiquity was installed as Grand Master. Amongst the named Officers were six Grand Stewards including William Preston; no self aggrandisement could be levelled against him in the venture. At the meeting it was stated by the new Grand Master that two lodges had applied for Warrants of Constitution and that the ceremonies would take place 'at such time as would be most convenient for himself and his Officers'. They were the only known Warrants granted—Perfect Observance No 1 and Perseverance and Triumph

No 2. Later that year William Preston was appointed Grand Orator and the following year Deputy Grand Master but it would seem that his was a token acceptance of that position. Records of their meetings are sparse and Preston was disillusioned by it all. He tendered his resignation on 17 October 1781 'in order to devote more time to his literary pursuits but a few years later his attendance at the other half of Antiquity was a prelude to a happy ending; it paved the way for a suitable apology to Grand Lodge on behalf of himself and his brethren and in 1790 Antiquity was re-united, although by that time Noorthouck and Bottomley's section of it had wilted. Of this reinstatement Preston wrote:

> ... I rejoice in the opportunity which the proceedings of the grand feast in 1790 have afforded, of promoting harmony, by restoring to the privileges of the Society all the brethren of the Lodge of Antiquity who had been falsely accused and expelled in 1779. By the operation of our professed principles, and through the mediation of a true friend to genuine Masonry, the late William Birch Esq., Past Master of the Lodge of Antiquity, unanimity was happily restored; the manifesto published by that in 1779 revoked; and the Master and Wardens of that ancient association, the first lodge under the English Constitution, resumed their seats in Grand Lodge as heretofore; while the brethren who had received the sanction of the Society as nominal members of the Lodge of Antiquity during the separation, were re-united with the original members of the real lodge, and the privileges of that venerable body limited to their original channel.
>
> Although I have considerably abridged my observations on this unfortunate dispute in the latter editions of this Treatise, I still think it proper to record my sentiments on the subject, in justice to the gentlemen with whom I have long associated; and to convince my brethren, that our re-union with the Society has not induced me to vary a well-grounded opinion, or deviate from the strict line of consistency which I have hitherto pursued.
>
> (*Illustrations of Masonry*, Twelfth Edition) 1812

The Grand Lodge South of the River Trent ceased to function becoming moribund in the 1780s and the last record pertaining to the Grand Lodge of All England at York was a scrap of paper referring to 'a meeting of the Grand Lodge of All England held at Brother Wolley's on Thursday the 23rd August 1792 ...' and it is thought faded from then on.

William Preston served Lodge of Antiquity so well until ill-health restricted his activity. From 1790 he was anually elected Deputy Master, except on two occasions in 1802 and 1807 when another took his place owing to illness. In 1809 when the Duke of Sussex accepted Mastership of that Lodge he appointed Preston as his Deputy and when Preston died a letter of full appreciation was sent by HRH the Duke of Sussex to the Lodge of Antiquity which included the following observation:

> ... Long has the Lodge of Antiquity been remarkable for its zeal in Masonry, and greatly is that Lodge and the Craft indebted to the diligence and example of my worthy Brother your Past Master Preston, whose name must be dear to every admirer and well wisher of our ancient Order. I have therefore only to recommend your following his steps when I may anticipate the most glorious result.

Preston's last attendance there was on 17 January 1816 and after a lengthy illness he died at his residence No 3 Dean Street, Fetter Lane, on 1 April 1818. He was interred in St Paul's Cathedral and after the funeral the 'Female Orphans belonging to the Freemasons' Charity in St. George's Fields returned to his house where they partook of wine and cake'. In his Will dated 1813 his masonic bequests were £500 Consols to the Girls' School, the same amount to the General Charity Fund, and £300 Consols to fund the Prestonian Lectureship which was designed to continue the dissemination of masonic knowledge he had started. The interest from the £300 was to be applied to 'some well-informed Mason to deliver annually a Lecture on the First, Second, or Third Degree of the Order of Masonry according to the system practised in the Lodge of Antiquity'. The first Lecturer to be appointed was Bro Stephen Jones, who was a prominent member of Antiquity as well as a fully instructed member of the Harodim Lodge and Harodim Chapter where Preston had taught his experts; Stephen Jones had married Preston's niece.

In 1923, after a lapse of some sixty years, it was decided that a new format for the Lectures was permissible, the lecturer thereafter being allowed to choose his own subject. Each year the statement is made 'The Board desires to emphasize the importance of these the only Lectures held under the authority of Grand Lodge.' In December 1984, the Grand Master, H.R.H. the Duke of Kent, authorised as a memorial to Preston and granted approval for a collarette and jewel (see page 86) to be worn by the appointed lecturer. At the end of his year of office, the brother would receive in exchange a modified jewel which would distinguish him as a Past Prestonian Lecturer. Those items of regalia remain the property of Grand Lodge (see also Appendix M.)

Past Prestonian Lecturer's Jewel to be worn on all masonic occasions with Craft regalia. It remains the property of Grand Lodge and must eventually be returned

Chapter 15

Towards the Union

There was no relationship between the Grand Lodges of the Antients and the Moderns—they simply did not recognize each other—but interchange between brethren on opposite sides was facilitated by the 're-making' procedure. Perhaps the project to have the biggest influence in causing some brethren to adopt a positive attitude for, or against, a particular allegiance was the attempt by the premier Grand Lodge to have the Society Incorporated as such. It commenced in 1763 with a speech by Thomas Edmonds, Junior Grand Warden, in which he proposed that a Charter be sought to Incorporate the Society as well as to build a Hall for the accommodation of the Moderns Grand Lodge. The Duke of Beaufort, Grand Master 1767–1771, became resolute in his efforts to press this home. The *Newcastle Journal* of November 1768 reported that the Incorporation was envisaged 'in order to annihilate the Society who stile themselves Antient Free Masons'. All attempts in the project tended to split brethren into two camps, for and against. The Caledonian Lodge organised a *Memorial* against it which was dated 2 January 1769 and on the 26th of that month Grand Lodge called a special meeting of Masters of lodges on the subject. A majority decided that the Grand Master be asked to provide a draft of the proposed Charter to put before their lodges. Owing to the efforts of Caledonian Lodge in that regard, Grand Lodge at their April meeting in 1769 agreed a motion that the lodge be erased, but at the meeting the Master craved pardon in the name of himself and of his lodge, which was granted. The opposition came principally from London Lodges and at another meeting of Masters and Past Grand Officers it was then resolved to support Caledonian to oppose the Charter. Because the members of Caledonian Lodge had written an 'indiscreet letter to a Past Grand Master of the Austrian Netherlands in support of their cause' they were expelled but re-instated six years later without loss of seniority. A Bill for Incorporation was presented in Parliament and read for the first time on 28 February 1772, but after its second reading the following month it was withdrawn.

Laurence Dermott's comment in his 1778 Edition of *Ahiman Rezon* was:

> The Modern Masons petitioned Parliament to grant them a Charter of Incorporation in order to give them the power and pleasure of punishing every Freemason in England that did not pay quarterage to them. Had they obtained the charter, it would have shut out all Masons of the neighbouring kingdoms, as they would receive no manner of benefit therefrom. The wisdom of Parliament treated the petition with just contempt; and it was reported in the public papers, that the honourable Speaker of the House of Commons said: 'That if the petition was granted, he made no doubt the chimney sweepers would soon apply for a charter.'

In his contribution in the multi authorship of *Grand Lodge 1717–1967*, Bro J. R. Clarke, who wrote on this period (pp 92–128) cited the brother who attended the Quarterly Communication of Grand Lodge on 22 November 1773 and then wrote to the *Leeds Intelligencer* that he was:

> ... extremely happy to find that all the differences which have for some years prevailed in that respectable Society, are now amicably adjusted, and the greatest harmony seems to reign among them.

In the first twenty years of the Antients' Grand Lodge there was tolerance between them and the Moderns, although a state of non-recognition existed between them. However, that began to deteriorate here and there and feelings of animosity emerged, but certain brethren had masonic ideals at heart and were anxious to find ways and means to create uniformity. One who may be brought to notice here is Captain George Smith, an Inspector at the Military Academy at Woolwich, an associate of William Preston, a Modern mason with leanings towards Antients practice. Although he was to reach high rank in the premier Grand Lodge it is obvious that his sympathies were also with the Antients as is shewn by his classifying the Royal Arch as follows:

> 8 April 1774 Grand Chapter (Minute Book No. 1)
> B^r Capt Smith read to the C^ns a Dissertation on the 4th Degree of Masonry contain^g many Instructive & Ingenious Remarks & rec'd the Unanimous Thanks of the C^ns from the Chair.

On 15 November 1776 Bro Smith sent a letter to James Heseltine the Grand Secretary raising the following points:

> 1. His Grace the Duke of Athol would wish to know by what authority the G.L. of England, pretends to a supremacy over the G.L. of Scotland instituted by Royal Charter granted by King James the Sixth to the family of Roslin in the year 1569 and then acknowledged to be the new head and first Lodge in Europe.
> 2. Why the G.L. of England has thought *propper* to alter the mode of Initiation, also the Word, *pass-word* & Grip of the different degrees in Masonry.

3. Whether Dermott constitutes Lodges in his own Name or in the name and Authority of the Duke of Athol, and whether anything can be laid to his charge, inconsistent with the character of an honest man and a mason.
4. Whether any mode of Union could be thought of, and in such a manner, that might appear probable to both parties.

It was a positive approach to try to sort out some of the elements of the 'differences' between brethren on both sides, but Smith was far too premature. We have no details of a reply, nor of any action or discussion on the subject from records of the Grand Lodge Committee, but his letter has to be viewed as a very early attempt to set a course towards agreement even though it was doomed to failure. It seemed to have had quite the opposite effect as the premier Grand Lodge passed a Resolution only a few months later, 18 April 1777, that has been quoted in the chapter above on 'Re-Making from One to Another'. That Resolution classified the Antients as belonging to 'a Pretended Grand Lodge in England'— they were 'not to be Countenanced or Acknowledged as Masons by any Regular Lodge or Masons under the Constitution of England'—that 'any Persons Initiated at these Irregular Meetings' were not to be admitted into any Lodge 'without being re-Made and paying the usual Making Fees'. The Resolution literally outlawed brethren under the Antients Grand Lodge. Yet Laurence Dermott, in his 3rd Edition of *Ahiman Rezon*, published the following year, (1778), ended his Address to the Fraternity with these words:

> I shall conclude this, as I did in former editions with saying, that I hope I shall live to see a general conformity and universal unity between the worthy masons of all denominations.

His desire was constant but he did not live to see it fulfilled; he died in June 1791 probably a saddened brother over that issue.

Among brethren from each side who chose to be friends, whose ideals transcended partisan claims, the 're-making process proved the compromise, although one incident in particular will show that human nature will swamp ideals when the occasion arises. From the records of Old Dundee Lodge No 18 we find:

> 1799, April 11. The R.W.M. having informed the Lodge that on the last Lodge Night Two Foreign Captains attended for the purpose of Visiting this Lodge, when upon examination it appeared from their Certificates they had been Initiated in England according to the Old Institutions; it was judged by the Members present to be inconsistent with the principals of Modern Free-Masonry to admit them. Br. Francis Daniel and Br. Masters being present as Visitors coinciding in the strongest terms in that opinion, they was refus'd admittance; when, upon the following day, Br. Daniel invited and permitted them to Visit the Royal Naval Lodge and strongly entreated them to become Members for the Unworthy Consideration of Seven Shillings and 6d. Brother

Masters being also present, and had previously indorsed their Certificates that they had visited the Lodge over which he presides at Ramsgate. Br. Moody proposed that Br. Francis Daniel, Apothecary, Wapping St,' Master of the Royal Navy Lodge *'never be permitted to Visit this Lodge again'* which was 2nd and carried. Br. Tayler, P.M. proposed that Br. Masters [Master of the Jacobs Ladder Lodge, Ramsgate] *'never be permitted to Visit this Lodge again'* which was 2nd and carried.

Sir Francis Columbine Daniel, surgeon and apothecary. Inventor of a 'Life Preserver' for which he was awarded the Royal Society's Medallion. Master for some twenty years of the Royal Naval Lodge No 59

Sir Francis Columbine Daniel (see page 90) provides the historian with interesting, one might say startling behaviour, and whilst his medical practice was located at Wapping adjacent to both Old Dundee and Royal Naval Lodges, in an area that provides much evidence of well developed masonic talent and activity, he extended his involvement in administration beyond Royal Naval Lodge in which he was the quasi-permanent Master. The members of Old Dundee Lodge, however, had his measure and never forgave his action. When he had made overtures to join the lodge he had the good sense to withdraw his name after they had black-balled several of his friends and thus avoided a similar fate. Also, in May 1826, they felt no obligation to accept a Petition for relief from his daughter for that was rejected. His Knighthood was looked upon somewhat dubiously when it was conferred in 1820 as it was thought he had been over-zealous in his exertions in that direction.

Seeing that an interesting, albeit rugged path towards the Union can be travelled by recounting some of the experiences of three brethren, Lord Moira, Thomas Harper, and Francis Columbine Daniel, let us stay with Daniel for a moment longer.

He was born on 2 April 1765 at King's Lynn, Norfolk; studied as a medical practitioner and came to London where he set up at Wapping, alongside the Thames, and at that time a thriving port. He was initiated on 4 March 1788 in Antients Lodge No 3 but 're-made' in Moderns Lodge No 344 later that year; he had a firm footing in both camps, as it were, and included in his memberships Antients Lodges No 23 (now United Mariners Lodge No 30) and Oak Lodge (now No 190) and Moderns Lodges, Emulation (now No 21) and Lodge of Felicity (now No 58). One might say that he almost 'took over' Royal Naval Lodge No 61 (now No 59) which he joined in 1791, as at that same meeting he proposed eleven others to join. It met at Wapping, as indeed did Old Dundee Lodge, and prospered under the mastership which he held for seventeen years; during that period it is said that he initiated over 600 American seamen and nearly 400 British Naval Officers. In 1792 he proposed 'That any Member for the time being who should bring forward Six Gentlemen that shall be made Masons in this Lodge shall receive for his assiduity in support of this Lodge a Medal to the value of Two Guineas.' It should be noted that they were 'to be made Masons' not to become members of it—but the 'Making Fee' had been raised to £3. 13. 6 which included the sum of 5s 0d. which was payable towards the expenses of the Cumberland School, one of the Charities in which he was interested. He invented a lifebelt which came to the notice of the Lords of the Admiralty; in all he seems to have been the complete extrovert.

Let us turn to Thomas Harper who also had a firm footing in both camps. He was initiated at Bristol seaport in 1761 in Lodge No 24 under Antients jurisdiction; that lodge lapsed a few years later. It is known that he went to America where he is listed as having joined with brethren in Charles Town, South Carolina in forming a lodge which received a Warrant from the Antients Grand Lodge dated 30 September 1774 on which Harper was named as the Junior Warden. It is not known how long the lodge had operated prior to the date of that Warrant, obviously there would have been a considerable time taken up between the application and receipt in those days of sailing ships; although communication was constant with the port of Bristol. No information is to hand regarding his return to England but he is listed in the membership of Antients Lodge No 5 in London together with Laurence Dermott (it is now Albion Lodge No 9), in the year 1785. The following year he was appointed Junior Grand Warden. The next year he joined Grand Master's Lodge which had been reserved for the No 1 place on the Antients Register from the inception of that Grand Lodge. He had numerous memberships in both sides, but, it is obscure regarding his first lodge on the Moderns List; he had several which included Preston's Harodim Lodge No 558 which eventually merged with the Lodge of Antiquity No 1 (now No 2) when that serious division in their ranks had been healed. But his most important membership in the Moderns in company with other prominent brethren from the Antients was in Globe Lodge (now No 23) in which the keys to open doorways to the Union were to be cut. In his *Memorials of the Globe Lodge No 23 1723–1861*, Henry Sadler made special reference on that point:

> ... It is indeed remarkable that the Globe, which derived its authority from the Grand Lodge of the Moderns, should have admitted to membership so many brethren who held prominent positions in the Grand Lodge of the Antients. Of the five brethren who signed the *Articles of Union* on behalf of the Antients, three were members of the Globe; they were Thomas Harper (Deputy Grand Master) the well-known Jeweller and Silversmith, *to whom I consider belongs the chief credit for the Union*, James Agar (Past Deputy Grand Master) and Robert Leslie (Grand Secretary). ...

The full list of Antients who were members together in Globe Lodge is impressive:

Thomas Harper joined in 1787	
was then	Senior Grand Warden
Robert Leslie joined in 1787	
was then	Past Junior Grand Warden
William Comerford Clarkson joined in 1790	Grand Treasurer (1798)

James Agar joined in 1790
   was then   Senior Grand Warden
John Bunn joined in 1791
   was then   Junior Grand Warden
Robert Gill joined in 1797
   was then   Past Senior Grand Warden
Peter Gilkes joined in 1798 member of   Prominent Preceptor in Masonic
   many Antients lodges   Ritual

Henry Sadler commented further that 'Globe Lodge contributed more than any other Lodge in the Craft to bring about the Union of the two Grand Lodges in 1813'. But membership of that lodge was to be a convenient peg upon which F. C. Daniel was to hang retaliatory measures against Thomas Harper, which we will deal with later, but first a brief glimpse of the background of Lord Moira our third guide on this journey.

Francis, Lord RAWDON, was appointed Acting Grand Master by His Royal Highness The Prince of Wales in 1790 and that position was held until just prior to the Union. He was engaged with the 4th Duke of Atholl in obtaining exemption for Free-masonry from the *Unlawful Societies Act* of 1799, which outlawed 'societies for seditious and treasonable purposes', providing that an annual return was made to the local Clerk of the Peace. It was that Act which caused the re-issue of Warrants as its wording was so construed to prevent new Lodges to come into existence.

The Earl of Moira, as he was, was untiring in his efforts and whilst the Antients had paid constant attention to the relationships with the Grand Lodges of Ireland and Scotland by acquainting them of the election or re-election of the Grand Master and current appointment of Grand Officers each year, together with normal correspondence—'as it breathes the true and genuine spirit of Free-masonry and also proves the good understanding that has hitherto, and we trust ever will subsist between the Grand Lodges of the whole Ancient communication . . .' as they expressed themselves in the Minutes of 27 December 1791; it fell to the Acting Grand Master to foster a new rapport on behalf of the Moderns. An account of his visit to the Grand Lodge of Scotland for that purpose is supplied by Alexander Lawrie, Grand Secretary, in his *History of Free Masonry in Scotland* (Edinburgh 1804 p 293):

> . . . the Brethren having assembled at the King's Arms tavern in the evening, to celebrate the festival of St. Andrew, were honoured with the company of his Excellency the Earl of Moira, Commander in Chief of his Majesty's Forces in Scotland, and Acting Grand Master of the Antient Grand Lodge of all England. From the presence of this Nobleman, the friends of the Grand Lodge of Scotland anticipated an union between that respectable body and the Grand Lodge of Scotland. . . .

That description, although somewhat misleading, refers, of course, to the Moderns Grand Lodge. Lord Moira was later to become Acting Grand Master of the Grand Lodge of Scotland (1806–8). It was also through his efforts that fraternal relations were opened with the Grand Lodge of Ireland as he wrote in the following terms to them in December 1808:

> I can answer for the cordial co-operation of the Grand Lodges of England & Scotland in maintaining the due authority (as far as their influence may operate) of the Grand Lodge of Ireland. For these bodies are deeply impress'd with the mischief which must arise to the Craft, as well as the danger to the State, if Masonic Lodges can be permitted to assume an independence of the Grand Lodge. (*History of the Grand Lodge of Ireland*, Lepper & Crossle, Lodge of Research CC, Dublin, 1925, p 382)

Staying for a moment on the subject of relationships, the Antients had shared Grand Masters with Ireland in the Earl of Blesington and the 6th Earl of Antrim, and with Scotland had shared the 3rd and 4th Dukes of Atholl. Their external relations extended overseas as we note in the 1807 Edition of *Ahiman Rezon*, pp 117–118:

> The same cordial zeal and brotherly affection subsists with us and the sister Grand Lodges of Canada, Pennsylvania, Maryland, South Carolina, New York, New England, Nova Scotia, and Massachusetts, at Gibraltar, and most of the Provinces and Islands in the East and West Indies: and from whom the most friendly communications are constantly and regularly received. At the request of the Ancient masons in Canada a Grand Warrant was granted on 7 March, 1792, constituting his Royal Highness Prince Edward (now Duke of Kent), Grand Master of Canada; to whose persevering zeal and condescending manners, the fraternity in that quarter are particularly indebted for much of their present strength and respectability.

Before he left Canada to return to England the Duke of Kent, who was astride both Grand Lodges, accepted a petition from brethren of both jurisdictions in that country urging him to foster the friendly relations that existed there hoping that through him unity would arise. He was to be installed as Grand Master of the Antients for the meeting on 27 December 1813 at which the Union was effected. The father of Queen Victoria set a pattern of royal patronage of extremely high standard.

There had been an undercurrent of activity on behalf of brethren on both sides, but it was counterbalanced by entrenchment on the part of others who seemed determined to maintain the partition; no equality of terms could be considered. A positive effort was made in the Antients Grand Lodge in December 1797:

> THAT a committee be appointed by this R.W. Grand Lodge to meet one that may be appointed by the Grand Lodge of Modern Masons, and with them to effect a Union ...

It was not carried. Indeed it only brought a subsequent hardening in attitude from some brethren; apparently it was premature. Five years later at the meeting of Grand Lodge on 2 March 1802, the Antients had this to say:

> ... The Ancient Grand Lodge of England has thought it due to its charac-
> ter to make this short and decisive declaration on the unauthorized attempts
> that have recently been made to bring about a union with a body of persons
> who have not entered into obligations by which we are bound, and who have
> descended to calumnies and acts of the most unjustifiable kind. They desire it
> therefor to be known to the masonic world, and they call upon their regular
> Lodges, their Past and Present Grand Officers, their Royal Arches and Master,
> their Wardens and Brethren, to take notice, that they cannot, and must not,
> receive any person who has not received the *obligations of Masonry, according to
> the Ancient Constitutions*, as practised by the United Grand Lodges of England,
> Scotland, and Ireland, and the regular branches that have sprung from their
> sanction—And this is our unalterable decree. By Order of the Grand Lodge.

Although there was no real difference between Robert Leslie, the Grand Secretary, and Thomas Harper they were not of one mind even though they were to be Joint Grand Secretaries for the period 1792–1800 and Harper to be Deputy Grand Secretary from 1800. But in 1801 a letter to Robert Leslie from the Duke of Atholl (4 February) appointed Thomas Harper as his Deputy Grand Master. It included the comment:

> ... in the firm persuasion that by such appointment the real Interest of
> the Craft will be promoted and I have no doubt that the knowledge which the
> Grand Lodge must have of the masonic virtues of Brother Harper will induce
> the Grand Lodge to think along with me that the Ancient Fraternity will
> derive from the choice I have made.

That letter was quoted in the Minutes which go on to record:

> ... R.W. Bro. Thomas Harper was thereupon immediately and due form
> Installed R.W. Deputy Grand Master for the year 1801, Proclaimed and Sal-
> uted according to Ancient Custom.

His occupation as Silversmith and Jeweller in Fleet Street, London has been commemorated in the survival of many and varied masonic jewels with the distinctive maker's mark of 'T.H.' registered at Goldsmiths' Hall on 27 May 1790. His former position as Joint Grand Secretary of the Antients Grand Lodge was filled by the appointment of his son Edwards Harper. Brethren holding positions of importance in the Antients Grand Lodge at that date are shown on the title page of the By-Laws (see page 96) which were approved and ordered to be printed and published in 1802.

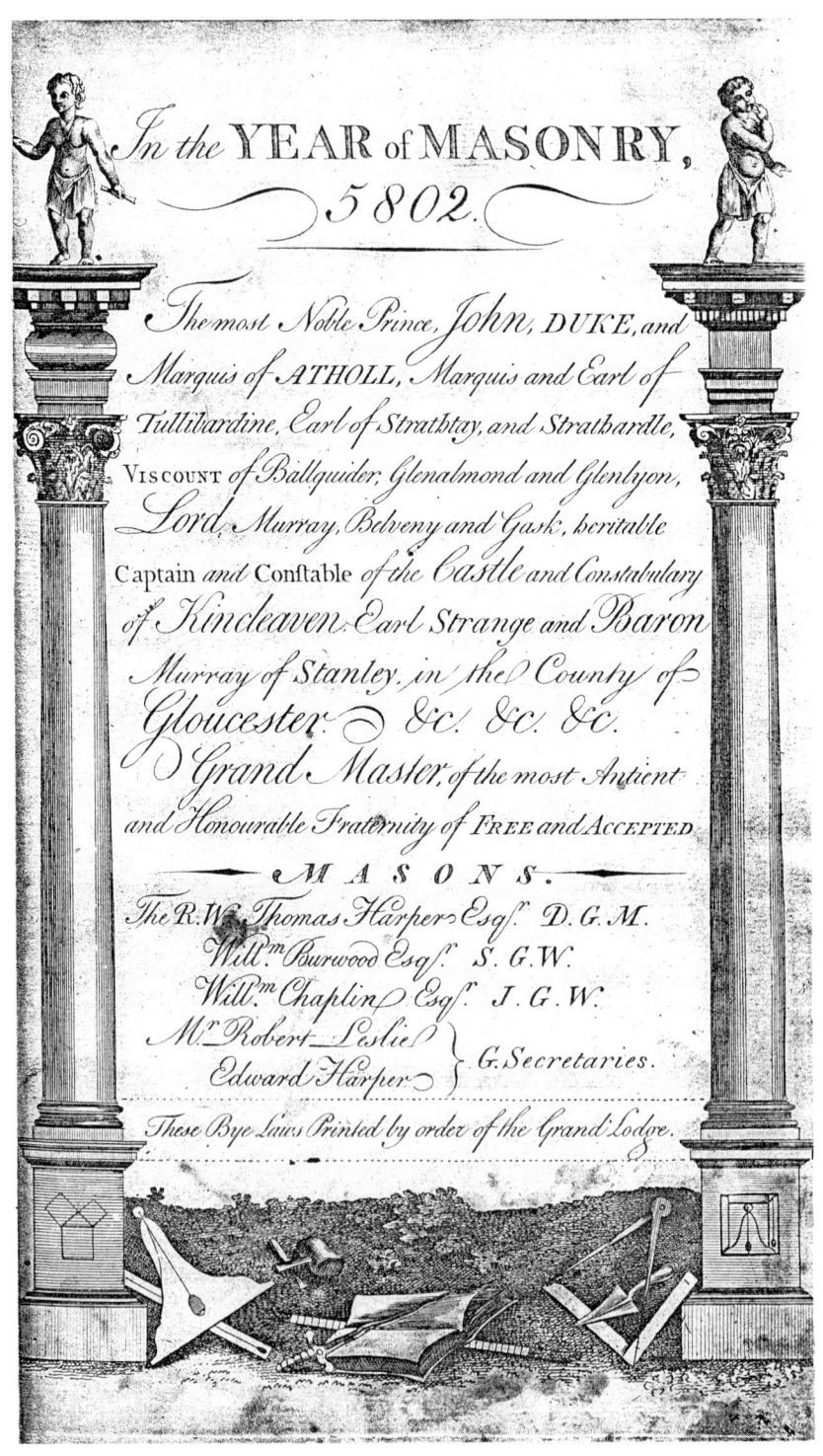

In the YEAR of MASONRY,
5802.

The most Noble Prince, JOHN, DUKE, and
Marquis of ATHOLL, Marquis and Earl of
Tullibardine, Earl of Strathtay, and Strathardle,
Viscount of Ballquider, Glenalmond and Glenlyon,
Lord Murray, Belveny and Gask, heritable
Captain and Constable of the Castle and Constabulary
of Kincleaven, Earl Strange and Baron
Murray of Stanley, in the County of
Gloucester. &c. &c. &c.
Grand Master, of the most Antient
and Honourable Fraternity of FREE and ACCEPTED
——— M A S O N S. ———
The R.W. Thomas Harper Esqr. D.G.M.
Willm Burwood Esqr. S.G.W.
Willm Chaplin Esqr. J.G.W.
Mr Robert Leslie ⎫
Edward Harper ⎭ G. Secretaries.

These Bye Laws Printed by order of the Grand Lodge.

Title page of the by-laws of the Antients Grand Lodge in 1802 showing the names of Thomas Harper and his son Edward (5) Harper

RULES
AND
ORDERS

Which are to be punctually observed and kept by the most Antient and Honourable Fraternity of FREE *and* ACCEPTED MASONS, *according to the old Constitutions granted by his Royal Highness Prince* EDWIN *at* YORK *in the Year of our Lord Nine Hundred Twenty and Six, and in the Year of Masonry Four Thousand Nine Hundred Twenty and Six.*

In order to prevent all Feuds, Controversies, illegal Arguments, or Debates which might in any Sort disturb or make void the true Intent and Meaning of this our unanimous Conjunction, We the Master, Wardens, Deacons and Secretary, together with the rest of the Members of our Lodge, N.º 277 (by and with the Approbation and Consent of the GRAND LODGE *) have thought proper to subscribe and establish the following Rules.*

The first page of the by-laws of an Antients Lodge

To return to Francis Columbine Daniel, ever the individualist, we find that whilst Royal Naval Lodge was under the jurisdiction of the Moderns Grand Lodge, like the brethren in Lodge of Antiquity, it followed a course more in keeping with the Antients, aptly described by Heron Lepper as 'Traditioner'. But Daniel went one stage farther in that he altered the name of the lodge to 'Royal Naval Lodge of Independence' and also issued Certificates of admission. One engraved Plate for that however kept to the proper name of the lodge (See Appendix E, and page 48). It was contentious and the matter came before the Stewards Lodge 21 January 1801:

> Received the Charge of Lodge No. 290 against Fran^s Daniel late of the United Mariners Lodge No. 23 Wapping for pretending to make and admit Wm Clark and divers Persons Brothers of the Most Ancient and Honourable Fraternity of Free Accepted Masons of England according to the Old Constitutions without the Grand Masters Warrant and granting certificates to the same Parties in imitation of Certificates of this Right Worshipful Grand Lodge Contrary to good faith and without any Warrant or Authority for so doing. Ordered that the Secretary Sum^s F.C. Daniel and all proper Parties to attend at the next Stewards Lodge.

Sir Francis Columbine Daniel author of the Address on the Subject of an Union *and a keen supporter of Masonic charities*

The Chair for that meeting was occupied by Robert Gill, SGW, with William Burwood, JGW, and ten others but Thomas Harper was not present. The Minutes for the February meeting continue with the story:

> ... The Lodge proceeded to the Examination of sev^l Brothers of said Lodge 290 and the Charges against Bro^r Daniel being thereby fully substantiated It was thereupon unanimously adjudged and determined that s^d Bro^r Fran^s Daniel be and he is hereby excluded the benefit of all his Masonic Rights and privileges of the Ancient Craft and of the Right Worshipful Grand Lodge according to the Old Constitutions. And that such exclusion be inserted in the Circular Letters of the Grand Lodge and Due Notice given to all Warranted Lodges to conduct themselves accordingly and according to the like usage in such cases.

The Chair on that occasion was taken by Robert Leslie with ten others in attendance but Thomas Harper was not present. That decision by the Stewards Lodge was confirmed in Grand Lodge on 4 March following. However, no time was lost by Daniel in his retaliation for he produced a contra charge involving Thomas Harper even whilst his case was under consideration. At the Committee of Charity, (the Moderns equivalent of the Antients administrative work done by their Stewards Lodge), the Minutes of 30 January 1801 record:

> A Complaint was preferred by Bro^r F.C. Daniel Master of the Royal Naval Lodge No. 57, Wapping, against Richard Barry of the Minories, Stationer, Francis Green of the Hermitage, Slopseller, Thomas Harper of Fleet Street, Jeweller, Robert Gill of Union Street, Bishopsgate, and William Burwood of Green Bank, Coal Dealer, for encouraging irregular meetings and infringing on the privileges of the Ancient Grand Lodge of all England assembling under the Authority of His Royal Highness the Prince of Wales. Ordered that the said Parties be respectively summoned to attend at the Committee of Charity to be held in November next to Answer to the said Complaint.

By general consent, at the next meeting of the Committee of Charity the matter was given priority on the agenda, thus, on 20 November 1801 we read:

> The Charge made by Brother Daniel at the last Committee was accordingly read and he was heard in support of it. The Resolution of the Grand Lodge on 7 April 1777 against all Lodges or Masons countenancing in any manner those under a pretended Authority from the Duke of Athol as Grand Master were also read.

> The parties summoned to attend were then heard in reply in which he admitted that he had been made a Mason in a regular Lodge in the Constitution of the Grand Lodge of England, that he had a long time back joined those holding under the authority of the Duke of Athol, that he had constantly attended their Meetings and at present held the situation of Deputy Grand Master under the Duke of Athol.

It is worthy of note here that as a member of Globe Lodge which was entitled to nominate a Grand Steward under the Moderns system, and was therefore a 'Red Apron' lodge, Harper had been approached on that matter but declined owing to his position as Deputy GM of the Antients. However, his fellow members persisted in their wish which caused Harper to seek advice in which he consulted James Heseltine the Grand Secretary who saw no objection. That resulted in his nomination as a Grand Steward in 1795 and he went on to join the Grand Stewards Lodge. Harper had previously served as Steward at the Grand Festival of the Antients Grand Lodge for the year 1785 when he represented Lodge No 190 (*The Grand Stewards and Red Apron Lodges*, A. F. Calvert, London, 1917 and *The Grand Stewards and their Lodge*, Colin Dyer, London 1985). But to return to the examination of the charge by F. C. Daniel against Thomas Harper:

> The Committee being disposed to act with all lenity, consistent with the Honor of the Grand Lodge, Mr. Harper was asked by the Grand Master in the Chair [Earl of Moira] if he was now willing to renounce his Connection with the said irregular Lodge and adhere to the Laws of this Grand Lodge, if not, that the Laws of the Society must be enforced against him. Mr. Harper said that on a question of such importance to him, he hoped that the Committee would indulge him with some time to give an Answer, particularly as he wished to consult with some others, and which might lead to a termination of the differences that had so long subsisted amongst Masons. Resolved THAT the further consideration of the Charge against Mr. Thomas Harper be deferred to the Committee of Charity to be held in February next and the like indulgence be extended to Mr. Robert Gill and Mr. William Burwood they standing in a similar situation.

Thus, the Deputy Grand Master together with the Senior and Junior Grand Wardens of the Antients Grand Lodge, all having memberships of lodges under the Moderns jurisdiction had been called forth under the Laws of that Society to renounce membership of an 'irregular Lodge' the judgement on which had been averted by Harper's wish to consult with colleagues with a view to finding ways and means of bringing unity in the Fraternity. At the following Committee held on 5 February 1802 the matter was pursued:

> ... The Grand Treasurer [James Heseltine 1785-1804, formerly Grand Secretary 1769-1783] took Notice of the Minute of the last Committee of Charity respecting Brother Thomas Harper by which he was to give his Answer at this Committee, whether he was willing to renounce his Connection with the Irregular Lodges held under the Authority of the Duke of Athol, and adhere to the Laws of the Grand Lodge. The Grand Treasurer then adverted to the Reasons which had induced the last Committee of Charity to suspend the Proceedings in regard to Brother Harper namely, THAT he as a principal Officer of the Society acting under the Authority of the Duke of Athol, would use his best endeavours to promote an Union of the two Societies, which had

long been the wish of many respectable Members of each Body. The Grand Treasurer stated that he had lately met and conversed with Brother Harper and James Agar Esqr late a principal Officer of the Society under the sanction of the Duke of Athol, and from the Friendly Sentiments and anxious desire expressed by those Brethren, THAT an Union of the two Societies might take place, upon liberal and constitutional grounds, it was suggested that the first step might be to appoint a Committee from each Society to meet for the purpose of considering and arranging a plan of fraternal Union, to be submitted to their respective General meetings; and in order to remove every impediment and prevent any unpleasant discussion which might arise out of the Minutes of the last Committee of Charity, as well as to enable the parties to meet with Cordiality and perfect satisfaction, it would be proper to dismiss the Suspended Motion respecting Brother Harper, he being one of the Officers who most probably must attend the proposed amicable Committee. On these grounds the Grand Treasurer moved and was seconded by Brother Francis Daniel that the said Order of the last Committee of Charity respecting the Complaint of Brother Daniel against Brothers Thomas Harper, Robert Gill, and William Burwood be dismissed and on the Question being put it was passed Unanimously in the Affirmative.

Ever the opportunist, Brother Daniel very quickly abandoned his Charge, or attempts at retribution so far as the Antients were concerned it was now plain that it would be that much better service to his ego to support all efforts towards establishing unity. But the wheels of the Antients were grinding exceedingly slowly for they produced very little between that Committee meeting in February and the next which was held on 19 November 1802 when the following was recorded:

> ... On a Motion duly made, the Minutes of the Committee of Charity and Grand Lodge which respected the Complaint against Brother Harper and others for their connexion with the Masons acting under the Authority of the Duke of Athol and the Minutes of the subsequent Proceedings thereon were read. The Earl of Moira then stated that the suggested idea of an Union of the two Societies fully met with the approbation of the Grand Master His R.H. The Prince of Wales. His Lordship and the Grand Treasurer acquainted the Committee that hitherto no proposition affecting an Union had been made by the other Society as had been expected from the Proceedings that had taken place in the Grand Lodge and the Declaration of Brother Thomas Harper on the subject, whereupon after mature deliberation it was Ordered that the Grand Secretary do write to Mr. Thomas Harper and acquaint him THAT he is to consider himself as standing under a peculiar engagement towards the Grand Lodge. THAT a judgment impending against him was done away solely upon a Condition suggested by himself and that the Grand Lodge after having met his suggestion with the most liberal disposition cannot but feel itself disappointed that Brother Harper has not offered any communication respecting that Union which it was hoped would have precluded the necessity of any Proceedings on the Charge exhibited against him. THAT Brother Harper's non-attendance at this Committee appears an indecorous neglect. In consequence of which an explanation is required from him before Wednesday next, such as may determine the Procedure which the Grand Lodge shall at that

meeting adopt, or that he may attend in person at that Grand Lodge to answer
to a revival of the Charge.

There can be no question other than 'was Thomas Harper at that
stage a victim of circumstances and by his silence was trying to be
discreet and thus obviate any heated discussion likely to arise'?, in
the view of the Antients nothing had been said by the Moderns
that they were willing to bring their Working and ceremonial into
conformity with ancient practice. Such a state maintained the
dividing line. At the next Committee of Charity held on 4 February
1803 the following was recorded:

> In consequence of a Complaint preferred by Brother F.C. Daniel against
> Brothers Richard Barry, Samuel Corbitt, Jeremiah Connellan, and Edward
> Butt for irregular Proceedings injurious to the Society, they were summoned to
> attend this Committee and the Grand Secretary read Letters he had received
> from them in answer. But on mature consideration the Committee were of
> opinion that it would be proper to defer any enquiry on this Complaint 'till
> after the decision of the Grand Lodge respecting Brother Thomas Harper. It
> was therefore Ordered to stand over 'till the next Committee in April.

At the next Committee of Charity held on 1 April 1803, the Resolution passed in Grand Lodge meeting on 9 February was the
main subject:

> Resolved. THAT the said Thomas Harper be expelled the Society, for counte-
> nancing and supporting a set of persons, calling themselves Ancient Masons,
> and holding Lodges in this Kingdom without authorisation from H.R.H. The
> Prince of Wales, the Grand Master duly elected by this regular Grand Lodge.
> Resolved also. THAT this resolution be inserted in the printed accounts of the
> Grand Lodge, to prevent the said Thomas Harper from gaining admittance
> into any regular Lodge. And it was further resolved that whenever it shall
> appear that any Masons, under the Constitution of this Grand Lodge shall in
> future attend or countenance any of the Lodges or meetings of persons calling
> themselves Ancient Masons, under the sanction of any persons claiming to be
> Grand Master of England, and not duly elected by this Grand Lodge, the
> Laws of the Society will be strictly enforced against them, and their names will
> be sent to the several Lodges under the Constitution of England.

Bro F.C. Daniel had sown the seed, it had germinated, sprouted,
and Thomas Harper was his victim; the decision was rescinded in
1810 but much was to happen in those seven years, in fact Daniel
undertook the next action of any consequence by writing *An Address
to His Grace the Duke of Athol on the Subject of an Union between the
Masons that have lately assembled under his Grace's Sanction and the
REGULAR MASONS OF ENGLAND* [under] *His Royal Highness
George Prince of Wales*. It was a pamphlet of 100 pages included with
other material and published under the title of *MASONIC UNION*
by Bro. Asperne, of Cornhill, London, another prominent freemason at that time. Daniel's *Address* was homiletic in character as

the following brief extract will show:

> ... can it, I say, be supposed that you, or any other nobleman, would lend his name to support or countenance a society, however praiseworthy its motives may appear, which holds its meetings in direct violation of the laws of the original establishment, and the government of the fraternity? No, my lord, your public character is too well known—your zeal for the welfare of the country is too manifest—and your attachment to the royal family too deeply rooted to admit of wilful deviation. Therefore, my lord, I trust your feelings coincide what honour, what peculiar satisfaction, and what heartfelt pleasure it would give you, to bring that society, which you have lately patronized, under the royal banner.

It was an action well in keeping with what we have seen so far of his activity; his feet were now firmly planted on just the one side. He now presumed to sermonise and point to the error of their ways through a discourse wending its way through information extracted from former records, an account of the newly created affinity with the Grand Lodge of Scotland, an Appendix which included a list of Regular Lodges, and Grand Patrons and Grand Officers, together with extracts from Masonic Sermons that had been delivered by the Rev Jethro Inwood of St Paul's church, Deptford, near to Wapping. It was all aimed to put the Grand Master of the Antients 'in the picture' as it were, almost on the lines 'well, somebody had to do it'!

Such was the nature of Bro. Daniel that he included as a Foreword a letter from the Rev Jethro Inwood which I feel gives a clear idea of how he communicated his initiative in this subject to others; for brethren of responsibility treasured the thought of that Union so dearly:

> It gave me no small degree of pleasure when informed that an union of the two Masonic Socities is in agitation and very likely to take place; and I think nothing can more impeach the Masonic character of every member of either Society than his throwing away any stumbling-block in the way of so desirable an object. Nay, I think it will impeach the character of every one, if he does not exert every ability he may be possessed of, to effect that much wished-for Union. Impressed with his idea, you have my humble labours in the Society of the Free and Accepted which you may esteem as having any tendency to propagate amongst, and impress upon the minds of the members of either party, that only true principle of either the MASONIC or CHRISTIAN profession, UNIVERSAL LOVE. It is the additional glory to us and our Society, that so amiable a character as the noble Earl MOIRA, should, amidst all his greatness of character, and multiplicity of greater and more important engagements, interest himself as he has formerly done, and still, it seems continues to be permanently established between the Grand Lodge of Scotland and England, by means of the Right Honourable the Earl of Moira. These are circumstances which must be highly gratifying to a virtuous mind, and which alone can make Masonry most eminently useful, and most eminently beautiful, namely a Union of the Brethren. And, surely, it may justly be impressed upon

the mind of every other character, that, with so excellent an example before
him he is unworthy the name of a Mason if he either espouses or countenances
any other principle but the principle of Union. My opinion then is, if any
member, whether of my own Society or the other, does anything, in word, or
deed, to increase the difference or enlarge the breach, he is (whether intention-
ally or not) absolutely an hindrance to the growth of brotherly love, and,
consequently subverts all the best efforts not only of the principles of Masonry,
but also of Christianity.

My hearty wishes, my dear brother, is, that this Union may soon be
effected, that the Masonic Temple of Universal Love and Concord may raise
its beautiful head, not only above all opposition of those who are acquainted
with its excellencies, but also that all its avenues of brotherly love may be filled
with brethren of one heart and one mind, all aiming, according to the true
principles of MASONIC UNION, to love each other with a pure heart fer-
vently; and the gazing world, admiring to see how we brethren love, may
anxiously desire to increase our numbers, and our means of doing good.

I remain,
Your affectionate Friend and Brother,
JETHRO INWOOD

Rectory House
St. Paul's Deptford.
Feb. 15. 1804

The climate of opinion was such that Daniel could take full advantage of all opportunities that arose. He managed to channel
masonic charity for clothing and educating sons of masons as well
as relief for needy widows from the original institution founded by
and in company with Burwood of the Antients Grand Lodge Ald-
house their Tyler, and others when they shared membership in
United Mariners Lodge. At the period when he changed the name
of Royal Naval Lodge to include 'of Independence'—he began a
neglect of payment for fees of registration and such was the state of
finance that on 28 November 1810 he was suspended by the Moderns Grand Lodge until settlement could be made. At that time he
joined the declining Lodge of Felicity, as one might expect was
elected to the Chair and the lodge commenced an era of prosperity;
the members undertook the responsibility for payment of the outstanding fees of £300 due from his activity in Royal Naval Lodge,
and the very next year paid off £105, eventually clearing the re-
mainder in 1815 when Bro. Daniel was conducted into the Grand
Lodge (United by then) admonished by the Grand Master, re-
invested with his Masonic clothing and allowed to take his seat as
Master of Lodge of Felicity. (E. L. Hawkins, *The Freemason* 22 & 29
May, 1909.)

During this time Thomas Harper had a rather low profile in
other than deliberations in the Antients Stewards Lodge and the

Grand Lodge connected with his prominent position which he upheld with the dignity that office required, as well as his attention to his business as silversmith and jeweller; there is ample evidence in both fields of activity. Also he published further editions of Dermott's *Ahiman Rezon*, first in 1801, an exercise which perhaps antagonised certain of the Moderns, then again in 1807. Those 6th and 7th editions were 'Revised by Thomas Harper' but still included the caustic remarks of Laurence Dermott's earlier efforts, as well as his *Address to the Fraternity*: it is worthy of notice that he also published the final edition of that work in 1813 in which was stated 'Revised and corrected with considerable additions, brought down to the present time, from the original of the late Laurence Dermott Esq., by Thomas Harper, D.G.M., Eighth Edition, London.' It was perhaps the final fling before the Union on 27 December of that year.

However, behind the scenes he must have been involved, unofficially or not, or certain actions taken by the Moderns Grand Lodge would not have occurred, the most effective being recorded in the Minutes of the Committee of Charity on 7 April 1809:

> Resolved unanimously THAT this Committee do not consider it necessary for the Grand Lodge any longer to continue in force those measures which were resorted to in or about the year 1739 respecting irregular Masons and do therefore recommend that the several Lodges be enjoined to revert to the Antient Land Marks of the Society.

It was confirmed in Grand Lodge and thus was removed one of the major hurdles that ever would have prevented 'an Union'; 'in or about the year 1739' was a rather late dating as all the references were in an earlier stage of the '30s' probably the action followed Prichard's *Masonry Dissected* which was published in 1730. It is appropriate here to recall the 8th Question and Answer in Dermott's *Address*:

> *8th.* Whether the present members of Modern Lodges are blameable for deviating so much from the old land-marks?
> *Ans.* No: because the innovation was made in the reign of King George the First, and this new form was delivered to them as orthodox to the present members.

King George I succeeded to the throne in 1714 and died in 1727 so Dermott may have been referring to certain changes indicated in the first Book of *Constitutions* compiled by James Anderson. However, it is of no consequence here to pursue their departure from the ancient Land-marks of the Society, or the 'differences' caused by abandonment of certain ceremonial procedure. For lists have been projected by various writers who have been inspired by hints from records on both sides, but nowhere is there an official list for such items would not have been placed on record.

The next major step was almost imperative for the Moderns and that occurred the following year in the Committee of Charity on 2 February 1810:

> Resolved THAT in consequence of late occurrences it be recommended to the Grand Lodge to rescind the Resolution of the Grand Lodge on the 9th February for the expulsion of Brother Thomas Harper.

It was confirmed in Grand Lodge only a few days later with the wording almost unchanged.

During the period of his expulsion from the Moderns the question of the Union was raised in the Stewards Lodge of the Antients, following the Moderns Resolution to 'revert to the Antient Land Marks'. For the second time Bro. Cranfield proposed the following, on 6 September 1809:

> That a Committee be appointed from the Grand Lodge to consider of and adopt such prompt and effectual Measures for accomplishing so desirable an Object as a Masonic Union.

Each time Thomas Harper was in the Chair, but according to the records in their Minute Book, he must have been an excellent example of diplomacy for the long debates were heated in exchange; the resistance may be measured by these remarks:

> The R.W. Bro. Charles Humphreys P.S.G.W., objected to the Motion being received as tending to annihilate the Ancient Craft.

Thomas Harper skilfully side-stepped in his 'verdict' which ended with:

> ... The R.W. Deputy Grand Master in the Chair after Maturely Considering hereon and as at present advised and according with his Duty as Dep! Grand Master conceiving it incompatible with his Situation in the absence of the Grand Master to receive such a Motion.

But persistence on the part of Bro Cranfield paid off because he raised the matter yet again on 6 December 1809, perhaps after a lot of lobbying, even in both camps, for at that meeting the Motion was accepted; the information was communicated to the Grand Lodges of Scotland and Ireland and, even before Harper's expulsion had been rescinded the Antients reached the following resolution:

> Grand Lodge, Crown and Anchor Tavern, London.
> Wednesday 7 March 1810
> THAT a Masonic union of the Grand Lodge under the present Grand Masters His Royal Highness the Prince of Wales and his Grace the Duke of Atholl, on principles equal and honourable to both Grand Lodges and preserving inviol-

ate the landmarks of the Ancient Craft would in the opinion of the Grand
Lodge be expedient and advantageous to both.

It was communicated to the Moderns Grand Lodge, and doubtless
with consultation among individuals, within a remarkably short
time had the desired effect:

> Grand Lodge (Moderns) held at Freemasons' Hall
> Great Queen Street April 11th 1810
> Resolved Unanimously that the Grand Lodge meets with unfeigned cordiality
> the desire expressed by the Grand Lodge under His Grace the Duke of Atholl
> for a Re-Union.

The expression 'Re-Union' was quite out of place as it implies that
the two Grand Lodges had formerly been united which was not the
case. But that resolution was followed by another:

> That the Grand Officers for the year, with the addition of the R.W.
> Masters of Somerset House, Emulation, Shakespeare, Jerusalem, and Bank of
> England Lodges, be a committee for negotiating this desirable arrangement.

The Masters of those lodges had been named in the Warrant for
the lodge set up in October the previous year 'for the purpose of
promulgating the Land Marks of the Society and instructing the
Craft in all such matters and forms ...'—yet another positive move
'to put an end to diversity and establish one true system' by the
Moderns Grand Lodge. Lord Moira communicated details of the
Committee to Thomas Harper who, following the next meeting of
the Antients Grand Lodge, gave details of their committee and
certain conditions:

> That Pastmasters should sit in the United Grand Lodge; and that Masonic
> Benevolence should be distributed monthly.
> That the Prince of Wales' Masons were to consent to take the same obligations
> under which the other three Grand Lodges were bound, and to work in the
> same forms.
> Also, the following were appointed members of the Atholl Committee, viz., the
> Present and Past Grand Officers, with Brothers Dewsnap, Cranfield, McCann,
> Heron, and Ronalds.

'the other three Grand Lodges' referred to Scotland, Ireland, and
themselves. The Moderns Committee assured the Antients that they
had already exerted themselves having formed a Lodge of Promulgation ... but were ready to concur in any plan for investigating
and ascertaining the genuine course ...'

Chapter 16

The Special Lodge of Promulgation

On 26 October 1809 Lord Moira issued a Warrant which re-stated the resolution passed in Grand Lodge on 12 April 1809:

> That this Grand Lodge do agree in opinion with the Committee of Charity that it is not necessary any longer to continue those measures which were reported to in or about the year 1739 respecting Irregular Masons, and do therefore enjoin the several Lodges to revert to the ancient Land Marks of the Society. We therefore for the better carrying into effect the intention of the said Grand Lodge DO hereby constitute [*then follows named brethren*] into a Lodge of Free and Accepted Masons to be opened at Freemasons Hall for the purpose of Promulgating the Ancient Land Marks of the Society and instructing the Craft in all such matters and forms as may be necessary to be known by them in Consequence of and Obedience to the said Resolution and Order ...

The Warrant empowered those who were named to co-opt others in the performance of their duties which were to last only until 31 December 1810. The named Master was James Earnshaw, with James Deans as SW and James Joyce as JW but at their first meeting on 21 November 1809, with those officers in place, Earnshaw was 're-elected' as Master, and he then appointed James Deans as Senior and William White as Junior Wardens. It was resolved that the lodge be called 'The Special Lodge of Promulgation'. They proceeded to elect twenty-three members amongst whom were the Master and Senior Warden of Lodge of Antiquity (No 1 on the Moderns List), HRH the Duke of Sussex and Bro Charles Bonnor.

At the meeting Bonnor was appointed Secretary and proved extremely helpful to them in that he was able to answer the question as to 'what were the Ancient Landmarks which they were required to restore?' The new Secretary proceeded to give a description of the practices that had been retained in Lodge of Antiquity which they, as 'Traditioners' to recall Heron Lepper's expression, had preserved.

The members placed themselves under an obligation 'not to reveal improperly any of the Secrets or Mysteries, Form or Ceremonies, of Ancient Masonry which have been or may hereafter be communicated to us'. Their exploratory efforts had quite a boost on 29 December 1809 when the Duke of Sussex attended and Charles Bonnor described certain details in regard to Past Masters. The Minutes include the following:

> ... a particular explanation of the Ancient practice of a respectable community of the Craft who have never entertained the modern practice was minutely set forth by the Secretary ... Whereupon certain deviations from the practice so explained were pointed out agreeable to the proceedings of the Athol Lodges, which deviations were ably descanted upon and discussed. Bro. H.R.H. the Duke of Sussex was pleased to contribute largely to the accumulation of valuable and important information by a luminous exposition of the Practices adhered to by our Masonic Brethren in Berlin.

The meeting of January 23 gave notice of arrangements for the next meeeting for January 26 which was to include 'an Oration applicable to the occasion by Bro. Corry, P.J.G.W. and the drinking of four toasts, to the King and the Craft; the Grand Master; the Acting Grand Master; and "The Heart that conceals and the Tongue that never improperly reveals" at intervals of the work.' The Minutes for the next meeting state:

> Bro. Corry addressed to the Brethren an Elegant Exordium applicable to the occasion ... then proceeded to explain (previous to a charge) the variations to be henceforth adopted in the manner of giving the honours and Drinking Toasts; and the Ancient mode of Adjourning to refresh and returning to Labour were also practised; and likewise the arrangements of the Wardens Columns;
> ...

It was followed by a verbal description and actual demonstration of 'the whole ceremony of Initiation according to Ancient Practice' and an Address by the Master that the lodge was 'first, to ascertain what were the Ancient Landmarks and the Ancient Practice, and then to communicate to the Craft at large'. The Minutes conclude with the remark that 'The routine of proceedings was occasionally relieved by the R.W.M.'s ordering Charges to the several Masonic Toasts, as they are usually drank in the Grand Lodge and were on this occasion with unabated fervour ...' A happy occasion indeed!

It is not the intention of this work to go through their deliberations in detail, a definitive Paper on the subject was compiled by Bro. W. B. Hextall and printed in *AQC* Vol 23 pp 37-71 for those who wish to pursue the matter. But the members had not completed their work within the term granted by the Warrant and extensions to it were approved up the end of March 1811. On the 5th of that month the Minutes have:

> The R.W.M. then took a retrospective view of the proceedings of the Lodge in the three Degrees of the Order ... and proceeded to point out the

material parts in and between the several degrees to which [their] attention would be requisite in preserving the Ancient Land Marks of the Order, such as the form of the Lodge, the number and situation of the Officers, their different distinctions in the different Degrees, the restoration of the pass-words to each Degree, and the making of the pass-words between one Degree and another, instead of in the Degree.

At that stage the ceremony of Installation, which they had previously acknowledged as 'one of the true Landmarks of the Craft and ought to be observed', was still occupying their attention. The Minutes end abruptly, without details of at least two further meetings, but on March 5 four pages are taken up with an account of the Installation of Lord Moira in Grand Lodge on 6 February 1811 performed by Bros Earnshaw as Grand Master, Deans as Senior Grand Warden, White as Junior Grand Warden, and Bonnor as 'IM' which may be interpreted as 'Immediate Master' because Earnshaw actually Installed Lord Moira. It was then that Lord Moira gave Notice of a Resolution as follows:

> That the thanks of the Grand Lodge be given to Bros. Earnshaw, Deans, White, and C. Bonnor, the Officers, and to the several other members of the Lodge of Promulgation for their labours respectively; and that a Blue Apron be presented to Bros. Deans and Bonnor, Officers of that Lodge who at present do not possess the same, and that they be requested to wear such Apron in all future meetings of the Society, and also that they be considered members of the Hall Committee.

That Resolution was duly passed in Grand Lodge on April 10 and the two brethren, not previously Grand Officers were granted that privilege. The following year Deans was appointed Junior Grand Warden, but Bonnor had a slightly stormy masonic career and, in 1816, 'lost' his Blue Apron, even following a temporary expulsion aggravated by his publishing a Paper with offensive material relative to masonry.

The appointment of Committees on each side was sound indeed, but the pathway was far from smooth and tempers at times became more than somewhat frayed. Human nature does not easily admit of compromise where specialists are concerned, and enthusiasm abhors tardiness. In effect the Moderns had to adopt forms and practices that the Antients claimed they had preserved; although one cannot assume that their performances could have been standardised as transmission verbally and visually must have suffered maltreatment from brethren who travelled from far and wide. However, with the comparative ease of inter-visitation in London, where there were chances for correction if necessary, procedure would have suffered far less. At the commencement of the 19th century one quite strong influence emerged in the person of

William Finch whose manuscript material and masonic books made an extensive contribution to masonic practice and were referred to over a very wide field. His activity extended beyond the Craft and Royal Arch for his researches and collation of material resulted in the spread of 'other degrees'. Ample evidence of his work has appeared in various parts of the country and his influence has been shewn in the work of his copyists.

A

MASONIC TREATISE,

WITH AN

ELUCIDATION

ON THE

RELIGIOUS AND MORAL BEAUTIES

OF

FREEMASONRY,

Ziydvjxyjpix, Zqjisgstn, Wxstxjin, &c.

RA—AM—RC—KT—MP—M &c.

FOR THE USE OF

LODGES AND BROTHERS IN GENERAL.

—»>◉<<—

DEDICATED, BY PERMISSION,

TO

WILLIAM · PERFECT, Esq.

PROVINCIAL GRAND MASTER

FOR THE

COUNTY OF KENT.

By W. FINCH, CANTERBURY.

(SECOND EDITION, with many valuable Additions.)

A LIST of Subscribers, with an Explanation to this and Two other PLATES, is given in the Book of Elucidations on the Plates.

—»>◉<<—

Please to observe that every Book has here on the Title Page,

ty Qxzf, and Oivjjxg Qvwgzjpix.

PRINTED BY J. ATKINSON, DEAL.

M.DCCC.II.

Title page from William Finch's Masonic Treatise. *He was a controversial character who attracted both support and fierce opposition*

William Finch was quite a controversial character, he seemed to attract both support and opposition, there was no half-way measure and it was inevitable that an official complaint should be raised and that was to happen in the Minutes of the Committee of Charity (Moderns) on 4 April 1806:

> It having been represented to the Committee by several Masters of Lodges that much Injury had arisen to the Craft from a Book published by William Finch entitled 'A Masonic Treatise with an Elucidation on the Religious and Moral Duties of Freemasonry' and the said Book having been produced to the Committee and inspected it was thereupon Resolved unanimously
> That by such Publication Bro. William Finch has been guilty of a Breach of his Obligation as a Mason and has violated the Laws of Grand Lodge.

That matter was reported to Grand Lodge and a few days later their Minutes shew:

> 9 April 1806 ... The Minutes of the last Committee of Charity were read when Brother Finch addressed the Grand Lodge at considerable length, on the Resolution of the Committee respecting his Publication entitled 'A Masonic Treatise etc' but on the question being put the Minutes were confirmed; however, in consequence of Brother Finch having expressed his great concern that he should have given offence to the Grand Lodge, by the said Publication, and having also promised to use every exertion in his Power to suppress the Sale of it, the Grand Lodge declined to proceed further on the Business.

But his opponents were not to be denied and another attempt was made the following year and we take up the story in the Minutes of 8 April 1807 of Grand Lodge:

> The following Charge against Brother William Finch was duly made by Brother T.H. Shaw of the Globe Lodge No. 14 and seconded by Brother Thomas Farrell, R.W. Master of the Lodge No. 203, viz. 'That Brother Finch has in repeated instances grossly violated his Obligation'. Whereupon on a Motion duly made and seconded it was Resolved That a Committee be appointed to take into consideration and examine the said Charge. That such Committee do consist of nine members [the names are listed, six of whom were prominent in the affairs of the Lodge of Promulgation which was yet to come] and that all Masters of Lodges be allowed to attend the said Committee.

It had arisen because whilst Finch had promised to suppress the sale of his book he was now supplying manuscript ritual matter but coded so as to make it unintelligible to the ordinary reader. The Report of that Committee was lengthy and exacting and ended as follows:

> ... on his being reminded that the Opinion expressed from the Chair of the Grand Lodge by the Most Worshipful Acting Grand Master at the last Grand Lodge perfectly coincided with that of your Committee, Brother Finch expressed his concern at having unintentionally given offence to the Grand Lodge stated his readiness to pay due deference and submission to such opinions and gave to your Committee his solemn promise that he would not write the

same or similar papers in consideration of which your Committee feel it their Duty humbly to recommend to the Grand Lodge that no further Censure be passed on Brother Finch at present nor unless he shall hereafter violate the promise now given to your Committee.

and the Report was accepted by the Grand Lodge. But it is of interest to note that according to his own account of that examination, Finch wrote that he produced a bundle of 'some 300 letters from most of the Lodges in the kingdom' and that after reading some of them the Chairman of the Committee, Earl Mount Norris, Prov. Grand Master for Huntingdonshire commented 'they certainly were much in Finch's favour'.

His instructions and guidance on freemasonry in general and ritual matters in particular went on and he felt so strengthened by the support and patronage that he received that he brought counter-charges against various brethren for making 'such groundless and vexatious charges' against him. The Committee of Charity on examination of his complaint found that it was 'of such a nature not to be proceeded on', but Finch was not satisfied. He sent what he called his *Manuscript Appeal* to the Grand Master and a long letter to Earl Moira, but no action came from those efforts. He became critical of both Grand Lodges for he wrote in *Freemason's Looking Glass*, published in 1807, that both Antients and Moderns had 'lost the true system' although he conceded that the Antients were nearer to it. He stated his desire 'to remove absurdities in our System and restore Truth' and went on to state 'and I mean to make apparent that the major part, if not 90 lodges out of 100 have in material points departed from the original genuine system and in its stead have introduced a medley of stuff, inconsistent with reason, truth, and history'.

Brethren were either for or against William Finch; he was a member of St Peter's Lodge No 249, at Southwark, where he did not see eye to eye with them and on 18 January 1811 they recorded:

Resolved unanimously that Br Finch be expelled this Lodge for his unmason like conduct.

Writing of that incident sometime later, Finch stated:

... a Pass Master reported to St Peter's Lodge that in consequence of the dissatisfaction of some of the members he had attended Grand Lodge to enquire of Earl Moira if he had done right in admitting Finch as a member of St Peter's Lodge; and that Earl Moira's answer was that 'Finch was eligible to enter any Lodge, for the Grand Lodge had not found anything in his Lectures that merited expulsion.'

The exact date of his death is not on record but apparently it was in the latter part of 1818, well after the Union. His work was revived by a non-mason, Richard Carlile who in 1825 published his extensive masonic 'exposure' material, and went on so doing for many years. He gave full credit to Finch as follows:

> I recollect that, in the year 1814 or 1815, a shower of rain once drove me for shelter on a Sunday, under a portal or steps of Finch's house, the sides of which were pasted all over with Masonic advertisements. ... It was Finch who laid the foundation of this, my Exposure of Masonry, and I may add my Instruction of Masons. He was the first individual to collect all the documents which he could collect conccerning Masonry for the press. But he has done it in the most obscure manner, making keys necessary to every document that he printed as really descriptive of Masonry.

Carlile's work was in plain English throughout and when printed in book form from 1850 onwards, with many editions to its credit, came to be regarded as a manual for several degrees, although officially condemned.

An extensive Paper, *William Finch*, was compiled by Col F. M. Rickard, and is available in *AQC* Vol 55 pp 163–283, and it attracted some valuable comment printed with it. Finch was, of course, trading in masonic publications but one of his efforts was described in a leaflet of his as follows:

> The author of the MASONIC KEY having nothing in view but a desire to see our excellent moral and religious lectures universally diffused for the general good of the Fraternity ... begs leave to acquaint the Fraternity in general, that the whole of the PROFITS arising therefore will be appropriated to the use of the GENERAL FUND of MASONIC CHARITY, or any other CHARITABLE PURPOSE that may be deemed proper by the Provincial Master and Officers of this County [Kent]. ...

and in regard to another he wrote:

> ... One third of the profits are to be appropriated to the Masonic Fund for Charity, one third to the General Fund, and the other third as a remuneration for my time and labour in this new plan for diffusing Masonic knowledge.

In letters, circulars, and advertisements, Finch used every opportunity to reach brethren in general, and he adapted his work from time to time to take into consideration the differences between the two jurisdictions. He kept pace with discussions and attempts to resolve the problems, even though he was quite critical of both. In Rickard's paper, Bro F. R. Radice (p 270–71) drew attention to a Finch advertisement which, although undated, was doubtless soon after the Moderns' Resolution regarding their reverting 'to the ancient Land Marks' which was passed on 12 April 1809. The first paragraphs from that will show something of his character including his sincerity of purpose for an amalgamation:

ADVERTISEMENT to BROTHERS

Every Mason who purchases one complete set of these Lectures on Freemasonry (four sealed packets) will receive, gratis, of Brother W. Finch, a
Written Synopsis; and likewise some Oral information on that which is of the
utmost consequence, for enabling him to understand, and conduct the whole
proceedings of Masonry, agreeable to the True Ancient System; and in conformity to the late injunctions of one of our Grand Lodges 'that all Lodges and
Brothers are to return immediately to the Ancient System' which unfortunately
for the long period of 92 years has been neglected. I cannot here be so explicit
as I could wish, let it therefore suffice, that there are 22 S.'s, T.'s, and W.'s, in
the three Degrees of Craft Masonry, as practised by most foreign Lodges;
where, those Masons at present designated by the term Modern, have but 12;
and the Antient, in England, but 16.

The absurdity of this great deviation for such a length of time has at last
roused the zealous and leading Members; and the Grand Lodge, much to their
honour, have commanded all Lodges in future, to conduct the business of
Masonry in the True Ancient manner, but as that is so little known, I have
found it expedient, with the concurrence of the Fraternity, for the general good
of our Society, to publish our Lectures; carefully avoiding every thing that is
improper for Masons to commit to paper. ... The better to effect that Union
so long wished for, the Moderns (as they are commonly called) must recover
these ten chief things that they have omitted, and the Antients recover six; and
the term Modern will no longer be known amongst us; but these two great
bodies of Masons, act in future, agreeable to the true Ancient laws of our
Order; to the satisfaction of all parties, and the admiration of the world. ...

Bro Radice commented on Finch 'his love for Masonry was indeed
a passion'. It is of interest to note that when used as an adjective
'ancient' was spelt thus, but when used as a noun it was 'Antient';
also, that 'practised by most foreign Lodges' were '22 S.'s, T.'s, and
W.'s', whereas 'the Antient, *in England*, but 16'. The italics are mine
as I feel it makes a significant point regarding a lack of uniformity
universally. Finch also stated that he had resorted to public advertisement in this case rather than send circulars to Lodges as that
would have resulted in the content being suppressed, or stifled as
he termed it, through jealousy and envy.

It is worthy of notice that on 1 January 1814, just four days
after the eventual Union between the two Grand Lodges he published a 'new set of Lectures' with just that title and this time his
advertisement stated:

The following Lectures, Laws, and Ceremonies have been carefully selected from the Genuine Manuscripts and ancient branches of the Royal Craft,
for the purpose of being incorporated with those commonly called Ancient and
Modern, and thereby render the system complete, and realise the grand object
and expectations of those Brethren who first promoted the UNION.

Before turning our attention to that major turning point in the
history of organised Freemasonry, let us make one brief reference
to the Minutes of the Antients Grand Lodge to take notice of the

tributes they paid to two of their brethren:

> Resolved Unanimously:-
>
> That the cordial thanks of this Grand Lodge be given to the Right Worshipful Brother Thomas Harper, Deputy Grand Master, for his indefatigable, zealous and honourable conduct during a period of more than twenty-eight years that he has been an Officer in this Grand Lodge; but more especially for his constant and unwearied attention for the last thirteen years, in the discharge of the arduous and important duties as Deputy Grand Master.
>
> Resolved Unanimously:-
>
> That the especial thanks of this Grand Lodge be given to our Right Worshipful Brother, Past Deputy Grand Master Perry, for the very distinguished services he has at various times and for a series of years rendered to the Craft.
>
> That the members of this Grand Lodge are led to the performance of this duty, peculiarly gratifying to them, from the high sense they entertain of the purity of the principles from which he has acted, from their unqualified admiration of the talents and eloquence which he has constantly displayed in their behalf, and from the pleasing anticipation of those happy and glorious consequences which his exertions have so eminently contributed to produce.
>
> The Grand Lodge was then closed with holy prayer till St John's Day next, to meet at Freemasons' Hall, at eleven o'clock in the forenoon.

Thus was their scene set for the great event to take place on St John the Evangelist Festival, 27 December 1813, to heal the division created in 1751 which lasted for nearly sixty-two years. Who shall say what course would have been steered but for the intransigence of the brethren who practised Freemasonry 'According to the Old Institutions'?

Chapter 17

Articles of Union

The Lodge of Promulgation, set up by the Moderns Grand Lodge on 26 October 1809 'for the purpose of promulgating the ancient Land Marks of the Society and instructing the Craft in all such matter and forms . . .', lasted until 5 March 1811. During that time it had provided terms of reference for brethren in London who had easy access and thus encouraged the revival of various Lodges of Instruction and the creation of others; thereby a greater interest was taken in matters of ceremonial. Inevitably, the official lodge had little influence, if any, upon the behaviour of brethren situated in the Provinces, they continued with their own attitudes of visitation or non-recognition according to local practice. However, the efforts of the Lodge of Promulgation confirmed the purpose and intention of the Moderns as was shown in the Minutes of Grand Lodge on 9 February 1811:

> THAT the Grand Lodge under His Roy! Highness the Prince of Wales had resolved to return to the Ancient Land Marks of Masonry and in Order to achieve a perfect Union of the two Grand Lodges they will consent to the same Obligation and Continue to abide by the Ancient Land Marks of Masonry when it should be ascertained what those Ancient Land Marks and Obligations were.

The Committees of both Grand Lodges met together, at times when the patience of the Moderns was severely strained, but firmer ground was reached by the end of that year as shown by the Antients Minutes of 13 December 1811;

> Received in due form the committee of the G.L. under H.R.H. the Prince Regent. Proceeded to business and among various items the following points were mentioned:
> The question was distinctly put to the Committee of the Grand Lodge under the Prince Regent whether in expressing their readiness to adopt the Ancient forms it was to be understood that the practice of the Grand Lodges of Scotland and Ireland, of America, and of the greatest part of the Continent, which in perfect Union with the practise of the Grand Lodge of England under the Duke of Atholl was to be the one adopted and acted upon by the United Grand Lodge so as to give complete Unity to the Masonic World. To this was Answered that undoubtedly it was their wish to put an end to all diversity and

to establish the one true system. But it should be essential that the true system should be ascertained. They had in fact for some time exerted themselves to Act by the Ancient forms; they had formed a Lodge of Promulgation; and they had the assistance of several Ancient Masons but in short they were ready to Concur in any plan for investigation and ascertaining the genuine Course, and when demonstrated to walk in it. . . .

Owing to the illness of King George III, HRH the Prince of Wales was created Prince Regent in February 1811 but he continued in office as Grand Master of the Moderns until 1813 and then was succeeded by his brother, Augustus Frederick, Duke of Sussex. In November of that year the Duke of Athol retired as Grand Master of the Antients Grand Lodge in favour of the Duke of Kent who was installed on 1 December 1813. Prior to that ceremony, in an adjoining room, the Duke of Sussex was 're-made' by being obligated as an Antient mason in order that he could take part.

The *Articles of Union* (see Appendix F) which had been compiled by the two Committees had been engrossed and taken to Kensington Palace on 25 November 1813 to be signed by the royal brothers. That document named the following from each side as commissioners for its implementation. On behalf of the Moderns:

> H.R.H. the Duke of Sussex
> Waller Rodwell Wright, Prov. Grand Master for Ionian Isles
> Arthur Tegart, Past Grand Warden
> James Deans, Past Grand Warden

and, on behalf of the Antients:

> H.R.H. the Duke of Kent
> Thomas Harper, Deputy Grand Master
> James Agar, Past Deputy Grand Master
> James Perry, Past Deputy Grand Master

The same brethren from each side were also later appointed as delegates to represent England at the Conference in June/July 1814 which formulated the International Compact between England, Ireland and Scotland.

Each Grand Lodge ratified the *Articles of Union* an action which was recorded by the Antients as follows:

> Dec. 1st 1813:
> . . . the R.W. Bro. Perry moved the following resolutions which were carried in the affirmative unanimously,
> 1. That the Articles of Union now read be Ratified and Confirmed.
> 2. That the Most Worshipful His Royal Highness the Grand Master be requested and empowered to affix the Great Seal thereto, and to exchange the same with His Royal Highness the Duke of Sussex as Grand Master of the other Fraternity.
> 3. That brotherly application be made to the Grand Lodges of Scotland and

Ireland, enclosing them copies of the above Articles, when ratified, and entreating them to delegate two or more enlightened members of their respective bodies to be present at the Assembly of Union on Monday the 27th December instant, pursuant to Article IV.

4. That the Grand Master do nominate nine worthy and expert Master Masons, or Past Masters, to discharge the duties set forth in Articles V, and XV.

5. That a special dispensation under the great Seal, be issued to those nine Brothers and their Secretary, to hold a Lodge of Reconciliation, in conjunction with an equal number to be appointed and empowered by His Royal Highness the Duke of Sussex, to fulfil the duties set forth and enjoined in the said Articles of Union.

6. That the Masters, Wardens and Past Masters of the warranted lodges do attend the said Lodge of Reconciliation according to notices to be addressed to them for the purposes of being obligated, certified, and registered, to entitle them to be present at the assembly of Masons for the Union of the two Grand Lodges of England on Monday the 27th December instant.

7. That the Secretaries of the said Lodge of Reconciliation shall keep a book, in which shall be entered the names of the regular Members of Lodges belonging to both Fraternities, so obligated and certified, that they may be registered without fee or reward in the books of the two Grand Lodges, and be thereby entitled to tickets of admission to the said Assembly of Union, and that a correct return of the whole be made to the Grand Secretaries on or before the 23rd of December instant.

Item 4 in those resolutions was in accordance with Article V of the *Articles of Union* (see Appendix F) and no time was lost in putting that into action in order that as many brethren as was possible could 'give and receive mutually and reciprocally the obligations of both Fraternities' and thereby become qualified to attend the great occasion. The Lodge of Reconciliation was under the authority of a special Warrant signed by the Duke of Sussex on 7 December 1813, his signature having been witnessed by the Duke of Kent. It is the only Warrant to bear the signatures of two Royal Grand Masters, but its function was to prepare the way for those who were to be engaged in the actual ceremonial and then to blaze the trail for:

> ... the most perfect unity of obligations, of discipline, of working the lodges, of making, passing and raising, instructing and clothing Brothers; so that one pure unsullied system, according to the genuine landmarks, laws, and traditions of the Craft shall be maintained, upheld, and practised, throughout the Masonic World, from the day and date of the said Union until time shall be no more. . . .

The Ceremony of the Union

December 27, the Festival of St John the Evangelist, in the year 1813 must assuredly be deemed a major turning point in the history of the organisation of Freemasonry. Then it was that the mother of all Grand Lodges, the premier Grand Lodge dating from 1717, conjoined with the Antients' Grand Lodge which dated from 1751 and thus came into existence 'The United Grand Lodge of Ancient Freemasons of England'.

In rooms adjoining the Grand Temple each Grand Lodge opened their own proceedings and then in procession entered the Grand Temple where the brethren from both sides, intermingled, had been assembled to receive them. The two Grand Masters took their seats, one on either side of the throne and the *Act of Union* was read. The following proclamation was made:

> Be it known to all Men, That the Act of Union between the two Grand Lodges of Free and Accepted Masons of England, is solemnly signed sealed, ratified, and confirmed, and the two Fraternities are one, to be from henceforth known and acknowledged by the style and title of THE UNITED GRAND LODGE OF ANCIENT FREEMASONS OF ENGLAND; and may the Great Architect of the Universe make their Union eternal!

The Grand Masters, Deputy Grand Masters and Wardens gathered round the Ark of the Masonic Covenant which had been made under the direction of Sir John Soane, Grand Supt of Works and had been placed before the Throne. Each distinguished brother gave three light knocks upon it with a maul and said the following:

> May the G.A.O.T.U. enable us to uphold the grand edifice of the Union, of which this Ark of the Covenant is the symbol, which shall contain within it the instrument of our brotherly love, and bear upon it the Holy Bible, square and compass, as the light of our faith and the rule of our works. May He dispose our hearts to make it perpetual.

The Act of Union was placed in the Ark and the whole consecrated in masonic manner.

Members of the Lodge of Reconciliation together with certain distinguished brethren from other Jurisdictions retired to an adjoining room and upon their return an announcement was made that 'the forms settled and agreed upon by the Lodge of Reconciliation were pure and correct'; it was later declared that they were 'the forms alone to be observed and practised in the United Grand Lodge and all Lodges dependent thereon, until time shall be no more'. The Rev Samuel Hemming, Master of the Lodge of Reconciliation, led the Obligation which was repeated by all present:

> By this solemn obligation we vow to abide, and the Regulations of Ancient Freemasonry now recognised strictly to observe.

The Grand Officers and those acting in the various offices then divested themselves of masonic regalia and James Perry, Past Deputy GM of the former Antients Grand Lodge took the Chair. The

Duke of Kent proposed his brother the Duke of Sussex to be Grand Master of the United Grand Lodge for the ensuing year, that was seconded by the Hon Washington Shirley, Past GW of the former Moderns Grand Lodge, and carried with acclamation. The Grand Master was obligated and placed upon the throne by the Duke of Kent. It was agreed that the formal Installation should take place on the next St George's Day, 23 April 1814, the Grand Officers of the year were then nominated and it was announced that the two Grand Lodges were at that point consolidated into one United Grand Lodge and declared to be open in due form according to ancient usage.

The Throne of the Grand Master, and the two Wardens' Chairs, used then and from that date on, had been made especially for the Prince of Wales after he had been installed as Grand Master of the Moderns in 1790. The feathers which were a prominent feature (see page 122) were replaced by a Ducal Coronet for the Duke of Connaught's installation as Grand Master in 1901. (see page 123). Grand Masters who have been enthroned in succession in that Chair, wherever the venue has been, are as follows:

1790–1813 HRH The Prince of Wales (afterwards King George IV)
1813–1843 HRH Augustus Frederick, Duke of Sussex
1844–1870 Thomas, 2nd Earl of Zetland
1870–1874 George Frederick Samuel, 1st Marquess of Ripon
1874–1901 HRH Albert Edward, Prince of Wales (afterwards King Edward VII)
1901–1939 HRH Arthur, Duke of Connaught and Strathearn
1939–1942 HRH George, Duke of Kent
1942–1947 Henry, 6th Earl of Harewood
1947–1950 Edward William Spencer, 10th Duke of Devonshire
1951–1967 Lawrence Roger, 11th Earl of Scarbrough
1967 HRH Edward George, Duke of Kent

We are indebted to the late Bro C.R.S. Foottit for a Paper entitled 'English Royal Freemasons' (*AQC* 81 pp 348–54) two paragraphs from which are particularly appropriate here:

Twenty-three Princes of the British Royal family have been members of the Craft since 1737 eight of whom honoured Freemasonry by accepting the office of Grand Master. In fact English Freemasonry has had Royal Grand Masters during 134 years in all. . . .

Of all the English Royal Freemasons, George, Duke of York (b 1895–d 1952) has the record of greatest masonic activity. After his accession as King George VI, Past Grand Master, he installed his brother the Duke of Kent in 1939, his brother-in-law the Earl of Harewood in 1943, and the Duke of Devonshire in 1948. Three years later, in 1951, he intended to instal the Earl of Scarborough as Grand Master but owing to illness was unable to be present. He died three months afterwards having won the hearts of all Freemasons, who mourned his passing and cherish his memory.

The Throne of the Grand Master made especially for the Prince of Wales. The feathers were a prominent feature

The Throne occupied by the Duke of Connaught in 1901 at his Enthronement. The feathers have been replaced by a Ducal coronet. Subsequent Grand Masters have been enthroned in succession in that chair wherever the venue has been

The Grand Lodge was called to refreshment and a Loving Cup was presented to the Grand Master who drank to 'Peace, Good Will, and Brotherly Love, all over the World', after which the Grand Lodge was recalled to labour to deal with a number of Resolutions, to receive an Address, and various Votes of Thanks to some of those who had played such strong parts in bringing the Union into being. Grand Lodge was then closed in Ample Form and the brethren retired to dine together at the Crown and Anchor Tavern in the Strand. At the banquet the recital included an ode especially written for the event by Bro. Waller Rodwell Wright, and an anthem composed by Samuel Wesley, Grand Organist (1813–17) with various songs, glees, and choruses.

In accordance with Article VIII lots were drawn for the positions of private lodges in the new Register and fate decreed that the Time Immemorial Lodge, the Lodge of Antiquity which was No 1 on the List of the Moderns and one of the four Founding Lodges of the premier Grand Lodge in 1717, became No 2. The Grand Master's Lodge which had been No 1 on the List of the Antients and had not come into existence until 1756, drew the first place and became No 1 on the new Register. Other lodges from both Jurisdictions followed alternately in like manner. The Grand Stewards Lodge which, on a Resolution passed in the Moderns Grand Lodge in 1792, was placed without number at the head of the *List of Lodges*, retained that position which it occupies uniquely to this day.

It is of interest to recall that Thomas Harper was confirmed in his rank as Deputy Grand Master, by the Duke of Sussex who must have deemed that to be an obvious courtesy gesture, and that the Grand Secretaries from each Jurisdiction were appointed as Joint Grand Secretaries for the United Grand Lodge and so remained until 1838. Certain other ranks and offices not then in existence were to be created in subsequent years.

The exact number of lodges on the Register of the former Grand Lodges is difficult to determine as some had failed to make a regular Return therefore one has to make allowance for what might be termed 'dead wood'; but the generally accepted figure of a combined total of 647, made up from 389 lodges on the Moderns side and 258 of the Antients is probably as near as one would get. From that combined figure London is credited with a total of 118. Those figures have expanded to a recorded total as at 1984 of London lodges—1,677, Provincial lodges 5,770, in Districts and abroad 775, making a combined total of 8,222.

The International Compact

In the period prior to the Union it is quite evident that the liaison between the Antients Grand Lodge and the Grand Lodges of Ireland and Scotland was close indeed. Grand Mastership between them had been shared as follows:

1756-1759 William, 1st Earl of Blesington who was GM of Ireland 1738-1739
1760-1765 Thomas Alexander, 6th Earl of Kellie who was GMM of Scotland 1763-1765
1771-1774 John, 3rd Duke of Atholl, who was GMM of Scotland, 1773
1775-1781 ⎫
1791-1813 ⎭ John, 4th Duke of Atholl, who was GMM of Scotland, 1778-79
1783-1791 Randal William, 6th Earl and 2nd Marquess of Antrim who was GM Ireland 1773 and 1779

For comparison, in that period the Moderns had the following although not simultaneously:

1757-1761 Sholto Charles, 15th Earl of Morton who was GMM of Scotland 1755-1756
1764-1766 Cadwallader, 9th Lord Blayney who was GM of Ireland for 1768

On record are many transcripts of communications exchanged between the Grand Lodges of Ireland and Scotland with the Antients but there are far less examples with the Moderns.

> Item IV of the *Articles of Union* stated:
> ... that brotherly application be made to the Grand Lodges of Scotland and Ireland, to authorize, delegate and appoint, any two or more of their enlightened members to be present at the Grand Assembly on the solemn occasion of uniting the said Fraternities; ... [and that all present] shall solemnly engage to abide by the true forms and obligations, particularly in matters which can neither be described nor written, in the presence of the said members of the Grand Lodges of Scotland and Ireland, that it may be declared, recognized, and known, that they all are bound by the same solemn pledge, and work under the same law.

That item was confirmed by the Antients before the Union at their Quarterly Communication held on 1 December when it was listed among the resolutions that were to be implemented; they are listed on pp. 118-19. Ireland was represented at the Grand Assembly, but no representative for Scotland attended. In pursuit of a mutual consultation a conference was called for 27 June 1814, at which were present the Grand Master Mason of Scotland, attended by a Past Depute Grand Master, the Grand Master of Ireland, attended by a Past Grand Master, and the Duke of Sussex, with Lord Dundas, Deputy Grand Master, together with five who had been appointed as Commissioners of the *Articles of Union*. The business not being concluded on that date, the conference was continued on 2 July.

The *Articles of Union* were read over and the following was recorded:

> Upon a strict examination on matters which can neither be written nor described, it was ascertained that the THREE GRAND LODGES were perfectly in unison in all the great and essential points of the Mystery and Craft, according to the immemorial traditions and uninterrupted usage of Ancient Masonry.

Various resolutions were agreed upon and that Conference laid the foundation for all future consultations. A document entitled *The International Compact between the Grand Lodges of England, Ireland, and Scotland* was drawn up, approved, and adopted subject to ratification by the Grand Lodges, and that was speedily forthcoming. It was thus the three sister Grand Lodges found a common basis and constructed agreed terms of reference.

Appendices (G and H) have transcripts of what is operative at the present time under the titles *Aims and Relationships of the Craft* and *Basic Principles For Grand Lodge Recognition*. Both provide perfectly clear statements of the practise of freemasonry as it is seen in the British Isles but the matter of Recognition so far as Grand Lodges in other parts of the world is concerned is subject to strict scrutiny. Unfortunately certain Grand Lodges do exist that do not qualify and freemasonry has, at times and by the uninformed, been measured by their behaviour.

Chapter 18

The Lodge of
Reconciliation

Item V of the *Articles of Union* provided for 'nine worthy and expert Master Masons, or Past Masters' to be appointed from each jurisdiction 'either to hold a Lodge under the Warrant or Dispensation to be entrusted to them, and to be entitled the LODGE OF RE-CONCILIATION, or to visit the several Lodges holding under both the Grand Lodges for the purpose of obligating, instructing, and perfecting the Masters, Past Masters, Wardens and Members, in both forms. . . .'

Mention has already been made of the Warrant, signed and witnessed respectively by the two Royal Brothers, which was issued on 7 December 1813. That Warrant appointed named brethren from the Moderns empowering them 'to meet unite and incorporate themselves with a Lodge of equal numbers to be constituted and appointed by His Royal Highness Edward Duke of Kent &c &c &c Grand Master of Masons according to the Old Institutions . . .' The named brethren under that Warrant were as follows:

Rev Samuel Hemming of the Lodge of Harmony (now No 255) who was appointed Master
William Meyrick, Lodge of Antiquity (No 2) to be SW
William Shadbolt, Grand Steward's Lodge, to be JW
Stephen Jones, Lodge of Antiquity (No 2)
Laurence Thompson, Lodge of Felicity (Now No 58)
Joseph Jones, Lodge of Sincerity (extinct)
J.H. Sarratt, Moira Lodge (now No 92)
Thomas Bell, Caledonian Lodge (now No 134)
James Joyce, Bank of England Lodge (now No 263)
and William Henry White to be Joint Secretary.

The named brethren appointed by the Duke of Kent, 'by a special dispensation under the great Seal' the 'nine worthy brethren' included two sons of Thomas Harper, are listed below:

R.F. Mestayer, Grand Master's Lodge (No 1)
Thomas Harper Jnr., of the same lodge
J.H. Goldsworthy, Lodge of Fidelity (now No 3)

William Fox, Royal York Lodge of Perseverance (now No 7)
James Ronalds, Robert Burns Lodge (now No 25)
William Oliver, Royal Jubilee Lodge (now No 72)
Michael Corcoran, Middlesex Lodge (now No 143)
Richard Bayley, of the lodge at 'the Lord Cochrane' (extinct)
James McCann, Lodge of Tranquillity (now No 185)
and Edwards Harper to be Joint Secretary

The pre-Union task of the Lodge of Reconciliation was to obligate as many as possible, in both forms, in order that brethren would be acceptable to each other for that great occasion. But its work was to go on although no time limit had been set for it. Eight meetings are on record prior to the Union, then there is a break until 9 February 1814 when the following is recorded:

B^r Wavell Secy of 249 [formerly No 200 on the Antients List] attended and received the obligation of a M. Mason as agreed and ratified on the 27th Dec. 1813.

Bro^r Thos. Harper Junr moved the following resolution, which seconded by Bro. St Jones and being put was carried unanimously:-

That it appears that several of the Lodges in the Country have sent deputations to London in the view of obtaining information as to the future mode of working at a considerable expense to themselves or the Lodges they represent, and as this Lodge is not yet qualified to give the required information, that a respectful representation be made to H.R.H. the M.W. Grand Master requesting that he will be generously pleased to give directions to the Grand Secretaries to notify all the Lodges that they will continue severally to work as heretofore until they receive further notice.

Resolved that this L. meet on Wednesday next at 7 o'clock punctually.

It drew forth a directive signed by the two Joint Secretaries, 'By command of the Most Worshipful HRH the Grand Master':

... It is earnestly recommended to the Provincial Grand Masters, and Masters of Lodges at a distance from London, to take the earliest opportunity of deputising, by written authority, some one or more of the most qualified Members of their respective Lodges, to attend the Lodge of Reconciliation which will be convened weekly at Freemasons Hall (the precise days of its Meeting may be hereafter learned upon application to the Grand Secretaries) that the acknowledged forms, to be universally used, may be made known to them for the information of their Brothers. In the meantime the Members of the two Fraternities are hereby empowered and directed to give and receive, in open Lodge, the respective obligations of each Fraternity; in order that they may cordially meet together and be placed all on the same level, and the better to receive the recognized forms, which are alone to be practised in the future.

The long interval that occurred between the meeting of the Lodge of Reconciliation held on 9 February 1814 and the next recorded meeting on 4 August 1814 is accounted for by its temporary suspension by the authorities as reported in the Report of the Quarterly Communication of the United Grand Lodge held in March:

> ... It having been thought advisable to postpone the Meetings of the Lodge of Reconciliation until after the arrival of the Brethren from Scotland and Ireland, you are requested not to depute etc etc ...

The members of the lodge probably met together unofficially for their own convenience but did not resume until August when six meetings were held for the instruction of deputations consisting of the Masters and Wardens of various lodges. The following month six more meetings took place in which month an interim report was drawn up to be presented to the Grand Master:

> The Lodge of Reconciliation respectfully beg leave to report to the Most Worshipful Grand Master that they have proceeded so far in performance of the duties entrusted to them, as to have thrice exhibited to the Lodges in the London District the newly arranged mode of Masonic instruction, as far as relates to the opening and closing of a Lodge in the three degrees, the several obligations therein required and the ceremonies of making, passing, and raising, together with a brief test or examination in each degree, and that they are also prepared to proceed in their system of elucidation, by such means as may be considered the best adapted for their purpose.
>
> [signed] Sam. Hemming S.G.W.
R.W.M.

The membership of the Lodge of Reconciliation did not stay constant with those who had been named, eg Thomas Harper Jnr 'having left England'; 'the non-attendance of Bros Ronalds and Corcoran'; 'from the improper conduct of Bro Goldsworthy allowing his name to appear in print arraigning the Conduct and mode of instruction adopted by this Lodge.' Other brethren, however, were added and the number increased as many expert and capable brethren became involved. But the rebellion that arose within its ranks stemmed from members of a group of lodges formerly under the Antients jurisdiction who were disenchanted with the system of working adopted and being communicated by the Lodge of Reconciliation. They set up a committee which met at The Crown Tavern, Clerkenwell Green, which was then the venue of one of the lodges concerned. The purpose was 'to devise measures for opposing the Innovations attempted to be introduced by the Lodge of Reconciliation', and the outcome was that a Memorial was prepared in Phoenix Lodge (now No 173), with which five other lodges associated themselves, which was sent to the Duke of Sussex. No action was taken by HRH other than to refer the matter to the Lodge of Reconciliation for examination and report. Various brethren were summoned to attend for examination on that subject, Bro Goldsworthy was 'no longer considered a Member' of the Lodge of Reconciliation, most brethren were mollified on the issue other than the brethren in Phoenix Lodge who, on 6 February 1815:

RESOLVED that the Lodge will not adopt or propagate the System introduced by the Lodge of Reconciliation.

In an attempt to obtain the co-operation of those brethren two members of the Lodge of Reconciliation presented themselves at their meeting called for 6 March 1815, Bro Bayley and RW Bro William Williams, Provincial Grand Master over Dorset. The following has been recorded of that event:

Brothers Bailey and Williams (both members of the L of Reconciliation and the latter Prov GM for Dorset) attended to be admitted into the Lodge, but not having taken the Obligation in the three Degrees of Ancient Masonry it was Resolved that they should not be admitted.

The WM produced a Summons he had received from the Grand Secretaries to attend the Board of General Purposes (on 22nd Feb) on the subject of the Resolution passed at the Last Lodge—THAT the Lodge would not receive or practise the System of Masonry adopted by the Lodge of Reconciliation and informed the Lodge that he had attended with his Wardens accordingly, and mentioned the result of what passed. . . .

One month later the Master informed the members that he had attended upon the Board of General Purposes together with three brethren from the lodge and upon that report it was resolved:

1st. That the Resolution passed in this Lodge on 6th February last, a copy of which was sent to the Grand Secretary, is strictly in unison with the Constitutions and Principles of Ancient Masonry.

2ndly. That from the report made by the W.M. assisted by Bros. Coates, Warne and Badger, who attended the B. of G.P. in consequence of the above Resolution of 6 February last, Agreeable tò Summons, it appears to us that without a manly and determined Opposition on the part of the Ancient Lodges the Noble and renowned fabric of Ancient Masonry will be greatly destroyed.

3rdly. That we will not assist in, or countenance the Subversion of Ancient Masonry, which the Measures of the L. of R. are strongly calculated to produce, countenanced and supported as those Measures are by the different Boards appointed by the Grand Master, and do therefore feel ourselves imperatively compelled to decline holding any intercourse until the Articles of the Union are fulfilled.

4th. That those Members of the L. of R. appointed by the Duke of Kent on the part of the Ancient Craft who have consented to and propagate the Measures adopted by the Grand Lodge, we consider to have sacrificed their Public Duty as Masons and countenanced Measures contrary to their Obligations and the Principles of Ancient Masonry, and therefore we declare those Members unworthy of our confidence, and in consequence that they shall not be permitted to visit this Lodge.

5th. That we will co-operate with any Ancient Lodge, who may resolve to defend and preserve true Ancient Masonry.

At an Emergency Meeting held on 5 May they decided to send a communication to the President of the Board of General Purposes in an attempt to heal the breach:

... the present unfortunate Dispute may be amicably adjusted and brought to a speedy and happy conclusion and the Articles of Union carried into full effect, this Lodge will undertake to recommend a certain Number of Masters or P.M. not exceeding Nine to be nominated on the part of the Ancient Craft to meet an equal Number to be appointed from the other Fraternity (but no Member of the Lodge of Reconciliation to be Nominated) to consider and compare the two Systems as practised before the Union in order that one Mode of M.P.R. and Lecturing may be established out of the two without the introduction of any new Matter or Language. ...

It failed to achieve the support they had hoped.

No written matter was permitted and only the demonstrations of the Lodge of Reconciliation, and its members, were allowed as the official means. But one member came under censure in that Laurence Thompson is shewn as having:

... offended against a known Masonic Rule, in printing certain letters, and marks, tending to convey information on the subject of Masonic instruction, should for this offence be reprimanded in such terms as the W. Master of the Lodge of Reconciliation might think proper.

The Master being in the chair did express accordingly the high sense of disapprobation which the Lodge felt at the unguardedness of his conduct, in having so done, but that in consequence of his candid acknowledgement of the Error into which he had fallen, and his determination to collect every Copy of the same that could be got at, and place them in the Custody of the Lodge of Reconciliation, to be destroyed according to their discretion.

The Master expressed his confidence that the reproof now exhibited would effectually prevent the recurrence of any such offence in future.

That subject received extensive study and research by Bro C.F.W. Dyer and his Paper, 'Laurence Thompson's Unauthorized Print', provides all the details. (*AQC* 84 pp 116–40).

The stated object of the Lodge of Reconciliation was: To promulgate and enjoin the pure and unsullied system, that perfect reconciliation, unity of obligation, law, working, language and dress, may be happily restored to the English Craft.

Its efforts lasted until 1816 but the 'happy restoration' was a little delayed, not only in London.

In his *Masonic Gleanings*, published in 1844, George Claret a ritual printer who achieved the distinction of being the first manual printer with any sense of credibility as he was also associated with the Lodge of Reconciliation as a staunch supporter, wrote the following account of one division:

We discovered that some of them had been busily engaged in an endeavour to do away with the ceremonies we had been practising and teaching nearly three years. The late Br. W. Williams Prov. G. Master for Dorsetshire, who took a very active part, and was often a visiter [sic] at their Lodges paticularly [sic] at No. 3 then held at the Crown Tavern, Clerkenwell Green, he was also on great intimacy with his R.H. the Duke of Sussex, the Grand

Master, it appeared that some of the brethren to whom I have before alluded who could not learn the present ceremonies, (as a last effort) sought to induce the Grand Master with the influence of Br. Williams, to alter that which had been settled so long before by the Lodge of Reconciliation. Those of us who were anxious to retain them, after consulting together came to the determination to memorialize the Grand Master, for which purpose, a committee was formed, meetings held in different parts of London, and in a short time we obtained nearly 700 signatures to the memorial, combining all the Masonic talent in London, it was presented by Br. Chinn, Stokoe, Steward, and Claret accompanied by Br. Isaac Lindo, Grand Officer [S.G.W.] on January 29th 1816. And we have reason to know that the memorial had the effect intended as the same ceremonies have been continued.

[A transcript of that Memorial appears as Appendix I.]

There was a possibility that George Claret had misinterpreted visits made by William Williams to any former Antients lodges, or elsewhere, for his valued services in the field of diplomacy received high commendation in Grand Lodge on 6 March 1816 when the following item was recorded:

> On a Motion duly made and seconded, it was RESOLVED UNANI-MOUSLY: That the Thanks of this Grand Lodge be given to the R.W. Brother William Williams, Prov. G.M. for the County of Dorset, for the distinguished Services which he has rendered to Masonry by his unceasing Exertions, in promoting the best Interest and Welfare of our Ancient Fraternity. Who, possessing the purest Principles of Brotherly Affection; with a Mind highly cultivated and enriched by Masonic Acquirements; with active Zeal and unexampled Labour, to conciliate the Members of the Order, has afforded most essential Service to the Craft; more especially in the various Arrangements consequent on the happy Re-Union of the Two Societies.

At a special meeting of Grand Lodge on 20 May 1816, members of the Lodge of Reconciliation opened a lodge in the First, Second, and Third Degrees respectively and demonstrated the ceremonies of Initiation, Passing and Raising. Official sanction for that came in the following meeting of Grand Lodge held on 5 June 1816:

> The Minutes of the Grand Lodge on 20th May last were read, when the Ceremonies and Practices recommended by the Lodge of Reconciliation were exhibited and explained; and alterations on two points, in the Third Degree, having been resolved upon, the several ceremonies, &c. recommended were approved and confirmed.

The final mention of their work came on 2 September 1816 when:

> ... the W Master, Officers, and Brethren were awarded the thanks of the Grand Lodge for their unremitting Zeal and Exertion in the cause of Free-masonry.

However, what was actually 'approved and confirmed' was not set down for posterity but was the subject of demonstration only, first by the official Lodge of Reconciliation, and by its members travelling to various parts of the country, or those who had attended conveying information upon what they had seen; it was then an age for Lodges of Instruction to arise or to be revived.

For a few years there were isolated incidents: some individuals who refused to conform, others remained detached from it all, whilst arguments came from those who apparently were teaching what they had learned from the demonstration only to be questioned on their material; individual interpretations and personality clashes were inevitable for there was no official ritual in print to which reference could be made. Two main teaching authorities were formed in London, Stability Lodge of Instruction founded in 1817 and Emulation Lodge of Improvement formed in 1823 out of two Lodges of Instruction that had been practising earlier. Others emerged only to fade over the years. Perhaps the nearest one can get to what was demonstrated in the Lodge of Reconciliation is from the published work of George Claret who, at first, supplied manuscript parts of the ritual but in 1838 printed all under the title *The Ceremonies of Initiation, Passing & Raising (with copious notes as regards the duties of the Master, Wardens, Deacons &c.) Opening and Closing in the Three Degrees, Questions and Answers of the Candidates previously to Passing and Raising with the Ceremonies of Installing the W. Master and his Officers.* It is of interest to note that the manual had 155 pages and was priced at One Guinea, which was a lot of money in those days! But even more interesting is the reference to '*Installing the W. Master and his Officers*' which was an item of ceremonial not dealt with by the Lodge of Reconciliation and, although raised as a subject in April 1813, did not receive attention until the special lodge set up in 1827. It was to become the reason for a confrontation and dissension between the authorities and certain Provinces and as recently as 1926 a ruling had been rescinded for an old custom to continue.

The Installation Ceremony

The Duke of Sussex issued a Warrant on 20 April 1813 for a Lodge of Installed Masters to be formed to practise and demonstrate a ceremony of Installation of Master; he stated 'in consequence of such neglect there are but few Past Masters competent to assist in the Ceremony'. Whilst his words would have applied to London brethren such was not the case in certain Provinces in the Moderns jurisdiction where brethren jealously guarded and maintained their own procedures.

After the Union the work of the officially Warranted Lodge of Reconciliation having ended it became a duty for its members

and other well informed brethren to convey the accepted forms
outside London wherever it was reasonable and possible to do so.
However, as we have seen, lodges at a distance from London did
not show a great deal of interest and it took a long time and much
hard work on the part of some Provincial Grand Masters and their
officers to make any impression. One item had not been dealt with
by the Lodge of Reconciliation and the form of Installation of
Master in private lodges remained controversial or ignored. A set
pattern had emerged based upon that which had been printed by
the Rev James Anderson in his *Constitutions* published in 1723 and
1738. It appeared in the former in the Postscript with the introduction '*Here follows the Manner of constituting a NEW Lodge as prac-
tis'd by his Grace the Duke of Wharton, the present Right Worshipful
GRAND-MASTER, according to the ancient Usages of Masons.*' Suitable
amendment was made in the 2nd Edition. Anderson was careful to
word one section of it '... with some other Expressions that are
proper and usual on that occasion, but not proper to be written.'
Possibly his work had provided guidelines for brethren in various
parts of the country and had brought them to installing masters
with dignified ceremonial, but, neglect of that ceremony was one
of the charges levelled against the Moderns by the Antients during
the time those authorities went their separate ways before the
Union was achieved.

At the meeting of the United Grand Lodge on 6 June 1827
the Duke of Sussex again raised the subject as the following was
Minuted for that occasion:

> ... there was much diversity in the Ceremonial of the Installation of
> Masters of Lodges, and feeling it to be most desirable that uniformity should
> exist, His Royal Highness had deemed it expedient to issue a Warrant to
> certain intelligent Brothers directing them, after due and careful consideration
> and examination, to hold meetings for the purpose of promulgating and giving
> instructions in this important ceremony that conformity might be produced,
> and also such meetings to instal any Masters of Lodges who had been duly
> elected to office. That he had limited the period for the continuance of this
> Board or Lodge of Installed Masters to the Quarterly Communication in De-
> cember next.

The Warrant was drawn up and issued on 6 February 1827 the
wording of which included '... this our Warrant shall continue in
force for the space of Twelve Calendar Months, and no longer'.
According to Henry Sadler (*Notes on the Ceremony of Installation*,
Kenning, London 1889) there were only 90 lodges in the London
District at that time and brethren from 57 of those attended one or
more of the meetings. Among their names are some who were
especially prominent in matters of ritual and instruction and

largely responsible for the main form in practise at the present time. One form that was to become known as the 'Extended Working in the Board of Installed Masters' was used in various Provinces and that had become their tradition. Indeed, that matter was brought to the attention of the authorities in 1889 and Grand Lodge ruled that it was 'irregular'. The subject was referred to in a letter from Col Shadwell H. Clerke, the Grand Secretary, to Col Alexander C. F. Gough, Deputy Prov GM in Charge (Staffordshire) in the following terms:

> ... I have to inform you that there is no doubt whatsoever that this so called ceremony is entirely irregular and was never recognized by or even known to Grand Lodge and that it formed no part of the Ritual authorized by Grand Lodge at the Union in 1813 and again in 1827 when the Installation of a Master was *specially* considered, and old Brethren who were present at the meetings in the latter years have declared that they [had] never heard of the ceremony—and there is strong reason to believe that it was imported from America. ...

When the matter was raised again with Sir Edward Letchworth the then Grand Secretary, he issued a letter in identical terms which was circularised to all Provincial Grand Masters to try to eradicate that practice. It was effective in certain places but failed in others. Comment was made that Sir Edward Letchworth had been influenced by a certain leading Lodge of Instruction in which various members of the Establishment were included.

The year 1926 saw the matter brought to a head when the President of the Board of General Purposes, who had again ruled that the ceremony was irregular, was prevailed upon to receive a deputation organised by brethren from Northumberland and Durham in particular. Diligent attention was paid to its history and evidence was produced that it had been part of the ceremonial in some lodges for over a century and, in one case, for more than 150 years. After much discussion in Committees and in Grand Lodge, it was ruled that the ceremony of the 'Extended Working' could be practised providing that a qualifying announcement regarding certain features in it was made in lodge at the time it was to be used. An extensive Paper on the subject with great detail was compiled by Bro Will Read, given to Quatuor Coronati Lodge on 1 January 1971 and appears in *AQC* 84 pp 26–68.

Chapter 19

Independent Lodges

From 1717 throughout the duration of the premier Grand Lodge, for various reasons lodges failed to conform to the Laws and Regulations that were passed from time to time, with the result that on occasions some had to be struck from the *List*. This was a subject dealt with by William Finch who, in the decade prior to the Union and in the following years printed masonic rituals. His work went to all parts of the country and at times he became the guide and mentor of some brethren whilst in the eyes of others he was nothing more than a purveyor of ritual exposures for personal gain and disloyal to the masonic obligation that was incumbent upon all who entered the fraternity.

On 1 March 1815 he published, *A LETTER TO HIS ROYAL HIGHNESS THE PRINCE REGENT* (*Printed by and for W. Finch No. 5, Charlotte Place, New Cut, Lower Marsh, Lambeth*), and a section of that work deals with Independent Lodges, as follows;

LIST OF INDEPENDENT LODGES

In the *MASONIC TELESCOPE*, [and] *THE LECTURES* &c, I have inserted a long list of the Lodges that seceded from the Grand Lodge, and set up Independent ones of their own; from the first period, 1722 to 1815, with the names of the Masters and Wardens of such Lodges, who manfully and zealously stood up for the rights and liberties of their brethren; also, the names of those brethren who took up their pens publicly in the independent cause; with remarks, &c. In the present letter to your Royal Highness, I shall merely insert the following, as most generally known.

3. Master—ANTHONY SAYER, P.G.M.
Wardens—John Turner and Mark Glover.
9. Master—GEORGE OWEN, M.D.
Wardens—Charles Brown and Edward Senex.
12. Master—J BEAL, M.D. & F.R.S.
Wardens—James Hemming and Thomas Payne.
19. Master—THOMAS PAWLET
Wardens—Samuel Anderson and Edward Vaughan.
20. Master—CHRISTOPHER WREN Esq. (son to the great Sir Christopher Wren, G.M.)
Wardens—F. Strong (P.J.G.W. before the establishment of the Modern Grand Lodge) and Wm. Douglas.
94. (This was the famous Lodge, called the Lodge of INDUSTRY held at the Ben Johnson's Head, Pelham Street)

R.W.M.—CHARLES MANNING
Wardens—Edward Bloomfield and Samuel Locke.
LODGE OF ANTIQUITY—with Brother PRESTON at the head of nearly
a hundred Independent Masons.
265. Master—C. CUMMINS
Wardens—Edward Butler and Thomas Handley.
353. Master—HENRY WOLFE
Wardens—Samuel Egerton and Wm. Bennett.
392. Master—ABRAHAM LEVI
Wardens—Joseph Monk and Thomas Clarke.
436. Master—EDWARD COUCHMAN
Wardens—Samuel Booth and Wm. Watson.
249. (St. Peter's Lodge, as it stood in the last revised list, before the Union).
Master—W. FINCH
Wardens—A. Frazier and T. Canvill.

I have now before me the engraved List of Lodges, for 1776, and the
Freemasons' Calendar for 1777, both published by authority of the Grand
Lodge; and from which I copy the following list of Lodges erased, &c. Thus
much from their official documents. If we look into the history of Masonry for
that time, we shall find that the independent Lodges were extremely warm
against the Grand Lodge; who were at war, not only with the Athol Masons,
but with the Grand Lodge at York; likewise with the Lodge of Antiquity, and
most of the following Independent Lodges. By these official publications from
the Grand Lodge, we find that out of the 337 Lodges in town and country,
then standing on their books, the 54, as below stated, were *erased*, as they term
it, from the Grand Lodge; but the fact is, 49 out of these declared for, and
obtained their Independence. Thus one sixth part under the Grand Lodge,
deserted them, besides many that were luke-warm in the cause, and most of
the others scarcely assembled together in sufficient numbers to constitute a
legal Lodge.

Lodges (at that time) erased for not conforming to the Laws.

INDEPENDENT TOWN LODGES.

40.	Chelsea, White Swan	316.	Billingsgate, Gun
265.	Goodman's Fields, Bear	41.	Bloomsbury, Orange St. 3 Kings
308.	Islington, King's Head	436.	Bow Street, Covent Garden
372.	Marylebone, Queen's Head	332.	British Society Lodge
353.	Piccadilly, Unicorn Coffee-House	159.	Chiswell St. Jack of Newbury
115.	Strand, Crown and Anchor	71.	Coleman St. Star
392.	Water Lane, Tower St. Ship	44.	Cornhill, Cock and Lion
32.	Barbican, Red Cross	270.	Doctor's Commons, Horn
17.	Bunhill Row, White Swan	12.	East Smithfield, 3 Crowns
402.	King St. Soho, Bunch of Grapes	318.	St. George's Field
27.	Rotherhithe, Eleph Stairs, Swan	375.	Old Gravel Lane, White Swan
272.	Snow Hill, Fountain	344.	Leadenhall Street, Ship
303.	Strand, Crown and Anchor	53.	St. Paul's Church Yard, Sun

*Out of these 26, 22 withdrew from the Grand Lodge and constituted Independent Lodges
of their own.*

INDEPENDENT COUNTRY LODGES.

234.	Portsmouth, King's Arms	299.	Shoreham, Dolphin

244. Stubbington, Hants
 69. Wolverhampton, Swan
199. Bristol, Thomas St. 3 Queens
201. Canterbury, King's Head
148. Cardiff, Glamorganshire, Bear
241. Chippenham, Hart
149. Cowbridge, Glamorganshr. Bear
 39. West Cowes, Isle of Wight
243. Dover, City of London
 95. Haverfordwest, 3 Cranes
120. Helston, Cornwall, Kings Arms
151. Loestoffe, Suffolk, Queens Head
355. Monmouth, Lodge at
254. Ross, Herefordshire

266. Sittingbourne, Rose
395. Warminster, Angel
 92. Bristol, Fountain reinstated 1776
356. Kingston-upon-Thames, Castle
362. Lewes, Sussex, White Hart
 67. Liverpool, African Coffee-House
348. Mansfield, White Lion
294. Milksham, Wilts, Kings Arms
333. Newcastle-under-Line Crown
227. Salop, Globe
198. Windsor, Bell and Castle
212. Wooler, All Saints' Lodge
232. Workington, Green Dragon
366. Blackwall, King's Arms
142. Leeds, Parrot

Out of these 31, 27 withdrew from the Grand Lodge, and constituted Independent Lodges of their own. For many years after this the standing toast in all these Independent Lodges was 'PROSPERITY TO THE 49 INDEPENDENT LODGES'.

That account from William Finch shows how widespread were lodges that could get along quite well without conforming, but his statement—'constituted Independent Lodges' is suspect and cannot be accepted in general terms. Certainly Preston's breakaway from Antiquity Lodge gave rise to the Grand Lodge South of the River Trent and because it did create lodges fell into that category; it was not unknown for a lodge to be formed as an unofficial 'daughter lodge' in some towns, but perhaps Finch may have intended his word 'constituted' to have been 'remained Independent Lodges on their own', for indeed that would have been nearer to the state of affairs. However, there were many brethren in lodges at a distance from London who, whilst they kept on the official Register objected to paying demands for the building fund for the new Grand Lodge premises in London; they felt remote from its affairs; that they had little voice in the management of the Craft; that the ritual now being imposed them with so many 'differences' had brought 'innovations' and further departures from the ancient landmarks which, although unspecified seemed to permit each brother to have his own sense of what amounted to an ancient landmark which varied according to location and lifestyle of the individual; furthermore, in certain areas, Lancashire in particular, the brethren being used to governing their own affairs under the Antients system, or at the most referring to the senior lodge in the town or city under that jurisdiction, were now being subjected to peremptory rulings from the Provincial Grand Master and his officers. That sense of grievance was to lead to the formation of another Grand Lodge at Wigan in 1823, and another in Stockport in 1837.

The Two Grand Lodges in Lancashire and Cheshire

The earliest mention of 'making masons' occurs in 1621 in the records of the London Masons Company but its exact meaning is open to question. The earliest account of a specific admission into a lodge of freemasons of a speculative nature on English soil was during the occupation of Newcastle by the Scots army when Robert Moray, Quarter Master General, was admitted by members of the Lodge of Edinburgh. The Introduction in this book gives the details of Elias Ashmole being 'made a Free Mason' on 16 October 1646 at Warrington in Lancashire, which confirms the existence of speculative freemasonry at that date in England, although the fraternity was not organised there or anywhere else in that period.

Prior to the Union of 1813, the County of Lancashire had various lodges and brethren who were either independent, or belonged to the Moderns, or to the Antients, or had been constituted by the old lodge at York, or even by the Grand Lodge of England South of the River Trent. The County could well be represented as a forum for contention yet it can be a matter of surprise that there are so few reports of animosity between brethren as there was quite a widespread practice of degrees beyond the three within the limitation imposed by the Moderns Grand Lodge. Thus, for many of the brethren who came under the banners of the two Grand Lodges for whom, having enjoyed their masonic freedom and possibly participated in a good deal of fraternisation, it must have been quite difficult to succumb to the new control exercised by the Provincial Grand Master and his officers anxious to bring conformity to the requirements of the newly United Grand Lodge.

Lodge No 31 which was previously on the Register of the Antients provided a rather petty incident that grew out of all proportion. It stemmed from a Motion from that lodge which was sent to the Provincial Grand Secretary requesting that the Grand Secretary obtain a ruling from Grand Lodge on the subject of the minimum number of members required for a private lodge to retain its Warrant prior to erasure; this enquiry that was aimed at another lodge in Liverpool with whom they had been in dispute, although the question had already been settled by the Provincial Grand Secretary, but not to their satisfaction. The Motion came before the Prov Grand Lodge, was passed, and forwarded to London in the name of the Prov Grand Lodge. It was received by the Board of General Purposes on 28 December 1818 and instead of raising the subject in Grand Lodge they replied that whilst it had been fully discussed by the Board it was thought better not to depart from 'that silence on the subject which had been observed

in all Books of *Constitutions*'. It was because the request had not
been dealt with in Grand Lodge that the sense of grievance of the
brethren became magnified and soon other complaints surfaced
which added to their resentment; it caused a rift between those
brethren and their Provincial Grand Master.

At the meeting of the Provincial Grand Lodge held at
Liverpool on 27 September 1819 the prime movers produced a
Memorial they had prepared which they proposed should be sent
to the Duke of Sussex. The Provincial Grand Lodge approved and
it was sent to London in their name making the points that, in
consequence of the remoteness of Lancashire from London the
brethren there were denied the enjoyment of being present at the
deliberations of Grand Lodge; they had no means of making their
sentiments known in that august Assembly other than through the
board of General Purposes; that Board, consisting of perhaps only
seven members, possessed the power of ignoring the sentiments of
sixty-two lodges on record; they felt that it failed to discharge what
they thought was its unquestioned duty. They stated further:

> they have ever been disposed to acquiesce with the Rules and Regulations
> adopted by that part of the United Grand Lodge which is held in London,
> provided always, that they continue to preserve the ancient Land-marks of the
> Order, as it is an incontrovertible truth that even the whole united Grand
> Lodge cannot legally alter those Land-marks.
>
> Notwithstanding this universally admitted fact, we perceive with regret,
> that some of the ancient Land-marks of the Order have been altered; and
> moreover, that a law is introduced in the Revision of the Constitution-Book,
> which appears to us calculated (at some convenient period) to compel an
> obedience to this violation.
>
> We here allude to Sec 21, Page 65, of the revised Edition of the
> Constitution-Book, under the head of Lodges of Instruction, where it is stated,
> that every Lodge shall be responsible that the mode of working therein
> adopted, has received the sanction of the Grand Lodge.
>
> If, therefore, an Obedience in this Law, consists in teaching every point
> which has been promulgated in this County by the Lodge of Reconciliation,
> then we shall know how to act; for we wish it to be perfectly understood, that
> we deny the power of any authority to compel us to adopt a System, which
> has hitherto been unknown, or not practised by the ancient Masons of this
> Kingdom.
>
> By the nature of our Masonic Ties, we are not at liberty to describe
> through this mode of communication, those points to which we particularly
> object; nevertheless, we feel it proper to state, that generally speaking we
> approve of the revised System, and have adopted it with the exception of such
> points as we know are not universal. . . .

Several other matters for complaint were included such as the im-
position of 'heavy contributions' to the building fund for Freemasons' Hall in London, and they observed that 'the Royal Arch

is a component part of Craft Masonry, and consequently requires no other authority than a Craft Warrant to render their Meeting perfectly legal and agreeable to ancient custom'.

The subject of their long drawn out complaint was adequately researched by two competent brethren, Bro Norman Rogers in his Paper 'The Grand Lodge of Wigan' (*AQC* 61 pp 170–210) and Bro Michael Spurr in 'The Liverpool Rebellion' (*AQC* 85 pp 29–60). It is not the purpose of this exercise to pursue the trials and tribulations of that area other than to bring to notice the establishment of a breakaway movement which resulted in the setting up of another Grand Lodge in Liverpool which shortly afterwards moved its headquarters to Wigan. It involved six lodges in its inauguration and Lodge No 31 became No 1 of the new Grand Lodge in 1823. In ten years only three lodges remained, the others having either become reconciled with the United Grand Lodge or having ceased to exist and eventually one founding lodge, the Lodge of Sincerity alone remained alone. It is worthy of note that William Finch became a member of Wigan Grand Lodge in 1825 presumably to line himself with their act of defiance. Also, it is from their records that we learn of yet another Grand Lodge formed in Cheshire, this one at Stockport with the title 'The Loyal Independent Order of Free Masons'. Relative correspondence is of interest in this connection.

To the W.M. & Brethren of the Lodge of Sincerity, Wigan.
Gentlemen,
About 2 years ago we commenced, being unaware at the time of the same Order in the County, we got a Seal & 1000 of Articles. We were applied to from Manchester when we open'd St. Alban's Lodge there. We are about opening 3 more Lodges, 1 in this month and the other on the 1st Monday in March. We have a very handsome Colour with all the emblems of Masonry inscribed. The reason of us not writing sooner as been in consequence of the W.M. and most of us having been inflicted with this prevailing disorder the influenza. We of St. John's are very glad to find others on the same footing and should like to have a communication as soon as possible, had we known sooner we certainly would have apply'd to you, but by Union & perseverance we rest assured of becoming a very numerous body soon. We have been at considerable expence and a great deal of trouble as the Old Masons have been very much against us, but we have some good staunch Men amongst us that is determined to persevere. We remain, Yours &c., in friendship, Love & Truth
James Tunstall, Scty.
P.S. We have removed from the White Bear to the Waggon & Horses Edward Street.

Ruben Hopwood	W.G.M.
Thos. Clayton	D.G.M. Manchester
Paul Jowell	S.G.W.
Joseph Williamson	J.G.W.
Nathan Birchenough	S.G.D.
Thos. Leigh	J.G.D.
James Tunstall	G. Secretary

It drew forth a reply from the Grand Secretary of the Grand Lodge at Wigan as follows:

> Wigan Feby. 9th 1837
>
> Sir & Br.
> I received your letter of the 6th Instant and the Laws of the Loyal Independent Order of Free Masons & Laid them before the Members of Lodge 492 when they expressed great pleasure at your Lodge seceding from the United Grand Lodge and requested me to send them to our D.G.M., M.A. Gage, Liverpool for his consideration, and as soon as I receive his Answer will communicate it to you in the mean time wishing your all prosperity.
> I am, Sir and Brother,
> Yours Respectfully
> Robt. Bolton.

Investigation has shewn that those brethren did not previously belong to any of the lodges meeting in Stockport, but it is not ruled out that they may have been members of lodges in Manchester.

The only other mention in the records of the Wigan Grand Lodge is the following:

> Septr. 20th 1837
> Being a Night of Emergency in consequence of Br. Reubin Hopwood of St. John's Lodge at Stockport, concerning a Union with them when a Letter was given to him in Open Lodge.

No other material has survived in that respect.

It now remains to review the career of Lodge of Sincerity as a whole. It was originally Warranted on 30 November 1786 by the Moderns Grand Lodge to meet at Wigan. It declared off the Register in 1823 and was formally erased by the Grand Lodge for non-payment of dues three years later. It worked consistently as No 1 of the Grand Lodge at Wigan until 1913 when a change of heart was occasioned by a sad incident the previous year. A newly raised brother a member of Sincerity Lodge received an invitation to visit another lodge and on presenting himself and shewing his Certificate was refused admission as the Certificate was deemed irregular. He wrote an abusive letter to the Secretary of Sincerity Lodge, labelling the lodge as a bogus institution and asserting that he had been the victim of a fraud. That changed the whole outlook of the members and on 1 April 1912 a special notice was ordered to be added to the next Summons regarding an Application to the [United] Grand Lodge. Four brethren were then appointed to 'inquire into the matter of affiliation with the Grand Lodge'. The next month they agreed 'that no more Candidates are accepted till the matter of joining the Grand Lodge be settled'. On 2 June it was then agreed 'That this Lodge do join the Grand Lodge of England as soon as all necessary arrangements are made' and the final Minutes of 12 July 1913 stated that 'The Lodge was Closed in greatest harmony & Peace'. They had petitioned for a Warrant 'to take the place of the Lodge erased in 1826'. On 11 June a Warrant for Lodge No 3677 was granted to seven Brethren for the Lodge of Sincerity to meet at the Masonic Hall, Wigan on the first Monday in every month; five were members of Lindsay Lodge at Wigan, No 1335 and one each from West Lancashire Lodge No 1403 and Holmes Lodge No 2708; the Master Designate was James Daniel Murray, PG Treas. None of these brethren were associated with the Lodge of Sincerity but obviously acted on their behalf. Conditions imposed were that the original Warrant should be surrendered and that all members of the Lodge of Sincerity should be accepted in the new Lodge.

This lodge was consecrated on 26 September 1913 by the Provincial Grand Master assisted by nine Provincial Grand Officers and fourteen others attending—but no brethren from Lodge of Sincerity. The first meeting of the new lodge was held on 6 October and twenty two Candidates were proposed all being members of the former lodge. At the second meeting held on 3 November, a Dispensation was read permitting the lodge to Initiate all twenty two Candidates. Two did not attend that meeting but of the remaining twenty, one was prepared and taken through the ceremony witnessed by his colleagues. At the following meetings in December and January eighteen brethren received the 2nd and 3rd degrees, *en bloc*. The Master Designate for that Warrant was presented with 'a Founder's Jewel to show the appreciation and esteem for the great work done by him in bringing them under the Grand Lodge of England' and so ended a term of separation that had lasted 90 years and one errant sheep had been returned to the fold of regularity. But before taking our leave, a few extracts from the Minute Book will show items of interest in their pattern of behaviour before that date:

22 Sept. 1889	(Sunday) Ten members took a waggonette to Skelmersdale to put Bro Roger Taylor through the Mark Degree.
24 Oct. 1897	Five members were 'made Mark Masons'.
29 Jan. 1900	Bro. J.P. Ashcroft was 'made a Past Master'.
13 May 1900	(Sunday) The Royal Arch degree with five Candidates.
30 Dec. 1901	Five Brethren 'took the degree of Past Masters'.
17 Dec. 1902	After two Brethren had been made Master Masons 'the Lodge was closed in greatest harmony & Peace at 9.15 when the Lodge was opened as the Grand Lodge of England under Prince Edwin of York' after which 3 brethren were made Past Masters.
30 Apl. 1904	Three brethren were 'passed the degree of the Royal Arch Chapter'.
30 May 1904	Two brethren received the Arch degree.

The Antients mode of Working has been taken into the next century by Lodge of Sincerity and shows that the format that is used in the American York Rite is probably the nearest to that which was normal in the Antients Jurisdiction and loyally performed by some of the non-conformists who broke away from time to time from the Moderns influence, preferring to stay with 'the Old Institutions' and the unspecified Landmarks; 'Innovations' were not for them—although somehow they accepted the developments that arose as time went on, the Royal Arch, the Mark, and other degrees that seemed to proliferate!

The Grand Lodge of Coloured Brethren

It is proper to make mention of another Grand Lodge which although self established in Boston, Massachusetts, stemmed from a lodge holding a Warrant dated 20 September 1784 that had been issued to them by the Grand Lodge of England (Moderns).

The background to the early existence of that lodge has been covered by various writers, but owing to the sparse evidence that is available have strayed somewhat from the factual and have allowed wishful thinking to close the gaps. However, from *Prince Hall Life and Legacy* (Charles H. Wesley, 1977, U.S.A.) and *Prince Hall Freemasonry* (George Draffen of Newington, *AQC* vol 89, pp 70–91) we get a brief but reasoned sequence of events.

Prince Hall always described himself as 'African' and there has always been a doubt about his exact age as nothing is known about his early life. It has been posed that he was seized by a slave trader somewhere on the West African coast, taken to Boston and sold there to William Hall; thus he was not freeborn. After he had worked for him for twenty-one years he was given a Certificate of Manumission dated 9 April 1770 signed by William Hall and his family and thus gained his freedom. That document is on record. In the archives of African Lodge is a sheet of paper dated 6 March 1775 stating:

By Marster Batt wose made these brothers	
Prince Hall	Thomas Sanderson
Peter Best	Buesten Singer
Cuff Bufform	Boston Smith
John Carter	Cato Spean
Peter Freeman	Prince Taylar
Fortune Howard	Benjamin Tiber
Cyrus Jonbus	Richard Tilley
Prince Rees	

Notes on that sheet show that fourteen men were made 'Marsters' three 'Crafts' and thirteen 'Prentices' but not necessarily on that date.

The date of admission was only a few weeks before the outbreak of the War of Independence. It would appear that those named brethren were initiated in a Regimental Lodge No 441 John Batt being its Master. He was stationed with the 38th Regiment of Foot (1st Battalion South Staffordshires) in Boston at that time. The ambulatory Warrant for Lodge No 441 had been granted by the Grand Lodge of Ireland; it was subsequently returned in 1840. No Minutes or records of its activity have survived regarding that period and no Return showing those new members was made to Grand Lodge. John Batt served his time and was discharged from the British Army when stationed in Staten Island in 1777 and, according to Bro Draffen, there is some evidence that he may have enlisted in the rebel forces.

Prince Hall and his brethren continued to meet as a lodge and eventually applied as follows to a London brother who was known to them:

> Dear Brother, I would inform you that this Lodge hath been founded almost eight years and we have had only a Permit to Walk on St. John's Day and to Bury our Dead in manner and form. We have had no opportunity to apply for a Warrant before now, though we have been importuned to send to France for one, yet we thought it best to send to the Fountain from whence we received the Light, for a Warrant; and now Dear Br. we must make you our advocate at the Grand Lodge, hoping you will be so good (in our name and Stead) to Lay this Before the Royal Grand Master and the Grand Wardens and the rest of the Grand Lodge, who we hope will not deny us nor treat us Beneath the rest of our fellowmen, although Poor yet Sincere Brethren of the Craft ... (from *Prince Hall's Letter Book*, W.H. Upton, *AQC* vol 13 pp 54–65)

That letter, sent from Boston, was dated 2 March 1784; a second letter was sent couched in similar terms on the 30 June.

Eventually, in April 1787, a normal English Warrant granted to African Lodge, No 459 on the Register, dated 20 September 1784 was received. It had taken that time to reach them, one year after the War of Independence had ended and the Peace Treaty had been signed.

African Lodge was erased from the Register of the Grand Lodge of England in 1813 as no Returns nor dues had been received for many years. The *Letter Book* has a record of correspondence having been sent but either they had not arrived in London or had been neglected.

In 1797 Prince Hall received a letter from a Bro Peter Manstone of Philadelphia who asked for a Warrant to be granted to himself and ten other brethren. He had made previous application elsewhere but had been refused on the grounds that 'black men living in Virginia would get to be masons too'. In reply Prince Hall wrote:

> Sir, I received your letter of the 2 which informed me that there are a number of blacks in your city who have received the light of masonry, and I hope they got it in a just and lawful manner. If so, dear Brother, we are willing to set you at work under our charter and African Lodge, we hereby and herein give you licence to assemble and work as aforesaid, under the denomination as in the sight and fear of God. I would advise you not to take in any at present till your Officers and Masters be installed in the Grand Lodge, which we are willing to do, when he thinks convenient, and he may receive a full warrant instead of a permit. . . .

Prince Hall was following a similar pattern to what had happened when, it is suspected, that John Batt gave him that 'Permit to Walk etc.' In a letter to William White, Grand Secretary in London, sent on 15 June 1802, Prince Hall wrote:

> . . . I have sent a number of letters to the Grand Lodge and money for the Grand Charity, and by faithful brethren as I thought, but I have not received one letter from the Grand Lodge for this five years, which I thought somewhat strange: but when I heard so many were taken by the French I thought otherwise, and prudent not to send. . . .

When the following Contributions were received for the Charity and Hall Funds:

	CHARITY	HALL		CHARITY	HALL
2 Somerfet-houfe Lodge, Freemafon's T.	4 4 0	4 4 0	318 L.of Induftry,B. Johnfon's H. Shoe-lane,	1 1 0	0 10 6
5 L.of Friendfhip,Thatched-h.St. James'sft.	3 3 0	3 3 0	325 L.of Friendfhip,Fore-ft.Plymouth-dock,		1 10 0
12 Lodge of Emulation, Paul's-head Tavern,		5 5 0	359 L.of Jehofaphat, Rummer-Tav. Briftol,	1 1 0	2 15 0
14 Fraternal-Lodge, Church-ft. Greenwich,	1 1 0	3 8 0	405 St. Peter's L. Bell, Upper Mount-ft.	1 1 0	5 5 0
19 Caftle-L of Harmony,Horn,DoctorsCom.	1 1 0	2 4 6	432 St. Michael's L. Alnwick, Northumb.	1 1 0	
21 The Globe, Fleet-ftreet,	1 1 0		453 Loyal Lodge, Globe Inn, Barnftable,	1 1 0	
29 Britannic Lodge,Starand Garter,Pall-mall,	3 3 0	3 3 0	459 African Lodge, Bofton, New England,	1 1 0	
35 King's Arms, Marybone-ftreet, Piccadilly,	1 1 0	5 5 0	469 L'Egalité, Frith-ftreet, Soho,	1 1 0	1 1 0
41 St. Paul's Lodge, Birmingham,		3 2 0	476 Thanet Lodge, Parade Hotel, Margate,	1 1 0	
46 Coal-hole, Fountain-court, Strand,	1 1 0	4 3 0	477 L. of Good Intent, Ship, Leadenhall-ft.	1 1 0	1 11 6
47 The STEWARDS' LODGE,			531 Old Globe Lodge, Scarborough,	0 10 6	4 17 6
† Ditto,	5 5 0	5 5 0	543 Royal Clarence Lodge, Brighthelmftone,	1 1 0	
104 Old Cumberland-L. Old Cavendifh-ft.		1 14 0	546 Royal York Lodge, Briftol,	5 5 0	1 0 0
122 Ancient French-Lodge, Leicefter-fields,	1 1 0	2 2 0	553 L.of goodFellowfhip,Chelmsford, Effex,	1 1 0	2 0 0
155 Beaufort-Lodge, Prince's Street, Briftol,	1 1 0	3 5 0	576 Silurean Lodge,Kington, Herefordfhire,	2 2 0	
160 L. of Fortitude, Half Moon, George-ft.		2 5 0	586 At Bulam, on Coaft of Africa, Conft.	2 2 0	2 2 0
201 Royal L. Thatched-houfe,St.James's-ft.	6 6 0	3 3 0	Conftitution-Book,	0 12 0	
221 Tontine, Sheffield, in Yorkfhire,	2 2 0	1 0 0	12 Certificates, at 6s. 6d.	3 18 0	
226 RoyalEdwin-Lodge, Bury St. Edmunds,	1 1 0		His R. H. the Prince of Wales, G. M.		21 0 0
238 L. of Unanimity, Wakefield, Yorkfhire,	1 1 0		Sir Peter Parker, Bart. D. G. M.		5 5 0
249 Sion-L. North Shields,	1 1 0		Thomas Swanton, Efq. S. G. W. 3 3 }		10 10 0
253 Union-Lodge, Caftle ditch, Briftol,	1 1 0	1 10 0	Ditto additional, 7 7 }		
256 L. of Morality, Old Compton-ftreet,	1 1 0	2 7 0	John Warre, Efq. J. G. W. 2 2 }		10 10 0
277 Caveac-Lodge, Angel, Hammerfmith,	1 1 0	2 2 0	Ditto additional, 8 8 }		
285 Qu. Charlotte's L. Hofier-l. Smithfield,		3 3 0	James Hefeltine, Efq. G. T.		3 3 0
292 Beaufort-Lodge, at Swanfea,	1 1 0		Mr. William White, G. S.		3 3 0
294 Lodge of Virtue, Market-place, Bath,	2 2 0	2 5 0	Chev. Bartholomew Rufpini, G. S. B.		1 1 0
296 L. of Hofpitality, Caftle-ftreet, Briftol,	1 1 0	0 15 0		£ 69 12 0	141 19 0

Grand Lodge Communication showing the Charity and Hall Funds contributions on 18 April 1792. African Lodge is No 459

At a QUARTERLY COMMUNICATION
OF THE MOST ANTIENT AND HONOURABLE
Society of Free and Accepted Masons,
UNDER THE CONSTITUTION OF ENGLAND,
HELD AT
FREE-MASONS' HALL, *LONDON*,
On *Wednefday, November* 22, 1797.
HIS ROYAL HIGHNESS
George Auguftus Frederick, PRINCE of WALES, &c. &c. &c.
GRAND MASTER.

Prefent

CHARLES MARSH, Efq. P. J. G. W. as G. M.
THEOPHILUS TOMPSON TUTT, Efq. P. J. G. W. as D. G. M.
BENJAMIN LANCASTER, Efq. P. J. G. W. as S. G. W.
JOHN MEYRICK, Efq. P. S. G. W. as J. G. W.

JOHN HUNTER, Efq. J. G. W.	Mr. WILLIAM WHITE, G. S.
WILLIAM FORSSTEEN, Efq. Prov. G. M. for Hartfordfhire.	Rev. JOHN FRITH, Mafter of the Stewards' Lodge, as G. S. B.
ADAM GORDON, Efq. Prov. G. M. for Herefordfhire.	JOSEPH SUMBEL, Efq.
GEO. DOWNING, Efq. Prov. G. M. for Effex.	The Wardens and Affiftants of the STEWARDS' LODGE, and the Mafters and Wardens of fundry
TERENCE GAHAGAN, Efq. D. Prov. G. M. for the Coaft of Coromandel.	Lodges.

When the following Contributions were received for the Charity and Hall Funds:

	CHARITY	HALL		CHARITY	HALL
The STEWARDS' LODGE,	2 2 0	1 10 0	325 Lodge of Honour, York-ftreet, Weftminft.	1 1 0	1 1 0
1 Lodge of Antiquity, Freemafons' Tavern,	5 5 0	1 1 0	330 Lodge of the Nine Mufes, St. James's-ftreet,	1 1 0	6 6 0
2 Somerfet-houfe Lodge, Freemafons' Tavern,	3 3 0	3 3 0	331 Union Lodge, York,	0 10 6	
3 Lodge of Friendfhip, St. James's Street,	3 3 0	3 3 0	332 Social Lodge, Bocking, Effex,	1 1 0	1 1 0
7 L. of St. Mary-la-bonne, Cavendifh-fq. c.h.	1 1 0	8 13 0	335 In the 6th, or Inni(killing, Reg. of Dragoons,	1 1 0	1 17 6
9 Dundee-armsLodge, Red-lion-ft. Wapping,	3 3 0	2 2 0	340 Pilgrim Lodge, Freemafons' Tavern,	1 1 0	5 5 0
10 Kentifh Lodge of Antiquity, Chatham,		1 0 0	351 Rodney Lodge, Kingfton-upon-Hull,		5 5 0
12 Lodge of Emulation, Cateaton-ftreet,	1 1 0	1 6 3	353 Lodge of Moral Reformation, Deptford,	1 1 0	9 9 0
13 Fraternal Lodge, Greenwich,	0 10 6	3 5 6	356 St.George'sL.inE.RidingReg.YorkMilitia,	1 2 6	2 17 6
16 White Swan, Norwich,	1 1 0		357 Lodge of Science, Salifbury,	1 1 0	1 5 0
25 Caftle Lodge, Manfel-ft. Goodman's Fields,	0 10 6	5 5 0	363 Minerva Lodge, Hull, Yorkfhire,		1 5 0
26 Corner-ftone Lodge, St. James's Street,	1 1 0	4 14 6	Ditto,	0 10 6	3 15 0
27 Britannic Lodge, Pall-Mall,	3 3 0	3 3 0	369 Harmonic Lodge, Dudley, Worcefterfhire,	1 1 0	1 17 6
29 Lodge of Fortitude, Eaft-Smithfield,	1 1 0	1 1 0	370 African Lodge, Bofton, New England,	1 5 0	
33 Anchor and Hope, Bolton-le-Moor, Lancafh.	1 15 0	0 15 0	371 Lodge of Truth, Richmond-green,	1 1 0	1 1 0
37 Lodge of Relief, Bury, Lancafhire,	0 10 6	1 0 0	379 Tyrian Lodge, Derby,	2 2 0	7 5 0
41 Strong Man, Eaft-Smithfield,	1 1 0	6 0 6	382 Trinity Lodge, Coventry,		1 1 0
47 Angel, Colchefter,		2 15 0	383 Lodge of Unanimity, Wells, Somerfetfhire,	1 1 0	0 15 0
48 King's Head, Norwich,	1 1 0	0 5 0	385 Lodge of St. George, New Windfor, Berks,	1 1 0	
50 Conftitutional Lodge, Lambeth-marfh,		1 11 6	389 Lodge of Perfect Friendfhip, Ipfwich,	0 10 6	1 4 6
51 Howard L. of Brotherly Love, Arundel, Suff.	1 1 0	1 1 0	390 Lodge of Unions, Pratt-ftreet, Lambeth,	1 1 0	
57 Royal Naval L. near Wapping Old-ftairs,	1 1 0	10 15 0	391 Lodge of Independence, Chefter,		0 10 0
58 Royal Chefter Lodge, Chefter,	1 1 0	1 0 0	394 L.Friendfhip & Sincerity,Shaftefbury,Dorf.	0 10 6	
60 Lodge of Peace and Harmony, Fifh-ftr.-hill,		5 5 0	397 St. John's L. Broomfgrove, Worcefterfh.	0 10 6	
61 Union Crofs, Halifax, Yorkfhire,	0 10 6	3 0 0	398 CarnaticMilitaryL.Vellore,No.2,C.Corom.		10 0 0
66 Lodge of Sincerity, Joiner-ftr. Southwark,	1 1 0	3 3 0	401 Lodge of Goodwill, Braintree, Effex,	0 10 6	
67 L. of Peace and Plenty, Horflydown-lane,	1 1 0	0 13 0	403 Lodge of Harmony, Ormfkirk, Lancafhire,	0 10 6	1 0 0
68 Grenadiers' Lodge, Brook-ftreet,		0 13 0	406 St. Matthew's L. Barton-upon-Humber,	1 1 0	0 5 0
72 Lodge of Unity, Suffolk-ftr. Hay-market,	1 1 0	3 13 0	410 L. Trade and Navigation,Northwich,Chefh.	3 3 0	2 15 0
76 Bear, Yarmouth, Norfolk,	1 1 0	1 10 0	423 Prince of Wales'sL.Gainfborough,Lincolnfh.	1 1 0	2 0 0
80 Labour-in-Vain, Norwich,	1 1 0		434 Salopian Lodge, Shrewfbury,	1 1 0	0 10 0
86 Unicorn, St. Mary's, Norwich,	1 1 0	0 5 0	438 Duke of York's Lodge, Doncafter,		0 7 6
88 Three Tuns, Great Yarmouth, Norfolk,	1 1 0	2 7 6	441 Lodge of Napthali, Manchefter,		5 12 6
99 Faithful Lodge, Norwich,	1 1 0	1 1 0	452 Royal Clarence L. Brighthelmftone, Suffex,	1 1 0	0 15 0
105 Caftle and Lion, Norwich,		1 5 0	454 Beneficent Lodge, Macclesfield, Chefhire,		2 5 0
108 St. James's Lodge, Uxbridge,	1 1 0	5 0 0	459 Independent Lodge, Congleton, Chefhire,	1 1 0	2 0 0
111 Lodge of Unanimity, Manchefter,	1 1 0		461 Lodge of Harmony, Halifax, Yorkfhire,	0 11 0	0 10 0
115 Sea Captains' Lodge, Liverpool,	5 5 0		462 L. of Good Fellowfhip, Chelmsford, Effex,	1 1 0	4 5 0
118 Lodge of Freedom and Eafe, Old-ftr.-road,	0 10 6	1 1 0	463 Lodge of Friendfhip, Oldham, Lancafhire,	0 10 6	2 15 0
120 Wounded Hart, Norwich,	1 1 0	0 15 0	488 Lodge of Amity, Rochdale, Lancafhire,	0 10 6	0 10 0
133 Lodge of Friendfhip, Norwich,	1 1 0	0 10 0	501 Shakefpear L. inWarwickfh.Reg.of Militia,	1 1 0	2 5 0
149 Royal Lancafhire Lodge, Colne, Lancafh.	0 10 6		502 L.Love and Honour,Shipton-Mallet,Somerf.	1 1 0	0 10 0
157. Royal Navy Lodge, Deal,	1 1 0		503 Royal Glocefter Lodge, Southampton,	1 1 0	0 15 0
162 Union Lodge, Nottingham,	1 1 0	3 14 6	508 Noah's Ark Lodge, Middlewich, Chefhire,	0 10 6	
165 At Richmond, in Yorkfhire,	0 10 6	1 0 0	511 Lodge of Harmony, Rofendale, Lancafhire,	0 10 6	0 5 0
168 Thorn, at Burnley, in Lancafhire,	0 10 6	1 5 0	512 Lodge of Fidelity, Leeds,		1 10 0
169 Union Lodge, Crifpin-ftreet, Spitalfields,	0 10 6	1 1 0	526 Union Lodge, Macclesfield,	1 1 0	1 15 6

As a result of the renumbering of the Register on 22 November 1797 African Lodge is now No 370 and £1.5.0 was the last amount received

The only remittances recorded were those made to the Grand
Charity with years between as shown below:

25 November 1789 (produce of 10 dollars)   £2. 2. 11
18 April 1792   1. 1. 0

Those were made under its number 459 but as a result of the
closing-up and renumbering on the Register in 1792 African Lodge
then became No 370 and under that number a remittance of
£1. 5. 0 is recorded on the Business Paper for Grand Lodge for 22
November 1797 (see page 147) and that was the last amount received. In 1806 Prince Hall again wrote complaining that he had
not received answers to his letters since 1792 but no payments in
respect of fees or dues of any kind had been received at Grand
Lodge and no Returns had been made. In its Obituary column on
Saturday 5 December 1807 the *Columbia Centennial* of Boston recorded:

> Yesterday morning Mr. Prince Hall, age 72, Master of African Lodge.
> Funeral on Monday afternoon at 3 o'clock from his late dwelling house which
> his friends and relations are requested to attend without a more formal invi-
> tation.

It was afterwards reported that 'a very large procession of blacks
followed him to the grave'. That grave has a marker (see page 150)
but the inscription on it bears an incorrect date:

> Here lies ye body of Prince Hall First Grand Master of the Colored Grand
> Lodge of Masons in Mass: Died Dec. 7 1807

A monument to his memory was erected some years later in Copp's
Hill Burying Ground, Boston, Mass: (see page 149). Prince Hall's
time on earth had obviously been well spent on behalf of others
and has enriched the lives of thousands who followed the trail that
he blazed. His immediate colleagues in African Lodge were under
the impression that the lodge was still a private lodge under the
Grand Lodge of England. Indeed it was certainly recorded in the
Freemasons' Calendar right up to the issue of 1814 shewing subordinate lodges on the Register up to 1813. That was printed by W.P.
Norris, London, and was the forerunner of what was later to become the official *Year Book*. But many dormant lodges and redun-
dant lodges continued to be listed until 1813 when the Union took
place and a renumbering for the new Register effectively weeded
out all those who had ceased to support the Grand Lodge.

The final letter from African Lodge was sent in 1824 and that
failed to bring response. On 17 June 1827 the Minutes of the lodge
state:

Monument to Prince Hall erected some years after his death in Capp's Hill Burying Ground, Boston, Massachusetts

The Worshipful Master, John T. Hilton was chosen to write and publish the Declaration of Independence, he was given the privilege to make a choice of whom he thought proper to assist him and also to write the independent charter.

The Declaration of Independence appeared the following day as it is dated 18 June 1827, signed by the Master and two Past Masters (see Appendix J) and thus came into being the first of many Prince Hall Grand Lodges as from that time onwards Prince Hall masonry spread its wings. The system is patterned upon those common in the USA which embrace much beyond the Craft and Royal Arch. Recognition from the United Grand Lodge of England and from other Sovereign Jurisdictions with whom England are in fraternal accord has not been achieved by Prince Hall Grand Lodges but, as we come to the close of the 20th century, the future remains unpredictable.

Prince Hall's Grave Marker but the inscription has an incorrect date

Chapter 20

The Royal Arch

Owing to lack of records, precisely when the Royal Arch came into being cannot be stated but it is quite clear that it was already well established before the earliest specific reference to it. There are indications that may well be deemed to be pointers and one such occurs in the records of the Court of Enquiry held by the Inquisition at Lisbon which started in July 1738, only two months after the Papal Bull, *In Eminenti*, had been issued. The statement of one witness has:

> ... and those who are Masters have a trowel, and there are two more classes which they call Excellent Masons, and Grand Mason, which are above all others and superior to that which he, the witness, exercised. ...

There is also the oft-quoted reference from D'Assigny's *Serious and Impartial Enquiry*, published in 1744, on the activity of freemasons in York:

> I am informed in that city is held an assembly of Master Masons under the title of Royal Arch Masons, who as their qualifications and excellencies are superior to others they receive a larger pay than working masons; (footnote on p 32)

D'Assigny commented upon an impostor who practised deception under the pretence of being 'Master of the Royal Arch' but was denounced:

> ... by a Brother of probity and wisdom, who had some small space before attained that excellent part of Masonry in London and plainly proved that his doctrine was false. ... [on the Royal Arch itself] it is an organis'd body of men who have passed the chair ...

Although the Royal Arch theme provided a logical sequence to follow the Hiramic legend, a development which the Moderns had adopted, anything other than the three Craft degrees was shunned by them. The repudiation of the Royal Arch was always well in evidence and examples from three successive Grand Secretaries are worth noting:

> 1 Samuel Spencer (G Sec 1757–1768) who wrote on 7 July 1767: ... the

Royal Arch is a Society which we do not acknowledge, and which we believe to have been invented to introduce innovations ...
2 Thomas French (G Sec 1768) answering a letter dated 28 Nov 1768: ... Relating to the behaviour of the Brother which mentioned in what concerns the Royal Arch masonry it comes by no means under our inspection tho his behaviour was certainly inconsistent with the character of a gentleman and a mason ...
Thomas French also wrote to another brother in October that year stating: ... there is one circumstance in your minutes which you are requested to correct and that concerns Royal Arch masonry which comes not under our inspection. You are desired never to insert the transactions thereof in your regular Lodge Book nor to carry on the business of that degree on your stated Lodge nights ...
3 James Heseltine (G Sec 1769-1780) who wrote in January 1774: ... With respect to the information you have rec'd as to the Grand Lodge of England's having Degrees and Mysteries superior to the three Degrees already communicated you may rest assured it has not the least foundation in truth. ... the Grand Lodge of England has not any other acknowledged Degrees. It is true that many of the Fraternity here belong to a Degree in Masonry say'd to be superior to the other three, called the Royal Arch. I have the honour to be a member of this Degree and its principles and proceedings are truly praiseworthy—but it is unknown in Grand Lodge, and all Emblems or Badges of distinction in that Degree are prohibited from being worn in G.L. ... the Royal Arch is a private and distinct Society. It is part of masonry but has no connection with the Grand Lodge ...

Bros Spencer and Heseltine were both Royal Arch masons but their private affairs did not conflict with official duty.

Laurence Dermott was initiated in Lodge No 26 at Dublin in 1741, in the early part of the year which under the Old Style calendar was still 1740. He was installed as Master of that lodge in 1746 and, according to a *Register of Members of the Royal Arch* compiled by the Antients Grand Lodge, entered the Royal Arch in 1746; it was attainable only by Masters or Past Masters as 'Excellent Masons'. It would be unreasonable to think that a brother of his acumen would have neglected any part of masonry known to him and would have wanted to practise freemasonry as he knew it from the time he settled in London in 1748. This 'fourth degree' must have formed part of the system constructed by the Antients from the time they formed their initial Committee in 1751, even though no mention was made of it until the next year when a complaint was received against two brethren because they:

> ... Initiated many persons for the mean consideration of a leg of mutton for dinner or supper to the disgrace of the Ancient Craft ... [that Dermott] upon examining some brothers they pretended to have made Royal Archmen the parties had not the least idea of that secret ... and they had not the least idea or knowledge of Royal Arch Masonry.

That Laurence Dermott was an expert is shown by the Minutes of the Grand Committee dated 2 September 1752:

> That this Grand Committee shall be formed immediately into a Working Lodge of Master Masons in Order to hear a Lecture from the Grand Secretary Laurence Dermott. The Lodge was Opened in Ancient form of Grand Lodge and every part of Real Freemasonry was traced and explained except the Royal Arch.

Dermott's fondness for that part of the masonic system is shown by his description:

> ... that Part of Masonry called the Royal Arch which I firmly believe to be the Root, Heart, and Marrow of Free-Masonry ...
>
> (*Ahiman Rezon*, 1756, p 47)

We may gather some idea of how the Antients felt the Royal Arch to crown the Craft system when we refer to *The Laws and Regulations* (*Ahiman Rezon* 1807 Edn):

> ANCIENT MASONRY consists of four Degrees—the three first of which are, that of the Apprentice, the Fellow Craft, and the sublime degree of Master; and a Brother, being well versed in these degrees, and otherwise qualified, as hereafter will be expressed, is eligible to be admitted to the fourth degree, the Holy Royal Arch.
>
> This degree is certainly more august, sublime, and important than those which precede it, and is the summit and perfection of Ancient Masonry ...

Although not referred to as Royal Arch, but sufficiently described to identify its similarity, the anonymous author of *Le Parfait Maçon* (translation reproduced in *Early French Exposures* edited by Harry Carr, QC Lodge London 1971) published the following in 1744, before Dermott was eligible to be Exalted:

> SECRET OF THE ECOSSAIS MASONS
>
> It is said among the Masons, that there are still several degrees above that of the Masters, of which I have just spoken; some say there are six in all, & others go up to seven. Those called *Ecossais Masons* claim that they form the fourth grade. As this Masonry, different from the others in many ways, is beginning to become known in France, the Public will not be annoyed if I relate what I have read about it in the same manuscript, which seems to give the *Ecossais* a degree of superiority above the Apprentices, Fellows, & ordinary Masters. ... Their work being much more arduous than that of the other Masons, they were also awarded a more favourable rate of pay ...

That writer probably saw a similar manuscript to that which, in the same year, influenced the D'Assigny publication previously referred to, as both have much in common. A footnote in the relative portion of the French publication is of interest:

> The *Ecossais* Masons all wear a wide red ribbon from which hangs a kind of buckler.

It was a comment on the sixth of a series of eight questions and answers:

> Q. Why do the Ecossais Masons carry the sword & the buckler?
> A. In memory of the order given by Nehemiah to all the workmen at the time of the rebuilding of the Temple, to have swords always at their sides, & their bucklers near at hand during the work, for use in cases of attack by their enemies.

Owing to the non-acceptance of the Royal Arch by their authorities, brethren under the Moderns jurisdiction felt deprived from what was enjoyed by those under the Antients; but, many had been obligated to become 'acceptable' and some had gone on to enter the Royal Arch. In the year 1761 a group of actors working a circuit of theatres in the Yorkshire area of York, Leeds, Hull, Halifax, etc received a Warrant from the Grand Lodge of the Moderns to found a new Lodge named the Lodge at the Punch Bowl No 259, taking the name from the meeting-place. That event led to a revival of the York Grand Lodge which had been dormant—but the two lodges worked in harmony, members from one becoming members of the other and frequent inter-visitations took place.

On 7 February 1762, one year after its constitution, four members of the Punch Bowl Lodge decided to perform the Royal Arch ceremony and formed themselves into a Chapter for there was no authority to whom they could apply for a Charter or Warrant. The Minutes of their first meeting commence with:

> A Most Sublime or Royal Arch Lodge Open'd at the Sign of the Punch Bowl in Stonegate, York on Sunday 7th Feb 1762.

It was attended by the four Founders and four Candidates who 'Petition'd to be raised to the 4th Degree of Masonry Commonly call'd the Most Sublime or Royal Arch'. That there was an affinity with the York Grand Lodge is shewn in the By-Laws passed on 1 May 1768:

> That the Fees for Making any Member of the Grand Lodge in York who may upon Ballot be admitted a Royal Arch Mason be five Shillings, and one Shilling to the Sword Bearer; every other person to pay half a guinea and one Shilling to the Sword Bearer.

That they assumed authority in the Royal Arch is shewn by the fact that four subordinate Chapters were constituted, three during the period 1768 to 1772 and one during 1778 to 1781, one at Ripon, another at Knaresborough, one in the Inniskilling Regiment of Dragoons, and the fourth at Rotherham; very little of the proceedings of any of those has survived. But it was not until their meeting of 8 February 1778 that the authoritative title was used:

In Consequence of Summonses sent to the Members of the Grand Royal Arch Chapter, the Brethren assembled, and a Most Sublime Royal Arch Chapter was opened.

The circumstances of the Royal Arch in York have been well documented by Bro G.Y. Johnson in his Paper—'The York Grand Chapter'—reproduced in *AQC* Vol 57 pp 196–255.

In London the intermingling between brethren from each Jurisdiction in certain lodges was quite an acceptable state and was effected by the simple process of being re-obligated to become 'regular' according to requirement. Ample records exist that this was normal in certain lodges and that it was not confined to the Craft; brethren from both sides could enter the Royal Arch and meetings for that purpose could be called by a newspaper announcement. The following, from the *Daily Advertiser* dated 11 January 1754 provides an example of that method:

> All Brothers who were made in the E.G. and R.C. commonly call'd the Royal Arch, are desired to attend on Sunday night, at Five in the evening, at Brother John Henry's the Crown and Anchor, in King Street, Seven Dials, in order for a Grand Installation, and to chuse the P.T.H.J.Z.L. and J.A. as Grand to proclaim the worthy S.O.J.N.R.S. with the two P.L.R.S. By Order of the P.T.H.J.Z.L. and J.A.
>
> W.L. Secretary
>
> Note: Removed from the Fountain in Monmouth Street.

The intriguing initials in that Notice may be interpreted as:

> E.G. and R.C. = Excellent Grand and Royal Chapter
> P.T.H.J. = Prophet Haggai (J and I being interchangeable)
> Z.L. = Zerubbabel
> J.A. = Jeshua
> S.O.J.N.R.S. = Sojourners
> P.L.R.S. = Pillars (two Scribes are deemed to be Pillars supporting the Arch represented by the three Principals)
> W.L. = William Lilly, Grand Pursuivant in the Antients Grand Lodge 1752–1756

It would have been no great step for some of the Moderns brethren, having entered the Royal Arch by courtesy of their friends on the Antients side, to set up a Chapter of their own and that is exactly what happened and one particular group are on record to that effect. They compiled a *Manifesto* which is dated 12 June 1765 (see Appendix K) and two of the twelve *Laws* from that are of interest here:

> 1st. We Resolve to Hold a Chapter at the Turk's Head Tavern in Gerrard Street, Soho, on the second Friday of every Month at Six O'clock in the Evening.
>
> 9. That a proper Coffer with two Locks and Keys, differing the one from the other, be provided for the preservation of the Robes, Jewells &c. belonging to the Chapter, which shall be reposited therein as soon as the Chapter is

closed, by the Janators with all care, and a Key of Lock No. 1 given to E:
Z.L.: and another alike to the Principal Sojourner. And a Kay of Lock
No. 2 to each of the Secretaries. And the Jewells &c. shall not be lent, or
carried out of the House where the Coffer is kept, unless with consent of
all the Officers. And if such a thing be done contrary to this Order, the
person or persons so offending shall forfeit one Guinea each, to the Common Stock, and make good any damage that such Jewells &c. may have
received by means of the said offence.

In their first Minute Book are notes to the effect that at least five
meetings were held prior to that date and it would appear that
their purpose was to Exalt brethren who were to become officers,
and to discuss a *Manifesto*; further *Laws* were recorded on 12 February 1766 from which we obtain some idea of their procedure. It
is of interest to note that Dr John James Rouby was Exalted in
that Chapter in 1765, and his breast jewel which is dated 1766 is
the earliest known Royal Arch jewel; it is exhibited in the Museum
at Freemasons' Hall, London.

The breast jewel of Dr John James Rouby
Exalted in the Royal Arch in 1765. The jewel
is the earliest known Royal Arch jewel

The Turning Point in the Royal Arch

Often to be found in early records are references to 'Grand Master' and 'Grand Lodge' but those terms were not meant in the context that applies today; they were frequently used in reference to the Master of an ordinary lodge whether on the Regular List or not, and non-freemasons today sometimes use the same titles in that regard thinking they are using the correct terms. Common titles in the Royal Arch were 'Grand Chiefs' or 'Excellent Masters' of the Royal Arch'; the first use of the title 'Excellent Grand Master' came in 1766. It was the turning point in the history of the Royal Arch when, on 11 June, twenty-seven Companions assembled at the Turk's Head Tavern, to witness the Exaltation of Lord Blaney the Grand Master of the Grand Lodge of England (Moderns). He accepted the office of First Principal at the next meeting on 22 July 1766 when the draft of a Charter was approved which described him as 'Most Excellent Grand Master of the Royal Arch of Jerusalem'. Thus was produced what is now deemed the parent of Royal Arch authority and of the Grand Chapters that appeared thereafter, but, as we have seen, it was not the first.

The text of the official document—*The Charter of Compact*—is reproduced in Appendix L and attention is drawn to the altered date from 1766 to 1767 which was done later in an attempt to discredit the entry of Lord Blayney into the Royal Arch whilst he was Grand Master. It was the subject of an item in *AQC* Vol 64 pp 136–7 by Bro J. R. Dashwood who stated:

> ... We know that, although most of the Grand Officers had been exalted into the Royal Arch, it was not favourably regarded by the 'Moderns' Grand Lodge. What, then, must have been the horror of its opponents when they heard that not only had the Grand Master allowed himself to be exalted during his term of Office, but he had also accepted the Titular Presidency of the Order as the natural corollary of his Craft Office, had presided at the meetings of the Chapter held since his exaltation, and had agreed to a Charter of Compact setting up a Grand Chapter with powers to grant Charters? I think that some person or persons unknown were determined to try to undo the worst of the damage, by making it appear that Lord Blayney had acted, not in his Official capacity as Grand Master, but in his private capacity after he had laid down that Office; the easiest way to effect this was by post-dating the Charter by a year to a time when his successor had been installed, and the insertion of the letter "P" to suggest that he was no longer in Office and was acting irresponsibly.

No real use was made of the power of that Charter for nearly three years. At the November meeting of Grand Chapter in 1768 a Committee was authorised to arrange further Laws and Regulations. But, during 1769, eight Charters to sanction new Chapters were granted. On 10 March of that year all attending the meeting signed the Charter of Compact in compliance with its Laws and Ordinances. It is a matter for regret that we have no explanation for the term 'the Birth of Virtue 5..3..7..9..' which has eluded modern students in this field. Whilst the photograph does not show that the final 7 is an alteration it is to be seen quite clearly on the document itself; the alteration of 5770 to 5771 is visible.

The work of Bro J.R. Dashwood has indeed set the record right in this respect and his Paper—'Notes on the First Minute Book of the Excellent Grand and Royal Chapter'—*AQC* Vol 62 pp 165–193, written earlier than the Note, just quoted has been of great value in this field.

The qualification for admission to the Royal Arch was stated in the *Charter of Compact* (see Appendix L):

> SIXTHLY That none but discreet and experienced Master Masons shall receive Exaltation to this sublime Degree in this or any other Chapter that may hereafter be duly constituted;

However, that in 1778 was changed to:

> ... must have passed the three probationary degrees of Craft; been regularly appointed and presided as Master, to be justly entitled to, and have received the Past Master's token and pass-word ...

but that proved to be too restrictive and four years later the words *been regularly appointed* as well as *to be justly entitled to and have received the Past Master's token and pass-word* were deleted; apparently a situation had developed causing dissension among those who had qualified as actual Masters and those who had not as the words 'Master Masons' in previous use had produced misunderstanding. Royal Arch members were originally classed as *Excellent Masons* but that title had included qualification as a Past Master. It is appropriate to recall a previous reference from *Le Parfait Macon* published in 1774 in which *Ecossais Masons* were said to be the fourth of a possible seven degrees:

> SECRET OF THE ECOSSAIS MASONS
>
> ... Instead of weeping over the ruins of the Temple of Solomon, as their brethren do, the *Ecossais* are concerned with rebuilding it. Everyone knows that after seventy years of captivity in Babylon, the Great Cyrus permitted the Israelites to rebuild the Temple & the City of Jerusalem; that Zerubabel, of the House of David, was appointed by him the Chief & Leader of that Temple for their return of the Holy City; that the first stone of the Temple was laid during the reign of Cyrus, but that it was not completed until the sixth year of that of Darius, King of the Persians. It is from this great event that the *Ecossais* derive the epoch of their institution, & although they are later than the other Masons by several centuries, they consider themselves of a superior grade. ... It is said among the Masons that there are still several degrees above that of

the masters ... Those called *Ecossais Masons* claim that they form the fourth grade.

There was no regularity for meetings of Royal Arch companions under the Antients jurisdiction, according to need a meeting would be called, even advertised in order to notify those who were qualified to attend, but the Minutes of such meetings were always read for approval in their Grand Lodge as the following example will show:

> Grand Lodge Minutes 1 December 1784
> Read and confirm'd the Minutes of the last Royal Arch Chapter and the Choice of Excellent Masters for superintending.

Wider power of control was exercised to include the deliberations of the Stewards Lodge:

> Read the Minutes of Royal Arch Committee and afterwards those of the Stewards Lodge of December, January, and February, and the same passed unanimously.

The function of the 'Stewards Lodge' of that period may be equated with what is exercised today by the Board of General Purposes and its various Committees. Whilst recommendations and proposals would be made by members of the Stewards Lodge following their examination of problems, a considerable amount of their time was spent on Appeals for relief which was afforded immediately if thought worthy by them.

Following the setting up of the Grand and Royal Chapter of the Royal Arch of Jerusalem by brethren from the Moderns jurisdiction, within a few years we find mention of 'Grand Chapter' in the Minutes of the Antients Grand Lodge. A typical entry is:

> Read the Minutes of the last Grand Chapter of the Royal Arch and same passed Unanimously.

But, the Royal Arch activity remained under the control of the Grand Lodge, it was indeed 'a rose by any other name!'

The qualification for entry to the Royal Arch was still a problem but on 4 December 1771 an attempt was made by Laurence Dermott to give guidelines and again we refer to the Minutes of the Antients Grand Lodge:

> The R! Worship! Deputy Grand Master informed the Grand Lodge of the proceedings of the *Royal Arch* meeting, Viz., on the 22nd October and 6th of November last and expatiated a long time on the scandalous method pursued by most of the Lodges (on S! John's Days) in passing a Number of Brethren through the Chair on purpose to obtain the sacred Mystery's of the *Royal Arch*, and proved in a concise manner that those proceedings were unjustifiable; therefore Moved for a Regulation to be made in order to suppress them for the future. The Deputy was answered by several Brethren, that there were many

Members of Lodges who from their Proffessions in Life (the Sea for Example) that could never regularly attain that part of Masonry, tho' very able and deserving Men, and humbly Moved that might be Considered in the New Regulations. The Grand Lodge in General thought such a Clause necessary and therefore the Question being put for the Regulation, it was unanimously Resolved: THAT no person for the future shall be made a *Royal Arch Mason* but the legal Representative of the Lodge [ie W Master] except a Brother (that is going abroad) who hath been twelve months a Register'd Mason; and must have the Unanimous Voice of his Lodge to receive such qualification—and in order to render this Regulation more Expedient it is further Order'd that all Certificates granted to Brethren from their Respective Lodges shall have Inserted the Day the Brother or Brethren joined or was made in said Lodge and that this Regulation take place on St John's Day the 27th Dec. 1771.

The subterfuge of 'Passing the Chair' for Master Masons to make them 'virtual Masters' however, still went on by both sides, although whenever it was detected steps were taken to censure those concerned:

> 11 November 1788. It was ordered by the W. Master and the Majority of the Lodge No. 6 to summons the Master and Wardens of No. 225 for a trespass committed by them in passing a member of Lodge No. 6 through the Chair in order to obtain a seat in the H.R.A. contrary to Constitution.

It was a procedure that had been practised so long that it was unlikely to be stopped. Although it became common for Master Masons to enter that way the Regulation passed in Grand Lodge (Antients) on 5 November 1783 ensured that Master Masons could not be elected to preside in a Chapter:

> RESOLVED. THAT Masters and Pastm^{rs} (bona fide) only ought to be admitted Master of the Royal Arch ...
> 4th RESOLVED That as it is Universally Acknowledged, That the Regular Masters of the Royal Arch (only) are in possession of the Supreme Degree of Freemasonry: THE GENERAL GRAND CHAPTER shall once in every year (for the future) when duly Congregated in conjunction with the Right Worshipful Grand Officers for the time being, Make choice of a Certain Number of the Most Excellent Masters amongst themselves. Which Number shall not exceed Nine persons, whose names and addresses shall be Return'd and Recommended to the General Grand Lodge. To Examine the abilities of all and every of the person or persons (of the Antient Lodges) who shall take upon him or them To Perform any of the secret Ceremonies Relative to the Royal Arch, the Installation of Grand Officers or Processions &c &c &c. And upon finding any such person or persons Master or Lecturer &c defective or unworthy, To report him or them to the Grand Master or his Deputy for the time being: So that such defective performer may be suppress'd and forbid to use his Craft until he or they shall be found more Capable. And in case of non-Compliance To be forever excluded. ...
> 7th RESOLVED That in Order to render those Regulations more Expedient and Effectual; no person (though a Regular Master or Pastmaster) shall be made a Royal Arch Mason (within thirty miles of London) without the Assistance or Concurrence of Six of the Masters whose Names are upon the Royal

Arch Record. Nor shall the name of any Mason be recorded amongst the Excellent Masters Without the Order of a General Chapter or a Certificate-sign'd by three (or more) of the Masters chosen (for that year) for Regulating the Craft as aforesaid. . . .

By the end of the 18th century Royal Arch Companions fell into two main groups, those who had received entry as bona-fide Masters or Pastmasters of Craft lodges and those brethren who had been made 'virtual Masters' having gone through the brief ceremony of 'Passing the Chair'; to some it was administered by their Grand Lodge to others it was entirely separated under a Grand Chapter; many anomalies came to the fore and much was neglected in the period of the approach to the Union of the two Grand Lodges during which the Royal Arch was overshadowed.

Recognition of the Royal Arch

Towards the end of the 18th century, when London's interest in a possible Union of the two Grand Lodges seemed paramount, there was much less activity in the Royal Arch which is apparent from the sparse records that have reached us. The printed *Proceedings* of the Antients, which were circulated to their lodges, carried a Note from 1792 onwards which was worded as follows, or similarly so:

Note: For Grand Lodge Certificates, and all business respecting the *Craft*, please apply or write to Mr. Leslie, Attorney and Notary, No. 28, Tokenhouse Yard; and upon matters relating to the *Holy Royal Arch*, to Companion Edwards Harper, No. 207, Fleet Street.

Thus, the administration of the Craft and the Royal Arch had been separated but nothing of any consequence has survived to guide us regarding their activity in the Royal Arch. The story for the Moderns Grand Lodge and Grand Chapter, however, contains continued rejection by the one and gross neglect of its affairs by the other. Following a complaint to the Grand Lodge against officers of the Grand Chapter, which occasioned an attempt at a schism in the ranks of the latter, the subject was dismissed by William White who, as Grand Secretary, stated:

That this Lodge do agree with its Committee that the Grand Lodge of England has nothing to do with the proceedings of the Society of Royal Arch Masons. That the circular letter sent to the several Lodges under the Names of some of that Society . . . has not been with the privity or under the sanction of this Grand Lodge.

We find reference to that subject dated six months later in the Proceedings of the (Moderns) Grand Chapter where on 10 May 1793 it was recorded:

That the Grand Lodge very properly observed on that occasion that it had
nothing to do with a Matter originating in another independent Society competent to judge of and determine its own affairs.

That competency was suspect as there is ample evidence from then
on that attendance at, and administration by, the Grand Chapter
had been stricken as may be seen by extracts from a letter dated
23 March 1793 sent by Comp Winzer, Grand Scribe N to John
Allen whom he addressed by his rank of Inspector General in the
Excellent Grand and Royal Chapter.

... The attendance of the Companions but especially of the Grand Officers
having been so seldom and at so late an hour that little or no business of
consequence could be transacted (if ever a chapter was formed) with the
regularity and solemnity appertaining to the government of a Royal Arch
Chapter of Jerusalem. ... We are now in the 4th month after the Gen Election
still without a possibility of completing a new List of the Grand Officers for the
present year, owing to the want of regular attendance & proper inclination to
act as Scribes which are the troublesome Offices in the Chapter. Many private
and regular Companions are now become disgusted and have withdrawn their
names—and others threaten to follow their example. ...

But whilst the top management was in a state of neglect the general
well-being of the Royal Arch in private Chapters in London and
throughout the country prospered.

We have noted that the Craft Union was accomplished with
two Royal brothers meeting together as the Grand Masters of the
two Grand Lodges, but it would not be out of place here to recall
that the Duke of Atholl had resigned as Grand Master of the
Antients to enable HRH the Duke of Kent, Prov Grand Master for
Lower Canada to become Grand Master. At a Special Grand
Lodge of Antients held on 18 May 1813, seven months before the
Union, it was recorded:

... the Grand Lodge received His Royal Highness upstanding, after the
custom of Master Masons, His Grace the Duke of Atholl being on the Throne,
congratulated the Grand Lodge & the fraternity on this cordial visit of our
Illustrious Brother, and paid a very high & just compliment to the active Zeal
& lively interest which H.R. Highness had always manifested for the Fraternity.

His Royal Highness made an elegant reply to the Most Noble & R.W.
Grand Master, & expressed in the warmest terms his unchangeable affection
and attachment to Masonry according to the Ancient Institution, and to the
Grand Lodge of England in which these principles were so purely & correctly
preserved. His R.H.[ss] further said, that upon every Occasion, he should be
happy to co-operate with them in exerting themselves for the preservation of
the Rights & Principles of the Craft and that however desirable an Union
might be with the other fraternity of Masons, it could only be desirable if
accomplished on the basis of the ancient Institutions, and with the maintenance
of all the rights of this Ancient Craft. ...

Those sentiments, so well expressed by HRH the Duke of Kent, describe the indomitable attitude of the Antients in general, and it is the author's considered opinion they account for the wording of Article 2 in the *Articles of Union* (see Appendix F) amounting to a compromise by the Moderns. The term 'pure and Ancient Masonry' meant the form and the system which was in being when the Antients Grand Lodge was founded in 1751; it had nothing to do with the history of freemasonry as 'ancient'; 'pure' meant the unadulterated system that had been continued in their ranks. The Royal Arch had at long last become recognised by the Moderns as part of the system.

Prior to the Union, at the meeting of the Moderns Grand Chapter on 10 May 1810, the Duke of Sussex having been proposed as head of the Royal Arch duly signified his acceptance of the position then designated as 'First Grand Master of Royal Arch Masons of England'. Also, at an Especial Grand Lodge of the Antients held on 1st December 1813, twenty-six days before the Union it was recorded:

> His Royal Highness, the Duke of Sussex, Grand Master of the other Fraternity of Masons, together with several of his Grand Officers, having been made Ancient Masons, in the Grand Master's Lodge No 1 (in a room adjoining) took their places in the Procession, which entered the Grand Lodge in the following order:—

then were detailed the brethren and items involved. It is interesting to note that the Banner of the Duke of Sussex was not carried in the procession but, at proper intervals, there were four which included:

> Banner of the Royal Arch.
> . . . . . .
> The Standard of Ancient Masons
> . . . . . .
> The Banner of the late [former] Grand Master [Duke of Atholl]
> . . . . . .
> The Banner of the Grand Master (HRH Duke of Kent) followed by the Royal Brothers.

At that meeting the *Articles of Union* were signed and the Great Seal affixed and it was stated:

> ... that brotherly application be made to the Grand Lodges of Scotland and Ireland enclosing them a copy of the above articles, when ratified and entreating them to delegate two or more enlightened members of their respective bodies to be present at the Assembly of Union, on Monday, the 27th December, instant, pursuant to Article V and XV. ...

On the 30 November 1813 at a Special Convocation of the Moderns Grand Chapter it was announced:

The M.E. Comp. Austin (3rd Grand Principal) stated that the Grand Lodge of England under H.R.H. the Duke of Sussex had entered into preliminary Articles with the Grand Lodge now under H.R.H. the Duke of Kent for an Union of the two Grand Lodges under one Grand Master. That by those Articles the Royal Arch was acknowledged as the perfection of the Masters Degree and those Articles had received the Unanimous approbation of the Grand Lodge. That H.R.H. the Duke of Sussex had commanded this Special Grand Chapter to be convened for the purpose of submitting this subject to their consideration in order that such measure might be adopted as would best accord with the general interest of Masonry.

Whereupon it was Resolved unanimously that as the Grand Lodge of England has through the M.W. Grand Master communicated its determination to acknowledge the Royal Arch this Grand Chapter does consider an Union of this Order with the Grand Lodge highly proper and desirable. Resolved that H.R.H. the Duke of Sussex M.E.Z. be invested with full and unlimited Powers to negotiate and conclude an Union on behalf of this Supreme Grand Chapter with the Grand Lodges under their Royal Highnesses the Dukes of Sussex and Kent in such a way as may appear to H.R.H. the M.E.Z. most conclusive to the General interest of Masonry. . . .

Recognition indeed, but it was to take a few more years yet!

Chapter 21

The United Grand Chapter

Recognition was one thing but inclusion of the Royal Arch within the system was another! Whereas the Moderns had an administrative authority for the Royal Arch, albeit somewhat neglected in the last decade of the 18th century and first part of the 19th, it would have been no problem for them to have mustered those whose attentions were focussed upon activity in the Craft towards the Union. For the Antients, however, it was a different matter as Royal Arch problems were dealt with at Stewards Committee level and Minutes of their Grand Chapter meetings were read for approval in their Grand Lodge; as we have seen in the later stage the Secretarial duties were delegated to Edwards Harper whose records have not survived, other than Lists that he made, ie entries of the names of those Exalted went on until 31 March 1819.

The last positive mention of the Royal Arch in Grand Lodge was at the meeting on 6 May 1792 in this Minute:

> Resolved Unanimously
>
> That it be recommended to His Grace the Duke of Atholl, Right Worshipful Grand Master of Masons, in England, according to the Old Constitutions, to inhibit and totally prevent all public masonic processions, and all private meetings of masons and lodges of emergency, upon any pretence whatsoever, and to suppress and suspend all masonic meetings, except upon the regular stated lodge meetings and Royal Arch Chapters, which shall be open to all masons, duly qualified as such.
>
> That when the usual masonic business is ended the lodge shall then disperse, the Tyler withdraw from the door, and formality and restraint of admittance cease. . . .
>
> It was ORDERED
>
> That the Grand Secretary shall immediately give Notice to every Lodge under the Ancient Constitution, as also to the Grand Lodges of Scotland, Ireland, &c, of these proceedings.
>
> read and confirmed on Wednesday 5th June 1799.

It is rather significant that the liason was strongly held with Scotland and Ireland but no specific mention of the premier Grand Lodge of England, the Moderns, although by that time brethren from both sides were anxiously talking about a possible union.

Some idea of the confused state of the Royal Arch that went on and on may be gained from a letter dated 15 October 1816, addressed to Edwards Harper who by that time was Joint Secretary of the United Grand Lodge, an appointment he held from the Union in 1813 until 1838. It came from St Johns Lodge No 670 of Chowbent, near Leigh, Lancashire:

> ... One part of our Brethren that are Arch-Masons were made under the Moderns system of an Arch-Warrant, the other under the Ancient system have been arched and the Craft. Now the former looks upon the latter as not legall; we wish to have youre advice on the subject how we ought to proceede, as many of our Brethren are desirous to take it; and some of them have taken it at the neighbouring Lodges, we wish to know if we shall be justifiable in Making Arch-Masons on the Ancient System; or if we could have a Dispensation from the Grand; untill such times as we can have an Arch-Warrant, if Warrants are to be granted for that degree; ...

Frontispiece of Thomas Harper's seventh edition of
Ahiman Rezon

Dedication to the Duke of Atholl from Thomas Harper's 1807 edition of Ahiman
Rezon.

THE

CONSTITUTION

OF

FREE-MASONRY,

OR

Ahiman Rezon,

CONTAINING,

AMONG OTHER USEFUL INFORMATION,

THE LAWS, CHARGES, & REGULATIONS

OF THE

FREE AND ACCEPTED MASONS,

ACCORDING TO THE OLD INSTITUTIONS;

To which is added, a

SELECTION OF MASONIC SONGS,
&c. &c. &c.

———◆———

REVISED AND CORRECTED, WITH CONSIDERABLE ADDITIONS, FROM THE
ORIGINAL OF THE LATE

LAURENCE DERMOTT, ESQ.

BY

THOMAS HARPER, D. G. M.

———◆———

SEVENTH EDITION.

———◆———

Londen:

PRINTED BY BROTHER T. HARPER, JUN.

Crane Court, Fleet Street.

For the Editor, No. 207, Fleet Street.

———

1807.

Title page from Thomas Harper's 1807 edition of Ahiman Rezon

Thomas Harper's Seventh Edition of *Ahiman Rezon*, dedicated to the Duke of Atholl, published in 1807 (see pages 166-8) had a very wide circulation, even among the Moderns, had the following as a preamble to the Royal Arch *Laws and Regulations*:

ANCIENT MASONRY consists of four Degrees—The first of which are, that of the APPRENTICE, the FELLOW CRAFT, and the sublime degree of MASTER; and a Brother, being well versed in these degrees, and otherwise qualified, as hereafter will be expressed, is eligible to be admitted to the fourth degree, the HOLY ROYAL ARCH.

This degree is more august, sublime, and important than those which precede it, and is the summit and perfection of Ancient Masonry. . . .

It must of consequence be allowed that every regular and warranted Lodge possesses the power of forming and holding Meetings in each of these several degrees, the last of which, from its pre-eminence, is denominated, among Masons, a Chapter.

The final meeting of the Antients Grand Chapter was held on the day of the Union of the two Grand Chapters, 18 March 1817. No record of that meeting has survived, indeed its Grand Chapter must have been, in effect, an *ad hoc* meeting of those who were qualified and had previously had dealings with such matters under their Grand Lodge. All supervision had disappeared when the Antients Grand Lodge ceased. However, we do have a record of the last meeting of the Grand Chapter of the Moderns which was written in the '*Rough Minute Book*' but not transcribed from there:

Supreme Grand Chapter of Royal Arch Masons of England.
Tuesday 18 March 1817.
. . . A Report was received from H.R H. the Duke of Sussex, M.E.Z. dated at Kensington-Palace this Day, in which His Royal Highness stated that, in Pursuance of the Powers vested in him, by the Grand Chapter on the 30 November 1813, he had made Arrangements for an Union of this Grand Chapter with the Grand Chapter over which His Royal Highness the Duke of Kent formerly presided; that those Arrangements had been made in such a way as to render the Connexion between the Grand Chapter and the United Grand Lodge as intimate as the Circumstances of the case will permit. For the purpose of forming the Junction of the Two Grand Chapters, His Royal Highness had caused not only this Chapter to be convened, but also the Members of the other Grand Chapter in a separate Apartment, and His Royal Highness proposed that so soon as this Grand Chapter should have concluded its necessary Business, it should, by Vote, adjourn itself to assemble immediately, in a third Apartment where he, the M.E.Z. would be ready to receive the Members of both Grand Chapters; and where Measures would be taken to constitute one United Grand Chapter.

. . . ORDERED That an Account of the Proceedings of this Meeting, and also of the last Grand Chapter, be printed, and transmitted to all subordinate Chapters, and that they be directed to transmit all future Communication to the United Grand Chapter.

A Communication being received from the Members of the other Grand

Chapter, announcing that they were ready to proceed into another Apartment, agreeably to the Directions of the M.E.Z. His Royal Highness the Duke of Sussex; Companion E., was deputed to go to the other Grand Chapter to inform them that, the members of this Grand Chapter would forthwith proceed to that Apartment to meet them; and, on a Motion duly made, the Chapter was adjourned accordingly.

The first Minutes of the newly formed United Grand Chapter give confirmation of the above procedure:

> The Members of the two former Grand Chapters having been summoned to meet this day they assembled in separate apartments; and the Chapter having been opened the Members proceeded to a Third Chamber where His Royal Highness the Duke of Sussex M.E.Z. was waiting to receive them; the United Grand Chapter was then formed as follows, viz:—

Then followed the names of the new officers and of those notables attending with the statement 'The Three Principals of the several Chapters in the London District'. It is regrettable that the Chapters were not listed, but a thorough examination of records nearest to that date shew that at least seventeen Chapters existed in 1823, probably there were more in 1817. Of the existing thirteen Chapters with approved date of formation prior to the Union of 1813, seven stemmed from the Antients and six from the Moderns Register. Owing to their jealous interest in the Royal Arch it is most unlikely that among 'The Three Principals of the several Chapters in the London District' the Antients were not well represented.

A Committee was set up to arrange Laws and Regulations and on 15 April 1817 the following were included among those adopted:

> That such regular Chapters as have existed prior to the said 27th December, 1813, without being attached to any regular Lodge, shall unite themselves to some Lodge.

Failure to do so, and non-payment of dues from then on, caused some Chapters to be erased from the List and that also contributed to the gaps that distress historians of the present day.

> That to this Order none ought to be admitted but men of the best character and education, open generous, of liberal sentiment, and real philanthropists, who have passed through the probationary degrees of Masonry, have presided as Masters, been duly proposed, recommended by two or more Companions of the Chapter, ballotted for, and approved of; the recommendation (unless on particular occasions) to be at least one Chapter previous to the ballot. The brother to be not less than twenty-three years of age at the time of exaltation, but none to be admitted, if, on ballot, there appear more than one negative. No Mason shall be exalted to this sublime degree unless he has been a Master Mason for at least twelve calendar months; ...

In the course of time from that groundwork various changes and amendments have been made to the laws and Regulations governing the Royal Arch.

On 3 September 1817 the Union was formally reported in the United Grand Lodge who passed the following resolution:

> That the Grand Lodge having been informed that the two Grand Chapters of the Order of the Royal Arch, existing prior to the Union of the Craft, had formed a junction, that rank and votes in all their meetings had been given to all the Officers of Grand Lodge, and that the Laws and Regulations of that body had been, as far as possible, assimilated, those of the Craft, it was *Resolved Unanimously* That the Grand Lodge will at all times be disposed to acknowledge the proceedings of the Grand Chapter, and so long as their arrangements do not interfere with the Regulations of the Grand Lodge, and are in conformity with the Act of Union, they will be ready to recognize, facilitate, and uphold the same.

Dignified reservations that kept dominance with the Grand Lodge!

Uniformity in the Royal Arch

In the years following the Craft Union brethren in London were preoccupied endeavouring to agree and to comply with the standard forms of ritual and ceremonial and it was not until 1827 that the last item, the Installation of Master, received official attention. During all those years the Royal Arch had, more or less, been left to its own devices, where attention to Secretarial work was minimal. A wide variety of practices in private Chapters continued even though the work of Finch and his copyist Carlile were available in print and widely circulated; while strongly condemned by the authorities, they nevertheless afforded some assistance. The Royal Arch Union of 1817 seemed to have just come and gone but eventually proper consideration for that part of Freemasonry did arise.

The matter came before Grand Chapter Convocations held in February, May, and June 1833 and in February 1834 it was announced that a Committee of nine had been appointed:

> ... to take into consideration the Ceremonies for the Installation of Principals as well as the various other ceremonies of the Order.

In November 1834 Grand Chapter records state:

> The Report of the Committee was submitted to the E. Companions in portions according to their several and respective ranks and fully explained; some few amendments were suggested and adopted unanimously. It was then moved that this Grand Chapter approves and confirms the arrangements of the several ceremonies as submitted by the Special Committee to the various classes which motion passed unanimously in the affirmative.

In May 1835 sanction was given for a Special Chapter of Promulgation to be formed to fulfil a task similar to what had been performed by the earlier Lodge of Reconciliation for arrangements in the Craft. At the first some Companions did not take kindly to the forms being promulgated and one event, in direct opposition, caused Grand Chapter to state:

> Some misconceptions having arisen as to what are the Ceremonies of our Order. It is hereby Resolved and declared that the Ceremonies adopted and promulgated by Especial Grand Chapter on the 21st and 25th November 1834, are the ceremonies of our Order which it is the duty of every Chapter to adopt and obey.

Unfortunately no official ritual was ever printed so terms of reference were unstable, being only the performances of the Chapter of Promulgation and what Companions who attended chose to remember. Once again, like the same situation in the Craft, the nearest that posterity will ever get to what was adopted and promulgated comes from the published work of George Claret. His first Craft ritual, referred to in an earlier chapter, was published in 1838 and after its title, which was descriptive of its contents, the following note appears:

> 'of whom also may be had the following Royal Arch Masonry, Opening & Closing, Ceremony of Exaltation, Passing the Veils, Prayers, Exortations [sic] and the R.A. Lecture.'

That manual was published within a mere three years after the demonstrations of the Chapter of Promulgation and Claret was making available Royal Arch working, probably only in manuscript, but knowing the character and dedication of this brother it would no doubt have been in keeping with what had been officially approved. His first manual for the Royal Arch appeared in 1844, the market by that time justifying publication. (A detailed study entitled *George Claret (1738–1850)—Ritual Printer*, by the author was published in *AQC* Vol 87 pp 1–22.)

Because it was necessary to be a Royal Arch Companion to qualify for admission to certain other Orders, it will not be inappropriate now to recall the latter part of Article II:

> ... But this Article is not intended to prevent any Lodge or Chapter from holding a meeting in any of the degrees of the Orders of Chivalry, according to the constitutions of the said Orders.

It was with this mind, certainly to encourage brethren to take 'higher degrees' that led to the downfall of RW Bro William Tucker, Provincial Grand Master for Dorset 1846–1853. He commenced his seventh year of office on 18 August 1853 with a service at the Parish Church at Wareham where he attended dressed in the full robes of a Sovereign Grand Inspector General of the 33rd

Degree. After the service the church bells rang out and a band led the procession from church to where the Provincial Grand Lodge was to be held, and there in distinct contravention of the Regulations on regalia contained in the book of *Constitutions* published in 1847 he conducted the meeting still wearing his robes. He also quoted Article II and said:

> ... Thus the chivalric Orders are allowed but not recognized; still their existence is fully admitted. This to a great extent cuts us off from Continental, and I may say, even from Scots and Irish Masonry ... To all young Masons, to all who take an interest in the history of our Order, I do most strongly recommend an advancing course. I recommend them to to take the higher Degrees, for on the Continent, and in Scotland and Ireland, they will find a greater respect paid to these Degrees than any other. ...

He was called to account and the correspondence is interesting; but he tried to maintain a stand that could only have one result. On the directions of the Grand Master, at that time the Earl of Zetland, the Grand Secretary wrote on 10 November 1853:

> ... because the proceedings were so completely at variance with the Ancient Constitutions and foundations of Freemasonry, and to the expressed and declared Laws of the Grand Lodge .... the opinions that you expressed are the convictions of your Mind, but the doctrines promulgated are so opposed to the universality of the Craft, which admits within its pale all who 'believe in the Glorious Architect of heaven and earth, and practise the sacred duties or morality'. ... You say, that, with your robe, and in addition to it, you wore your full clothing as Prov. G.M.; that it is which makes it obnoxious to the law; out of Lodge everyone may wear whatever decorations he chooses, and express whatever opinions may please him; it is only within the Lodge walls that the laws forbid the introduction of aught which might excite differences of feeling and be a prelude to personal discord and contention. ... the publicity you have given to opinions so opposed to those which have ever been held and pronounced by the Grand Lodge of England, and by the Ancient Craft, imposes upon the Grand Master the necessity of these remarks, and at the same time of relieving you of the burthen of an office, the duties of which it is manifest you cannot longer discharge without a sacrifice of your convictions. The G.M. cannot refrain from reiterating how deeply he is pained by the course which he is compelled to adopt, at the same time assuring you, that personally his sentiments of regard remain unaltered. ...

That sad story was told in great detail by Bro F.J. Cooper, in his Paper *R.W. Bro. William Tucker* and was published in *AQC* Vol 83 pp 125–148. It shows the staunch and inflexible adherence by Grand Lodge to basic freemasonry, a stand that is still maintained yet not fully appreciated by brethren in some of the other jurisdictions.

No Other Degrees

Often questioned is why the Mark degree failed to be part of the system practised in England? The more so when history shows that links with the craft of the stonemason and his behaviour pattern in Guild procedure were closely formed. The Minutes dated 20 December 1643 of the Lodge of Kilwinning No 0, were supplied in modern transcript by the late Harry Carr in his history of the Lodge (QC Lodge 1961 p 20) and one item there makes the point quite clearly regarding masons' marks:

> Item that no fellow of craft nor master be received nor admitted without the number of six masters and two entered apprentices, the Warden of the said Lodge being one of the six and that the day of receiving the said fellow craft or master to be orderly booked, and his name and mark to be inserted in the said book, with the name of the six admitters and the entered apprentices; and the names of the Intenders 'that shall be chosen to every person' shall also be inserted therein. Providing always that no man shall be admitted without ... 'ane essay and sufficient tryall of his skill and worthiness in his vocatioune and craft ...'

Bro Carr wrote that the item was a restatement of traditional practice and almost word for word of the relevant clause in the Schaw Statutes of 1598 as it appeared in the minute book of the Lodge of Mary's Chapel, Edinburgh (p 23). A personal mark for a mason of the craft became a feature in speculative Freemasonry. It is no small surprise that as an aspect it was not overlooked and developed into a masonic degree. The popularity of the Mark degree was such that it spread wherever freemasonry travelled in the 18th century. The earliest reference to it appears at Newcastle and is dated January 1756, it tends to show that the connection with Freemasonry was then tenuous. The most interesting reference is the cypher entry in the minutes of the Chapter of Friendship at Portsmouth when in September 1769 they recorded:

> The Pro. G.M. Thomas Dunckerley bro't the Warrant of the Chapter, and having lately rec'd the 'MARK', he made the Bre'n 'MARK MASONS' and 'MARK MASTERS', and each chuse their 'MARK' ... He also told us this man'r of writing which is to be used in the degree w'ch we may give to others as they be F.C. for Mark Masons, and Master Masons for Mark Masters.

From 1723 the premier Grand Lodge had adopted a system that would not permit innovation unless accepted and approved in Grand Lodge; they remained firmly rooted in that decision. With the proliferation of degrees that sprang up in the mid 18th century, with others following in the 19th, it has been estimated that well over one thousand so-called 'masonic degrees' became available so it is no small wonder that the authorities although themselves at one time guilty of departing from ancient 'landmarks', stayed with basic freemasonry. The Antients, however, whilst claiming that those basic degrees were kept 'pure and ancient' did not refrain from practising other degrees and were permitted to do so by virtue of the Warrants granted from their Grand Lodge; the Mark degree was popular with their brethren.

The subject was examined by representatives of Grand Chapter which on 1 February 1856 passed the following resolution:

> That the Grand Chapter concur in the opinion expressed by their Committee, that the Mark Mason's Degree forms no portion of Royal Arch Masonry, and they therefore leave the further consideration of the subject in the hands of the Grand Lodge of England.

A Joint Committee was set up with representatives from both the Grand Chapter and Grand Lodge and in due course they reported that the Mark degree '... is not essential to Craft Masonry; ... that it might be considered as a graceful addition to the Fellow Craft's Degree.' Their recommendation resulted in the following being proposed:

> The Board submit to the consideration of Grand Lodge the propriety of declaring that the degree of Mark Man, and Mark Master is not at variance with the Ancient Land Marks of the Order, and that the degree shall be an addition to, and form part of the Fellow Craft degree, and may consequently be conferred by all regular Warranted Lodges, under such regulations as may be suggested by the Board of General Purposes, approved and sanctioned by the M.W. Grand Master.

That was as far as it went for the next Communication of Grand Lodge, held on 4 June 1856, it was recorded:

> The Minutes of the Quarterly Communication of 4 March last having been read, the question was proposed that the same be confirmed. Upon which an amendment was moved: 'That such portion as related to the subject of the Mark Masons be not confirmed'. After some discussion the amendment was carried. Upon Motion made, the remaining portion of the Minutes were then confirmed.

Very little time was lost before interested brethren got together, and on 23 June 1856 'The Grand Lodge of Mark Master Masons of England and Wales and the Colonies and Dependencies of the British Crown' was formed. After minor 'teething troubles' it became well-established and has since made great contributions to Freemasonry in general having given shelter to Grand Councils since formed to govern certain degrees, the fate of which might otherwise have been in the balance.

The Mark degree was accepted as part of the system in many other jurisdictions, amongst whom it is an essential step to be taken prior to entry to the Royal Arch. It is sometimes conferred in a Mark Lodge under its Mark authority, in others under that from the Grand Chapter, but the degree, and all else, remains outside the English Craft system.

Chapter 22

Recognition, Aims, and Basic Principles

Details of the aims and basic principles of Freemasonry as well as terms governing relations with other Grand Lodges with whom they were in fraternal accord were published in August 1938 in a statement issued jointly by the Grand Lodges of England, Ireland, and Scotland. (see Appendices G & H).

It is a matter for profound regret that in some countries there exists so called Freemasonry which does not conform with the terms expressed in that joint statement; an example having been made evident in recent years with the activity of the Lodge 'P 2' in Italy in which Freemasonry was manipulated for nefarious ends (See: *In God's Name*, David Yallop, J. Cape, London 1984). The Craft has ever been a useful tool employed for malpractice. In this regard Freemasonry, as a whole, has to bear the brunt of censure from those who do not understand that there are 'regular' and 'irregular' bodies, those who are recognised by the three sister Grand Lodges and those who are unrecognised who often style themselves as freemasons. It is not possible to prevent a change in the character of an individual who may choose to dishonour an obligation thought by his colleagues to have been taken in all sincerity.

It is for this reason that constant reminders are issued by the United Grand Lodge to its members that they should not become involved with masonic bodies which are not recognised as 'Regular', nor with those which accept as visitors brethren from Grand Lodges which are not recognised. It is part of the duty of its members not to associate masonically with members of unrecognised Constitutions and should such a situation occur 'they should tactfully withdraw even though their visit may have been formally arranged'. To avoid such an occasion, and its potential embarrassment to all concerned brethren are urged not to make masonic contact overseas without first having sought guidance from the authorities at Freemasons' Hall, London. In order that such an important warning should reach all members it is officially recommended that it should be repeated in Lodge to all new brethren and printed in the business paper for lodge meetings once a year.

From the inception of organised Freemasonry occasioned by the setting up of the premier Grand Lodge in London in 1717, the Craft has been subject to attack for countless reasons. From the inauguration onwards there developed a wide variety of attacks, skits on Freemasonry, mock processions in public, so-called 'exposures' of masonic ritual and proceedings, with the introduction of imitative forms purporting to be Freemasonry. Over the years the vast range of books for and against Freemasonry, in whatever language and in whatever country would fill a huge library. But throughout all this the authorities remained faithful to their adopted motto, *Audi—Vidi—Tace*, 'Hear—See—be Silent' which had proved most effective. However, we live in a changing world and in this present era of instant communication around the world, the constant trials by television interviewers and the media in general, the impertinence from them all knowing no bounds, the authorities have met it all with commendable fortitude. Free-masonry has been graphically displayed on television, fully 'ex-plained' on radio, preached at and discussed by all and sundry to such an extent that there can be nothing left secret beyond its modes of recognition from one to another, the more tangible forms of which have been plagiarised. The essence of Freemasonry is not something that is seen or felt, it is that which is developed within the member himself and only he would recognise in another brother who has been endowed with similar motivation and spirit. The present authorities have shewn themselves prepared to discuss masonic matters quite openly and constructively, to answer all who have a genuine interest; they encourage brethren to behave in that manner to individuals who are sincere in a quest for information, keeping within the published aims and principles available for that purpose.

The United Grand Lodge of England describes itself as a Sov-ereign and independent Body practising Freemasonry only within the three Degrees and only within the limits defined in its Consti-tution as "pure Antient Masonry". It has sustained freemasonry in a simple form.

In the preceding pages we have seen how the term 'pure An-tient Masonry' emerged and how well the Craft in England has been kept in an uncomplicated form.

According to the faith of the individual candidate for free-masonry the Holy Book that he reveres is the one used in an obligation to provide sanctity of purpose when embarking upon a masonic career; but that kind of religious tolerance is an anathema to orthodoxy. In 1723 the Craft set a course by opening its doors to all men of goodwill who confirm their belief in a Supreme Being. The position was made clear in the *Charges* under the sub-heading 'Concerning God and Religion' and printed in the first Book of *Constitutions*, approved by the Grand Lodge in 1723, stating:

> A Mason is oblig'd, by his Tenure, to obey the moral Law; and if he rightly understands the Art, he will never be a stupid Atheist, nor an irreligious Libertine. But though in ancient Times Masons were charg'd in every Country to be of the Religion of that Country or Nation, whatever it was, yet 'tis now thought more expedient only to oblige them to that particular Religion in which all men agree, leaving their particular Opinions to themselves; that is, to be *good Men and true*, or Men of Honour and Honesty, by whatever Denominations or Persuasions they may be distinguish'd; whereby Masonry becomes the *Center of Union*, and the Means of conciliating true Friendship among Persons that must have remain'd at a perpetual Distance.

Freemasonry is not a religion, nor is it a substitute for religion. It provides no system of faith peculiar to itself and it proscribes discussion of religion and politics at its meetings. In the world at large, sectarianism in each and every form of religion has produced disagreement, dissension, opposition and open warfare, which for generation after generation has denied 'Peace on Earth, Goodwill towards Men' and it has all happened whilst men have outwardly been offering 'Glory to God on High'. But, as the Bard of Avon might well have put it—*'twas ever thus.*

William Smith's *Pocket Companion* (See page 34) contained *A Short CHARGE to be given to new admitted BRETHREN* which, although written before 1735 is just as appropriate today as it was then, a few extracts will make that point:

> You are now admitted by the unanimous Consent of our Lodge, a *Fellow* of our Antient and Honourable Society; *Antient*, as having subsisted from times immemorial, and *Honourable*, as tending in every Particular to render a Man so that he will be conformable to its glorious Precepts. ... Monarchs in all Ages ... have been Encouragers of the *Royal Art* ... not thinking it any lessening to their Imperial Dignities to Level themselves with their *Brethren* in Masonry ... Religious Disputes are never suffered in the Lodge; for as Masons, we only pursue the universal Religion or the Religion of Nature. This is the Cement which unites Men of the most different Principles in one sacred Band, and brings together those who were the most distant from one another. There are three general Heads of Duty which Masons ought always to inculcate, viz., to *God*, our *Neighbours* and *ourselves*. To *God*, in never mentioning his Name but with that Reverential Awe which becomes a Creature to bear to his Creator ... To our *Neighbours*, in acting upon the Square, or doing as we would be done by. To *ourselves*, in avoiding all Intemperances and Excesses ... In the State, a Mason is to behave as a peaceable and dutiful subject, conforming cheerfully to the Government under which he lives. ... He is to be a Man of Benevolence and Charity, not sitting down contented while his Fellow Crea-

tures, but much more his *Brethren*, are in Want, when it is in his Power (without prejudicing himself or Family) to relieve them. ... He is not to neglect his own necessary Avocations for the sake of Masonry, nor to involve himself in quarrels with those who through Ignorance may speak evil, or ridicule it. ... If he recommends a Friend to be made a Mason, he must vouch him to be such as he believes will conform to the aforesaid Duties ... Nothing can be more shocking to all faithful Masons, than to see any of their *Brethren* profane or break the sacred Rules of their Order, and such as can do it they wish had never been admitted.

Two hundred and fifty years later the situation is unchanged, but now it seems that people outside Freemasonry should not be left to flounder when seeking information regarding the Order.

On this journey from some of the roots which affected the rise and development of organised Freemasonry, we arrived in the mid 19th century when administration became virtually stabilised. The route shows that the human element intrudes at all times and in all things, yet there is always a common interest to protect the highest good; the *Summum Bonum* which has ever been man's greatest struggle to achieve.

In this modern, computerised, microchip age, set into an unbalanced world bewildered by constant distractions, attitudes of a different calibre have emerged; but to be happy, and to find a pathway to communicate happiness to others is still an unending search which starts only when the individual arrives at his own question on life itself. A Brotherhood of Man under the Fatherhood of God is the highest ideal and somewhere along the line freemasonry has an opportunity in that enterprise. However, from his first step it is made quite clear that any freemason will get out of Freemasonry only that which is commensurate with what he puts into it, to be measured by the plumbline, the level, and the square.

The author has only one recommendation to the reader who may wish to seek further information on any facet of Freemasonry which has interest for him and that is to refer to the librarian of any major Freemasons' Hall in whatever city, or whatever country, remembering that Freemasonry is world-wide, and informed guidance and assistance will be readily forthcoming for any genuine enquiry.

APPENDICES

Appendix A

The earliest Antients' Warrant which is still in use. The text was prepared for five Warrants in 1752, but they were all held over until 'proper Grand Officers' could be appointed. Each Warrant bore the same date of 'Constitution', 17 July 1751 which was the date of the General Assembly from which the Antients' Grand Lodge arose. The original Lodge No 6 soon lapsed and their seniority was promptly purchased by Lodge No 37 who, on 18 July 1755, received this Warrant. It was then signed by the Grand Master and Deputy Grand Master which completed the transaction. In 1819 they took the name 'Enoch' and the Lodge remains on the Register but now at No 11.

E. A. VAUGHAN G.M.

W. HOLFORD D.G.M.

J. Jackson S.G.W.   Saml Galbraith J.G.W.

No. 6   TO ALL WHOME IT MAY CONCERN

WE, the Grand Lodge in Ample form Assembled do hereby Authorize and Impower our Truly and Well beloved Brethren Willm Cowen Master, William Osborn Senr Warden and John Nelson Junr Warden with their lawful Assistants To form & hold a Lodge of Free & Accepted Ancient Masons and in such Lodge Admit Enter and Make Masons according to the Ancient and honourable Custom of the Royal Craft in all Ages and Nations throughout the known World And we do hereby further Authorize and Impower our said Trusty and Well beloved Brethren William Cowen William Osborn and John Nelson (with their Lawful Assistance To nominate Chuse and Instal their Successors whom they are to invest with their Power and dignity and such Successors shall in like manner Nominate Chuse and Instal their Successors &c. &c. &c. such Instalations to be on every St. John's Day during the continuance of the Lodge for EVER.

Providing that the Above named Brethren and their Successors always pay due Respect to this Ancient Grand Lodge otherwise this Warrant to be of no force nor Virtue.

Given under our hands and Seal of the ANCIENT GRAND LODGE London, this 18th Day of June (in the Year of our Lord 1755 and in the year of Masonry 5755).

Constituted July 17   [signed]

1751   5751   [signed]

Lau. Dermott G. Sec^y

Appendix B

This in another example of an original Warrant, issued to Lodge No 93 which was erased on 5 March 1777. It was reissued on 18 March 1813, the new lodge retaining No 93 on the Register. After the Union it became No 116; on the closing-up of numbers in 1832, by a strange coincidence it again became No 93. The lodge was named 'Pythagorean' in 1834 and, on the final closing-up in 1863, it was numbered 79.

ATHOLL GRAND MASTER

Archibald Herron S.G.W.   *Thomas Harper* D.G.M.   *Jeremiah Cranfield* J.G.W.

TO ALL WHOM IT MAY CONCERN

Nº 93

WE the GRAND LODGE of the most Ancient and Honourable Fraternity of Free and Accepted Masons according to the old Constitutions granted by His Royal Highness Prince Edwin at York Anno Domini Nine hundred twenty and Six, and in the Year of Masonry Four thousand Nine hundred twenty and Six in ample form assembled, viz. The Right Worshipful The Most Noble Prince John, Duke Marquis and Earl of Atholl Marquis & Earl of Tullibardine Earl of Strathsay and Strath Viscount Balquider Glenalmond and Glenlyon Lord Murray Belvery and Gask, Constable of the Castle of Kindaven Lord of Man and of the Isles Earl Strange and Baron Murray of Stanley in the County of Glouster &c. &c. &c. Grand Master of Masons, The Right Worshipful Thomas Harper Esqʳ Deputy Grand Master, The Right Worshipful Archibald Herron Esqʳ Senior Grand Warden and the Right Worshipful Jeremiah Cranfield Esqʳ Junior Grand Warden with the approbation and Consent of the Warranted Lodges held within the Cities and Suburbs of London and Westminster Do hereby authorise and Impower our trusty and Well beloved Brethren viz. the Worshipful John Stow one of our Master Masons the Worshipful Samuel Packwood his Senior Warden and the Worshipful John Satterly his Junior Warden, to form and Hold a Lodge of Free and Accepted Masons aforesaid at the Mitre Tavern in Greenwich or Elsewhere in the County of Kent upon the first and third Monday being first duly Registered Pursuant to the Statute and on all seasonable Times and lawful Occasions: And in the said Lodge when duly congregated to admit and make Free Masons according to the most Ancient and Honourable Customs of the Royal Craft in all Ages and Nations throughout the known World. And We do hereby further authorise and impower our said Trusty and Well beloved Brethren John Stow, Samuel Packwood and John Satterly with the Consent of the Members of their Lodge to nominate Chuse and install their Successors to whom they shall deliver this Warrant, and invest them with their Powers and Dignities as Free Masons. And such Successors shall in like manner nominate chuse and install their Successors &c. &c. Such installations to be upon or near every Sᵗ John's Day during the Continuance of this Lodge for ever. Providing the above named Brethren and all their Successors always pay due Respect to this Right Worshipful Grand Lodge, otherwise this Warrant to be of no Force nor Virtue.

Given under our hands and the Seal of our Grand Lodge in London this eighteenth Day of March in the Year of our Lord One thousand Eight hundred and thirteen and in the Year of Masonry five thousand eight hundred and thirteen.

(signed) Robᵗ Leslie

Note: This Warrant is registered
in the Grand Lodge Vol 3
Letter C & E 27th October 1761

*An engraved Plate by William Skelton of HRH the Duke of Sussex Grand Master
United Grand Lodge of England 1813–1843*

Appendix C

THE MANIFESTO OF THE LODGE OF ANTIQUITY A.D. 1778

To all regular free and Accepted Masons.

WHEREAS the Society of free Masons is universally acknowledged to be of ancient standing and great repute in this Kingdom, as by our Records and printed Constitutions, it appears that the first GRAND LODGE in England was held at YORK, in the year 926, by Virtue of a Royal Charter, granted by King ATHELSTAN—And, under the Patronage and Government of this Grand Lodge, the Society considerably increased; and the ancient charges and regulations of the Order so far obtained the sanction of Kings and Princes, and other eminent Persons, that they always paid due Allegieance to the said Grand Assembly.

AND WHEREAS it appears, by our Records, that in the year 1567, the Increase of Lodges in the South of England being so great as to require some NOMINAL PATRON to superintend their Government, it was resolved that a Person under the Title of Grand Master for the South should be appointed for that purpose, with the Approbation of the Grand Lodge at York, to whom the whole fraternity at large were bound to pay Tribute and acknowledge subjection— And, after the appointment of such Patron, Masonry flourished under the guardianship of him and his successors in the South, until the Civil Wars and other Intestine commotions interrupted the Assemblies of the Brethren.

AND WHEREAS it also appears that, in the year 1693, the Meetings of the fraternity in their regular Lodges in the South became less frequent, and chiefly occasional, except in or near Places where great Works were carried on—At which time the Lodge of Antiquity, or (as it was then called) the Old Lodge of St. Paul, with a few others of small note, continued to meet under the Patronage of Sir Christopher Wren, and assisted him in rearing that superb structure from which respectable Lodge derived its Title.

AND WHEREAS, of late years, notwithstanding the said solemn engagement in the year 1721, sundry innovations and encroachments have been made, and are still making on the original plan and Government of Masonry, by the present nominal Grand Lodge in London, highly injurious to the Institution itself, and tending to subvert and destroy the ancient Rights and Privileges of the Society, more particularly of those Members of it, under whose sanction, and by whose Authority, the said Grand Lodge was first established and now exists.

AND WHEREAS, at this present time, there only remains one of the said four Original ancient Lodges, the Old Lodge of St. Paul, or as it is now emphatically styled, The Lodge of Antiquity, Two of the said four Ancient Lodges having been extinct many years, and the Master of the other of them having, on the Part of his Lodge, in open Grand Lodge relinquished all such inherent Rights and Privileges, which, as a Private Lodge acting by Immemorial Constitution, it enjoyed. But, the Lodge of Antiquity, conscious of its own Dignity, which the Members thereof are resolutely determined to support, and justly incensed at the violent Measures and Proceedings which have been lately adopted and pursued by the said Nominal Grand Lodge wherein they have assumed an unlawful Prerogative over the Lodge of Antiquity in Manifest breach of the aforesaid 39th Article, by which means the peaceable Government of that respectable Lodge has been repeatedly interrupted, and even the Original Power thereof, in respect to its own Internal Government, disputed:

THEREFORE, and on account of the Arbitrary Edicts and Laws which the said nominal Grand Lodge has, from time to time, presumed to issue and attempted to enforce, repugnant to the ancient Laws and Principles of free Masonry, and highly injurious to the Lodge of Antiquity. But on completing this edifice in 1710, and Sir Christopher Wren retiring into the Country, the few remaining Lodges, in London and its Suburbs, continued without any Nominal Patron, in a declining State for about the space of seven years.

AND WHEREAS, in the year 1717, the fraternity in London agreed to cement under a New Grand Master, and with that view the Old Lodge of St. Paul, jointly with three other Lodges, assembled in form, constituted themselves a Nominal Grand Lodge pro Tempore, and elected a Grand Master to preside their future general Meetings, whom they afterwards invested with a power to constitute subordinate Lodges, and to convene the fraternity at stated Periods in Grand Lodge, in order to make Laws with their consent and approbation for the good Government of the Society at large. But subject to certain conditions and restrictions then expressly stipulated, and which are more fully set forth in the 39th Article of the General Regulations, in the first *Book of Constitutions*. This Article with 38 others was afterwards at a Meeting of the Brethren in and about the Cities of London and Westminster in the year 1721, solemnly approved of ratified and confirmed by them and signed in their presence by the Master and Wardens of the four old Lodges on the one part and Philip Duke of Wharton then Grand Master, Dr. Desaguliers D.G.M. Joshua Timson and William Hawkins Grand Wardens, and the Master and Wardens of sixteen Lodges which had been constituted by the fraternity betwixt 1717 and 1721, on the other part. And these Articles the Grand Master engaged himself and his Successors, when duly Installed, in all time coming to observe and keep sacred and inviolable—By these prudent Precautions the Ancient Land Marks (as they are properly styled) of the four Old Lodges were intended to be secured against any encroachments on their Masonick Rights and Privileges.

WE, the Master, Wardens, and Members of the Lodge of Antiquity, considering ourselves bound in duty, as well in honour, to preserve inviolable the ancient Rights and Privileges of the Order, and as far as in our Power, to hand them down to Posterity in their Native Purity and Excellence, do hereby, for ourselves and our Successors, solemnly disavow and discountenance such unlawful measures and proceedings of the said Nominal Grand Lodge; and do hereby declare and announce to all Our Masonick Brethren throughout the Globe, that the said Grand Lodge has, by such Arbitrary conduct, evidently violated the conditions expressed in the aforesaid 39th Article of the general regulations, in the observances of which Article the permanency of their Authority solely depended.

And in consequence thereof, We do by these Presents retract from, and recall, all such Rights and Powers, as We, or our Predecessors, did conditionally give to the said Nominal Grand Lodge in London; and do hereby disannul and make void all future Edicts and Laws which the said Grand Lodge may presume to issue and enforce, by virtue of such sanction, as Representatives of the Ancient and honourable Society of free and Accepted Masons.

AND WHEREAS We have, on full enquiry and due examination, happily discovered, that the aforesaid truly ancient GRAND LODGE at YORK does still exist, and have authentic records to produce of their Antiquity, long before the establishment of the nominal Grand Lodge in London, in the year 1717. WE DO, therefore, hereby solemnly avow acknowledge, and admit the authority of the said Most Worshipful GRAND LODGE at YORK, as the truly ancient and only regular governing Grand Lodge of Masons in England, to whom the fraternity all owe and are rightfuly bound to pay Allegiance.

AND WHEREAS the present Members of the said Grand Lodge at York have acknowledged the ancient Power and Authority of the Lodge of Antiquity in London as a Private Lodge, and have proposed to form an Alliance with the said Lodge, on the most generous and disinterested Principles—We do hereby acknowledge this generous Mark of their friendship towards us, and gratefully accept their liberal, candid and ingenuous offers of Alliance:— And do hereby, from a firm persuasion of the Justice of our Cause, announce a general Union with all Regular Masons throughout the World who shall join us in supporting the original Principles of Free Masonry,—in promoting and extending the authority of the said truly ancient Grand Lodge at York,—and under such respectable auspices in Propagating Masonry on its pure, genuine and original Plan.

AND LASTLY, We do earnestly solicit the hearty concurrence of all regular Lodges of the fraternity in all Places where Free Masonry is legally established, to enable us to carry into execution, and at the present critical juncture, so essentially necessary to curb the arbitrary power which has already been exerted, or which hereafter may be illegally assumed, by the Nominal Grand Lodge in London, and so timely prevent such unmasonick Proceedings from becoming a disgrace to the Society at large.

By Order of the right Worshipful Lodge of Antiquity in Open Lodge assembled, this 16th Day of December, A.D. 1778, A.L. 5782

J. Sealy, Secretary.

As a few expelled Members of the Lodge of Antiquity have presumed to associate as Masons at the Mitre Tavern, in Fleet Street, under the denomination of this Lodge—Notice is hereby given, that the Right Worshipful Lodge of Antiquity, acting by an Immemorial Constitution, is removed from the Mitre Tavern, to the Queen's Arms Tavern, in St. Paul's Church Yard; where all Letters to the Lodge are requested to be directed.

Appendix D

The Constitution Granted to the Lodge of Antiquity Creating Them a Grand Lodge

Wm. SIDDALL, G.M. To all Masonic Brethren to whom these present shall come. WE the Grand Master and Members of the most Worshipful Grand Lodge of all England of free and accepted Masons legally assembled at the City of York, Send Greeting, Whereas it has been represented to us, that there now exists in London a regular Lodge of free and accepted Masons under the Denomination of the Right Worshipful Lodge of Antiquity which acts by an Immemorial Constitution Independent of the Nominal Grand Lodge in London held at the Hall lately erected in Great Queen Street Lincolns Inn Fields called Free Masons Hall, And Whereas on due enquiry to discharge the Duties of Masonry in a regular and Constitutional manner by virtue of their said Immemorial Constitution, And Whereas the Members of the said Lodge of Antiquity have expressed a Desire of establishing a friendly Alliance and Communion with us wherein We on our Part are willing to concur.

NOW BE IT KNOWN to all regular Masons throughout the World That for sundry good and sufficient Reasons us thereunto moving We do for ourselves and our successors acknowledge and declare that we do allow of and admit the power and authority of the said Right Worshipful Lodge of Antiquity to act as a private Lodge of free and accepted Masons so long as the Government thereof corresponds with and is consonant to the ancient charges and noble principles of our venerable Institution And as a Token of our friendship and regard for and of the confidence we repose in the members of the said Lodge of Antiquity We do hereby admit of ratify and confirm Our Alliance with them and do hereby declare and publish the same And further at the request of the Master Wardens and Brethren of the said Right Worshipful Lodge of Antiquity We do hereby for ourselves and our successors by virtue of the authority inherent in us as the Most Worshipful and only legal Grand Lodge of all England of free and accepted Masons admit them to a participation of our Government as hereinafter mentioned, and to act as a Grand Lodge throughout that part of England which is situated SOUTH OF THE RIVER TRENT, so long as they do faithfully observe and keep inviolable the ancient Charges and Regulations of our Order and do acknowledge in manner hereinafter mentioned the Allegiance and Homage due to us as the most ancient Patrons of the Masonic Art. And for this purpose Be it further known to all whom it may anyways concern That out of our Good Will and favour and for the Honour and Increase of our Truly ancient Instutution upon the original plan of its establishment and from the great Trust and confidence We repose in our well beloved Brothers—John Wilson, Benjamin Bradley, Daniel Nantes, Samuel Bass, William Preston, James Donaldson, Gilbert Buchanan, John Sealy, Thomas Shipton, Hugh Lloyd, John Savage, William Sheppard, James Cookson, Samuel Goddard, Samuel White, John Wells, the present members of the Right Worshipful Lodge of Antiquity anciently and now held at the Queen's Arms Tavern in St. Paul's Church Yard London. WE do give and grant unto them (Independent of the Power and Authority which they already possess as a private Lodge of Masons acting by an Immemorial Constitution) full power and authority at all times hereafter to assemble as a Grand Lodge of free and accepted Masons and when regularly convened as a Grand Lodge Do vest in and give and grant unto them full and sufficient power and authority to issue Warants of Constitution for all that part of England which is situated South of the River Trent aforesaid and also to any place or places in foreign Countries upon Application being regularly made to them for that purpose, Also to make and enforce Laws and to do and perform every other Act and Deed requisite and necessary for the support of their Authority as a Grand Lodge in friendly communion and Alliance with us And we do promise all countenance and protection as far as shall be required of us to all Lodges which shall be constituted by them And we do hereby authorize and command that the first Meeting of the said Grand Lodge hereby created under the title of THE RIGHT WORSHIPFUL GRAND LODGE OF FREE AND ACCEPTED MASONS OF ENGLAND SOUTH OF THE RIVER TRENT, consisting of the aforesaid Members of the Right Worshipful Lodge of Antiquity or such of them as shall be then living together with the Master and Wardens of all such other Lodges as shall be constituted by them to be held at the Queens Arms Tavern aforesaid on the feast day of St. John the Baptist now next ensuing And do nominate and appoint our dear and well beloved Brother John Wilson Esquire to preside at such Meeting as Grand Master, Brother Samuel Bass as Deputy Grand Master, Brother Benjamin Bradley as Senior Grand Warden, Brother Daniel Nantes as Junior Grand Warden, Brother James Donaldson as Grand Treasurer, Brother John Sealy as Grand Secretary and [left blank] as Grand Chaplain. And at the said Meeting do impower the said Brethren in Grand Lodge assembled to proceed to the election of Grand Officers for the ensuing twelve months and do order the election of Grand Officers to take place annually on the feast Day of Saint John the Baptist And that as soon thereafter as may be the Names of such Grand Officers be transmitted to us to the Intent that the same may be duly commemorated by us and entered in our Records. And the more effectually to carry our design into execution. We do further enjoin that the said Grand Lodge so constituted by us as hereinbefore mentioned Do meet in quarterly assembly four times at the least in every year at such times and places as shall be most convenient for them And we do require that all Lodges to be constituted by the said Grand Lodge do pay due Allegiance to them and that the names of all such subordinate Lodges as shall from time to time be constituted by the said Grand Lodge shall be annually transmitted to us in order that the same may be duly entered on our Records And our request and expectation is that as a token of the Allegiance and Homage due from the said Grand Lodge to us as the most ancient Patrons of the Masonic Art they do pay into our Treasury at the City of York an annual consideration in money and the sum of two guineas for every Constitution which shall be so granted by them in their said Grand Lodge as aforesaid. And also that in every Warrant and Constitution to be granted by them they do specify and express that the same is so granted under the Authority delegated to them by the Most Worshipful Grand Lodge of all England held at York And further that they do remit to us such Payments as aforesaid annually on the feast day of St. John the Baptist or as soon after as may be And lastly in consideration of the Premises and for other sufficient Inducements as hereunto moving We do solemnly engage and promise that we will from henceforth for evermore patronize and cherish as far as in us lies or We lawfully may or can the said Grand Lodge in all their regular proceedings as long as the same shall correspond with and be conformable to the ancient usages of the Order and do promise faithfully to maintain a strict and regular Alliance and correspondence with them Given under the seal of our truly Ancient and Most Worshipful Grand Lodge of all England, legally assembled at the City of York this Twenty ninth Day of March A.D. 1779 A.L. 5783.   John Browne Gr. Secretary

Appendix E

Royal Naval Lodge Certificate (1803)

During the Mastership of F. C. Daniel a new engraved Plate had the newly adopted title of the lodge but retained the text in English on the left side and Latin on the right. Although a 'Modern' lodge the Seal affixed to the Certificate bore the Arms of the Antients.

The Light Shineth in Darkness and the Darkness comprehendeth it not.
(Angel figure with trumpet)
Lodge 57
ROYAL NAVAL LODGE OF INDEPENDENCE
WAPPING
Of the Most Ancient and Most Honorable
Society of Free & Accepted Masons of all England
(According to the OLD YORK CONSTITUTIONS)
To all whom it may concern these are
to certify that our well beloved Brother
William Bull
aged Thirty Eight Years who hath
signed his Name   in the
Margin hereof being well recommended
to us was Regularly Initiated into the
First Passed to the Second and Raised
to the SUBLIME Degree of a MASTER MASON
in this our Lodge & we are happy to annou
nce that during his continuance amongst us
hath distinguished himself as a TRUE
& FAITHFUL BROTHER. We therefore after due
Examination most earnestly recommend
him to your Friendship & protection & to
admit him into all Regular Lodges Thro
ughout the Universe. In Testimony
whereof we have subscribed our Names
& affixed the Seal of our Lodge
aforesaid the 2^{d} Day of
May in the Year
of our Lord 1803 and of
Masonry 5803
(Signed) F. C. Daniel W.M.
(Signed) C. J. Dession
(Signed) Fra^{n} Green
(Signed)
C. F. Gelle
        Secty.

Witness (signed) C. J. Dession. (signed) Wiliam Bull ne variatur

Appendix F
The Articles of Union (1813)

IN THE NAME OF GOD, AMEN.

The Most Worshipful His Royal Highness Prince AUGUSTUS FREDERICK, Duke of Sussex, Earl of Inverness, Baron Arklow, Knight Companion of the Most Noble Order of the Garter, and Grand Master of the Society of Free and Accepted Masons under the Constitution of England; the Right Worshipful WALLER RODWELL WRIGHT, Provincial Grand Master of Masons in the Ionian Isles; the Right Worshipful ARTHUR TEGART, Past Grand Warden; and the Right Worshipful JAMES DEANS, Past Grand Warden; of the same Fraternity: for themselves and on behalf of the Grand Lodge of the Society of Freemasons under the Constitution of England: being thereto duly constituted and empowered:—on the one part,

The Most Worshipful His Royal Highness Prince EDWARD, Duke of Kent and Strathearn, Earl of Dublin, Knight Companion of the Most Noble Order of the Garter and of the Most Illustrious Order of Saint Patrick, Field Marshal of His Majesty's Forces, Governor of Gibraltar, Colonel of the First or Royal-Scots Regiment of Foot, and Grand Master of Free and Accepted Masons of England, according to the Old Institutions; the Right Worshipful THOMAS HARPER, Deputy Grand Master; the Right Worshipful JAMES PERRY, Past Deputy Grand Master; and the Right Worshipful JAMES AGAR, Past Deputy Grand Master; of the same Fraternity: for themselves and on behalf of the Grand Lodge of Freemasons of England, according to the old Institutions: being thereto being constituted and empowered:—on the other part,

HAVE AGREED AS FOLLOWS—

I. There shall be, from and after the day of the Festival of Saint John the Evangelist next ensuing, a full, perfect, and perpetual union of and between the two Fraternities of Free and Accepted Masons of England above described; so as that in all time hereafter they shall form and constitute but one Brotherhood, and that the said community shall be represented in one Grand Lodge, to be solemnly formed, constituted, and held, on the said day of the Festival of Saint John the Evangelist next ensuing, and from thenceforward for ever.

II. It is declared and pronounced, that pure Ancient Masonry consists of three degrees, and no more; *viz.* those of the Entered Apprentice, the Fellow Craft, and the Master Mason, including the Supreme Order of the Holy Royal Arch. But this article is not intended to prevent any Lodge or Chapter from holding a meeting in any of the degrees of the Orders of Chivalry, according to the constitutions of the said Orders.

III. There shall be the most perfect unity of obligation, of discipline, of working the lodges, of making, passing and raising, instructing and clothing Brothers; so that but one pure unsullied system, according to the genuine landmarks, laws, and traditions of the Craft, shall be maintained, upheld and practised, throughout the Masonic World, from the day and date of the said union until time shall be no more.

IV. To prevent all controversy or dispute as to the genuine and pure obligations, forms, rules and ancient traditions of Masonry, and further to unite and bind the whole Fraternity of Masons in one indissoluble bond, it is agreed that the obligations and forms that have, from time immemorial, been established, used, and practised, in the Craft, shall be recognized, accepted, and taken, by the members of both Fraternities, as the pure and genuine obligations and forms by which the incorporated Grand Lodge of England, and its dependent Lodges in every part of the World, shall be bound: and for the purpose of receiving and communicating due light and settling this uniformity of regulation and instruction (and particularly in matters which can neither be expressed nor described in writing), it is further agreed that brotherly application be made to the Grand Lodges of Scotland and Ireland, to authorize, delegate and appoint, any two or more of their enlightened members to be present at the Grand Assembly on the solemn occasion of uniting the said Fraternities; and that the respective Grand Masters, Grand Officers, Masters, Past Masters, Wardens and Brothers, then and there present, shall solemnly engage to abide by the true forms and obligations (particularly in matters which can neither be described nor written), in the presence of the said Members of the Grand Lodges of Scotland and Ireland, that it may be declared, recognized, and known, that they all are bound by the same solemn pledge, and work under the same law.

V. For the purpose of establishing and securing this perfect uniformity in all the warranted Lodges, and also to prepare for this Grand Assembly, and to place all the Members of both Fraternities on the level of equality on the day of Re-union, it is agreed that as soon as these presents shall have received the sanction of the respective Grand Lodges, the two Grand Masters shall appoint each nine worthy and expert Master Masons, or Past Masters, of their respective Fraternities, with warrant and instructions to meet together at some convenient central place in London, when each party having opened in a separate apartment a just and perfect Lodge, agreeably to their peculiar regulaions they shall give and receive mutually and reciprocally the obligations of both Fraternities, deciding by lot which shall take priority in giving and receiving the same; and being thus all duly and equally enlightened in both forms, they shall be empowered and directed, either to hold a Lodge under the warrant or dispensation to be entrusted to them, and to be entitled the LODGE OF RECONCILIATION, or to visit the several Lodges holding under both the Grand Lodges for the purpose of obligating, instructing and perfecting the Master, Past Masters, Wardens, and Members, in both the forms, and to make a return to the Grand Secretaries of both the Grand Lodges of the names of those whom they shall have thus enlightened. And the said Grand Secretaries shall be empowered to enroll the names of all the Members thus remade in the Register of both the Grand Lodges, without fee or reward: it being ordered that no person shall be thus obligated and registered whom the Master and Wardens of his Lodge shall not certify by writing under their hands, that he is free on the books of his particular Lodge. Thus, on the day of Assembly of both Fraternities, the Grand Officers, Masters, Past Masters, and Wardens, who are alone to be present, shall all have taken the obligation by which each is bound, and be prepared, to make their solemn engagement, that they will thereafter abide by that which shall be recognized and declared to be the true and universally accepted obligation of the Master Mason.

VI. As soon as the Grand Masters, Grand Officers, and Members of the two present Grand Lodges, shall, on the day of their Re-union have made the solemn declaration in the presence of the deputation of Grand or enlightened Masons from Scotland and Ireland, to abide and act by the universally recognized obligation of Master Mason, the Members shall forthwith proceed to the election of a Grand Master for the year ensuing; and to prevent delay, the Brother so elected shall forthwith be obligated, *pro tempore*, that the Grand Lodge may be formed. The said Grand Master shall then nominate and appoint his Deputy Grand Master, together with a Senior and Junior Grand Warden, Grand Secretary, or Secretaries, Grand Treasurer, Grand Chaplain, Grand Sword Bearer, Grand Pursuivant, and Grand Tyler, who shall all be duly obligated and placed; and the Grand Incorporated Lodge shall then be opened, in ample form, under the stile and title of the UNITED GRAND LODGE OF ANCIENT FREEMASONS OF ENGLAND.

The Grand Officers who held the several offices before (unless such of them as may be re-appointed) shall take their places, as Past Grand Officers, in the respective degrees which they held before; and in case either, or both of the present Grand Secretaries, Pursuivants, and Tylers, should not be re-appointed to their former situations, then annuities shall be paid to them during their respective lives out of the Grand Fund.

VII. The UNITED GRAND LODGE OF ANCIENT FREEMASONS OF ENGLAND shall be composed, except on days of Festival, in the following manner, as a just and perfect representative of the whole Masonic Fraternity of England; that is to say, of

> The GRAND MASTER,
> Past Grand Masters,
> Deputy Grand Master,
> Past Deputy Grand Masters,
> Grand Wardens,
> Provincial Grand Masters,
> Past Grand Wardens,

Past Provincial Grand Masters,
Grand Chaplain,
Grand Treasurer,

Joint Grand Secretary, or Grand Secretary if there be only one, Grand Sword Bearer,

Twelve Grand Stewards, to be delegated by the Stewards' Lodge, from among their Members existing at the Union; it being understood and agreed that, from and after the Union, an annual appointment shall be made of the Stewards if necessary,

The actual Masters and Wardens of all Warranted Lodges,

Past Masters of Lodges, who have regularly served and passed the Chair before the day of Union, and who have continued without secession regular contributing Members of a Warranted Lodge. It being understood that of all Masters who, from and after the day of the said Union, shall regularly pass the chair of their respective Lodges, but one at a time, to be delegated by his Lodge, shall have a right to sit and vote in the said Grand Lodge; so that after the decease of all the regular Past Masters of any regular Lodge, who had attained that distinction at the time of the Union, the representation of such Lodge shall be by its actual Master, Wardens, and one Past Master only,

And all Grand Officers in the said respective Grand Lodges shall retain and hold their rank and privileges in the United Grand Lodge, as Past Grand Officers, including the present Provincial Grand Masters, the Grand Treasurers, Grand Secretaries, and Grand Chaplains, in their several degrees, according to the seniority of their respective appointments; and where such appointment shall have been contemporaneous, the seniority shall be determined by lot. In all other respects the above shall be the general order of precedence in all time to come, with this express provision, that no Provincial Grand Master, hereafter to be appointed, shall be entitled to a seat in the Grand Lodge, after he shall have retired from such situation, unless he shall have discharged the duties thereof for full five years.

VIII. The Representatives of the several Lodges shall sit under their respective banners according to seniority. The two first Lodges under each Grand Lodge to draw a lot in the first place for priority; and to which of the two the lot No. 1 shall fall, the other to rank as No. 2; and all the other Lodges shall fall in alternately, that is, the Lodge which is No. 2 of the Fraternity whose lot it shall be to draw No. 1, shall rank as No. 3 in the United Grand Lodge, and the other No. 2 shall rank as No. 4, and so on alternately through all the numbrs respectively. And this shall for ever after be the order and rank of the Lodges in the Grand Lodge, and in Grand Processions, for which a plan and drawing shall be prepared previous to the Union. On the renewal of any of the Lodges now dormant, they shall take rank after all the Lodges existing at the Union, notwithstanding the numbers in which they may now stand on the respective rolls.

IX. The United Grand Lodge being now constituted, the first proceeding after solemn prayer shall be to read and proclaim the act of Union, as previously executed and sealed with the great seals of the two Grand Lodges; after which the same shall be solemnly accepted by the Members present. A day shall then be appointed for the installation of the Grand Master and other Grand Officers with due solemnity; upon which occasion the Grand Master shall in open Lodge, with his own hand, affix the new great seal to the said instrument, which shall be deposited in the archives of the United Grand Lodge, and be the bond of union among the Masons of the Grand Lodge of England, and the Lodge dependent thereon, until time shall be no more. The said new great seal shall be made for the occasion, and shall be composed out of both the great seals now in use; after which the present two great seals shall be broken and defaced; and the new seal shall be alone used in all warrants, certificates, and other documents to be issued thereafter.

X. The regalia of the Grand Officers shall be, in addition to the white gloves and apron, and the respective jewels or emblems of distinction, garter blue and gold; and these shall alone belong to the Grand Officers present and past.

XI. Four Grand Lodges, representing the Craft, shall be held for quarterly communication in each year, on the first Wednesday in the months of March, June, September, and December, on each of which occasions the Masters and Wardens of all the warranted Lodges shall deliver into the hands of the Grand Secretary and Grand Treasurer, a faithful list of all their contributing Members; and the warranted Lodges in and adjacent to London shall pay towards the grand fund one shilling per quarter for each Member, over and above the sum of half a guinea for each new made member, for the registry of his name, together with the sum of one shilling to the Grand Secretary as his fee for the same, and that this contribution of one shilling for each Member shall be made quarterly, and each quarter, in all time to come.

XII. It shall be in the power of the Grand Master, or in his absence of the Past Grand Masters, or in their absence of the Deputy Grand Master, or in his absence of the Past Deputy Grand Masters, or in their absence of the Grand Wardens, to summon and hold Grand Lodges of Emergency whenever the good of the Craft shall, in their judgment, require the same.

XIII. At the Grand Lodge to be held annually on the first Wednesday in September, the Grand Lodge shall elect a Grand Master for the year ensuing, (who shall nominate and appoint his own Deputy Grand Master, Grand Wardens, and Secretary), and they shall also nominate three fit and proper persons for each of the offices of Treasurer, Chaplain, and Sword-Bearer, out of which the Grand Master shall, on the first Wednesday in the month of December, chuse and appoint one for each of the said offices; and on the Festival of St. John the Evangelist, then next ensuing, or on such other day as the said Grand Master shall appoint, there shall be held a Grand Lodge for the solemn Installation of all the said Grand Officers, according to antient custom.

XIV. There may also be a Masonic Festival, annually, on the Anniversary of the Feast of St. John the Baptist, or of St. George, or such other day as the Grand Master shall appoint, which shall be dedicated alone to brotherly love and refreshment, and to which all regular Master Masons may have access, on providing themselves with tickets from the Grand Stewards appointed to conduct the same.

XV. After the day of the Re-union, as aforesaid, and when it shall be ascertained what are the obligations, forms, regulations, working, and instruction, to be universally established, speedy and effectual steps shall be taken to obligate all the members of each Lodge in all the degrees, according to the form taken and recognized by the Grand Master, Past Grand Masters, Grand Officers, and Representatives of Lodges, on the day of Re-union; and for this purpose the worthy and expert Master Masons appointed, as aforesaid, shall visit and attend the several Lodges, within the Bills of Mortality, in rotation, dividing themselves into quorums of not less than three each, for the greater expedition, and they shall assist the Master and Wardens to promulgate and enjoin the pure and unsullied system, that perfect reconciliation, unity of obligation, law, working, language, and dress, may be happily restored to the English Craft.

XVI. When the Master and Wardens of a warranted Lodge shall report to the Grand Master, to his satisfaction, that the Members of such Lodge have taken the proper enjoined obligation, and have conformed to the uniform working, cloathing, &c., then the Most Worshipful Grand Master shall direct the new Great Seal to be affixed to their warrant, and the Lodge shall be adjudged to be regular, and entitled to all the privileges of the Craft: a certain term shall be allowed (to be fixed by the Grand Lodge) for establishing this uniformity; and all constitutional proceedings of any regular Lodge, which shall take place between the date of the union and the term so appointed, shall be deemed valid, on condition that such Lodge shall conform to the regulations of the Union within the time appointed; and means shall be taken to ascertain the regularity, and establish the uniformity of the Provincial Grand Lodges, Military Lodges, and Lodges holding of the two present Grand Lodges in distant parts; and it shall be in the power of the Grand Lodge to take the most effectual measures for the establishment of this unity of doctrine throughout the whole community of Masons, and to declare the Warrants to be forfeited, if the measures proposed shall be resisted or neglected.

XVII. The property of the said two Fraternities, whether freehold, leasehold, funded, real or personal, shall remain sacredly appropriate to the purposes for which it was created; it shall constitute one grand fund, by which the blessed object of Masonic benevolence may be more extensively obtained. It shall either continue under the trusts in which, whether freehold, leasehold, or funded, the separate parts thereof now stand; or it shall be in the power of the said United Grand Lodge, at any time hereafter, to add other names to the said trusts; or, in case of the death of any one Trustee, to nominate and appoint others for perpetuating the security of the same; and in no event, and for no purpose, shall the said united property be diverted from its orginal purpose. It being understood and declared that, at any time after the Union, it shall be in the power of the Grand Lodge to incorporate the whole of the said property and funds in one and the same set of Trustees, who shall give bond to hold the same in the name and on behalf of the United Fraternity. And it is further agreed, that the Freemasons' Hall shall be the place in which the United Grand Lodge shall be held, with such additions made thereto as the increased numbers of the Fraternity, thus to be united, may require. And it is understood between the parties, that, as there are now in the Hall several whole length portraits of Past Grand masters, a portrait of the Most Worshipful His Grace the Duke of ATHOLL, Past Grand Master of Masons according to the Old Institutions, shall be placed there in the same conspicuous manner.

XVIII. The fund, appropriate to the objects of Masonic benevolence, shall not be infringed on for any purpose, but shall be kept strictly and solely devoted to charity, and pains shall be taken to increase the same.

XIX. The distribution and application of this Charitable Fund shall be monthly, for which purpose a Committee, or Lodge of Benevolence, shall be held on the third Wednesday of every month, which Lodge shall consist of twelve Masters of Lodges (within the Bills of Mortality); and three Grand Officers, one of whom only (if more are present) shall act as President, and be entitled to vote. The said twelve Masters to be summoned by the choice and direction of the Grand Master, or his Deputy, not by any rule or rotation, but by discretion; so as that the Members, who are to judge of the cases that may come before them, shall not be subject to canvass, or to previous application, but shall have their minds free from prejudice, to decide on the merits of each case with the impartiality and purity of Masonic feeling: to which end it is declared, that no Brother, being a Member of such Committee or Lodge, shall vote, upon the petition of any person to whom he is in any way related, or who is a member of any Lodge, or Masonic society, to which he himself actually belongs, but such Brother may ask leave to be heard on the merits of such petition, and shall afterwards, during the discussion and voting thereon, withdraw.

XX. A plan, with rules and regulations, for the solemnity of the Union, shall be prepared by the Subscribers hereto, previous to the Festival of St. John, which shall be the form to be observed on that occasion.

XXI. A revision shall be made of the rules and regulations now established and in force in the two Fraternities, and a code of laws for the holding of the Grand Lodge, and of private Lodges; and, generally, for the whole conduct of the Craft, shall be forthwith prepared, and a new Book of Constitutions be composed and printed, under the superintendence of the Grand Officers, and with the sanction of the Grand Lodge.

Done at the Palace of Kensington, this 25th Day of November, in the Year of our Lord, 1813, and of Masonry, 5813.

AUGUSTUS FREDERICK, G.M.	L.S.	EDWARD, G.M.	L.S.
		THOMAS HARPER, D.G.M.	L.S.
WALLER RODWELL WRIGHT,		JAMES PERRY, P.D.G.M.	L.S.
P.G.M. Ionian Isles.	L.S.		
ARTHUR TEGART, P.G.W.	L.S.	JAMES AGAR, P.D.G.M.	L.S.
JAMES DEANS, P.G.W.	L.S.		

In Grand Lodge, this first day of December, A.D. 1813, Ratified and Confirmed, and the Seal of the Grand Lodge affixed.

AUGUSTUS FREDERICK, G.M.

In Grand Lodge, this first day of December, A.D. 1813, Ratified and Confirmed, and the Seal of the Grand Lodge affixed.

EDWARD, G.M.

Great
Seal.

WILLIAM H. WHITE, G.S.

Great
Seal.

ROBERT LESLIE, G.S.

Appendix G

Aims and Relationships of the Craft

Accepted by Grand Lodge, September 7, 1949

In August, 1938, the Grand Lodges of England, Ireland, and Scotland each agreed upon and issued a statement identical in terms except that the name of the issuing Grand Lodge appeared throughout. This statement, which was entitled 'Aims and Relationships of the Craft', was in the following terms:

1. From time to time the United Grand Lodge of England has deemed it desirable to set forth in precise form the aims of Freemasonry as consistently practised under its Jurisdiction since it came into being as an organized body in 1717, and also to define the principles governing its relations with those other Grand Lodges with which it is in fraternal accord.

2. In view of representations which have been received, and of statements recently issued which have distorted or obscured the true objects of Freemasonry, it is once again considered necessary to emphasize certain fundamental principles of the Order.

3. The first condition of admission into, and membership of, the Order is a belief in the Supreme Being. This is essential and admits of no compromise.

4. The Bible, referred to by Freemasons as the Volume of the Sacred Law, is always open in the Lodges. Every Candidate is required to take his Obligation on that book or on the Volume which is held by his particular creed to impart sanctity to an oath or promise taken upon it.

5. Everyone who enters Freemasonry is, at the outset, strictly forbidden to countenance any act which may have a tendency to subvert the peace and good order of society; he must pay due obedience to the law of any state in which he resides or which may afford him protection, and he must never be remiss in the allegiance due to the Sovereign of his native land.

6. While English Freemasonry thus inculcates in each of its members the duties of loyalty and citizenship, it reserves to the individual the right to hold his own opinion with regard to public affairs. But neither in any Lodge, nor at any time in his capacity as a Freemason, is he permitted to discuss or to advance his views on theological or political questions.

7. The Grand Lodge has always consistently refused to express any opinion on questions of foreign or domestic state policy either at home or abroad, and it will not allow its name to be associated with any action, however humanitarian it may appear to be, which infringes its unalterable policy of standing aloof from every question affecting the relations between one government and another, or between political parties, or questions as to rival theories of government.

8. The Grand Lodge is aware that there do exist Bodies, styling themselves Freemasons, which do not adhere to these principles, and while that attitude exists the Grand Lodge of England refuses absolutely to have any relations with such Bodies, or to regard them as Freemasons.

9. The Grand Lodge of England is a Sovereign and independent Body practising Freemasonry only within the three Degrees and only within the limits defined in its Constitution as 'pure Antient Masonry'. It does not recognize or admit the existence of any superior Masonic authority, however styled.

10. On more than one occasion the Grand Lodge has refused, and will continue to refuse, to participate in Conferences with so-called International Associations claiming to represent Freemasonry, which admit to membership Bodies failing to conform strictly to the principles upon which the Grand Lodge of England is founded. The Grand Lodge does not admit any such claim, nor can its views be represented by any such Association.

11. There is no secret with regard to any of the basic principles of Freemasonry, some of which have been stated above. The Grand Lodge will always consider the recognition of those Grand Lodges which profess and practise, and can show that they have consistently professed and practised, those established and unaltered principles, but in no circumstances will it enter into discussion with a view to any new or varied interpretation of them. They must be accepted and practised wholeheartedly and in their entirety by those who desire to be recognized as Freemasons by the United Grand Lodge of England.

The Grand Lodge of England has been asked if it still stands by this declaration, particularly in regard to paragraph 7. The Grand Lodge of England replied that it stood by every word of the declaration, and has since asked for the opinion of the Grand Lodges of Ireland and Scotland. A conference has been held between the three Grand Lodges, and all unhesitatingly reaffirm the statement that was pronounced in 1938: nothing in present-day affairs has been found that could cause them to recede from that attitude.

If Freemasonry once deviated from its course by expressing an opinion on political or theological questions, it would be called upon not only publicly to approve or denounce any movement which might arise in the future, but would sow the seeds of discord among its own members.

The three Grand Lodges are convinced that it is only by this rigid adherence to this policy that Freemasonry has survived the constantly changing doctrines of the outside world, and are compelled to place on record their complete disapproval of any action which may tend to permit the slightest departure from the basic principles of Freemasonry. They are strongly of opinion that if any of the three Grand Lodges does so, it cannot maintain a claim to be following the Antient Landmarks of the Order, and must ultimately face disintegration.

Appendix H

Basic Principles for Grand Lodge Recognition

Accepted by Grand Lodge, September 4, 1929

THE M.W. The Grand Master having expressed a desire that the Board would draw up a statement of the Basic Principles on which this Grand Lodge could be invited to recognize any Grand Lodge applying for recognition by the English Jurisdiction, the Board of General Purposes has gladly complied. The result, as follows, has been approved by the Grand Master, and it will form the basis of a questionnaire to be forwarded in future to each Jurisdiction requesting English recognition. The Board desires that not only such bodies but the Brethren generally throughout the Grand Master's Jurisdiction shall be fully informed as to those Basic Principles of Freemasonry for which the Grand Lodge of England has stood throughout its history.

1. Regularity of origin; i.e. each Grand Lodge shall have been established lawfully by a duly recognized Grand Lodge or by three or more regularly constituted Lodges.

2. That a belief in the G.A.O.T.U. and His revealed will shall be an essential qualification for membership.

3. That all Initiates shall take their Obligation on or in full view of the open Volume of the Sacred Law, by which is meant the revelation from above which is binding on the conscience of the particular individual who is being initiated.

4. That the membership of the Grand Lodge and individual Lodges shall be composed exclusively of men; and that each Grand Lodge shall have no Masonic intercourse of any kind with mixed Lodges or bodies which admit women to membership.

5. That the Grand Lodge shall have sovereign jurisdiction over the Lodges under its control; i.e. that it shall be a responsible, independent, self-governing organization, with sole and undisputed authority over the Craft or Symbolic Degrees (Entered Apprentice, Fellow Craft, and Master Mason) within its Jurisdiction; and shall not in any way be subject to, or divide such authority with, a Supreme Council or other Power claiming any control or supervision over those degrees.

6. That the three Great Lights of Freemasonry (namely, the Volume of the Sacred Law, the Square, and the Compasses) shall always be exhibited when the Grand Lodge or its subordinate Lodges are at work, the chief of these being the Volume of the Sacred Law.

7. That the discussion of religion and politics within the Lodge shall be strictly prohibited.

8. That the principles of the Antient Landmarks, customs, and usages of the Craft shall be strictly observed.

Appendix I
Memorial sent to the Duke of Sussex (1816)

THE MEMORIAL

To His Royal Highness the Duke of Sussex Grand Master, of the United Grand Lodge of Ancient Free Masons of England.

The Humble Memorial of the Masters, Past Masters Officers and Brethren of divers Lodges assembled under the government of your Royal Highness.

Sheweth

That in pursuance of the union which has been happily effected under the auspices of your Royal Highness and your August Brother the Duke of Kent, eighteen brethren were selected to form a lodge, under the name or title of 'The Lodge of Reconciliation' to revise the different modes of Workmanship, and from them to form a system for the general use and government of the Craft.

That the Lodge of Reconciliation having been formed accordingly, and having 'arranged the various points referred to their consideration,' the brethren of the lodges of both Fraternities, were by the Command of your Royal Highness, frequently summoned to attend the meetings of the said lodge, in order that your Memorialists 'might be instructed in the Forms and Ceremonies to be in future, used throughout the Craft.'

That signal success attended their labours, which combine purity of language with a strict adherence to the Ancient Landmarks of our Honorable order, and while they attract the attention of the Scholar, they are not above the Comprehension of every Brother who has received a common Education.

That from the moment of its being made public to the Society, a general spirit of Emulation pervaded the whole Masonic Body, and such have been the commendable industry and laudable atention of the Brethren in general, that the number of expert Masters has increased in the proportion of nearly five to one.

That the system so promulgated by the lodge of Reconciliation is not only firmly established in London, but has been eagerly received by the Brethren in most of the Counties of England and Wales, in Scotland and Ireland, and has even been extended to East and West Indies.

That with the most painful concern we lament to state to our gracious and venerated Grand Master, that a few individuals have lately insinuated to the Fraternity that the whole of what they have been so instructed in and taught by the Lodge of Reconciliation, ought not to be practised, as another system would soon be presented to them, under the sanction of your Royal Highness. This Intelligence has been received by your Memorialists and the Members of their respective lodges with the utmost astonishment and grief, and if persisted in will assuredly be attended with more injurious consequences than the unhappy division of 1752.

Your Memorialists therefore most humbly solicit, that your Royal Highness will be pleased to declare your Sanction to the System of Free Masonry practised taught and promulgated by the Lodge of Reconciliation prior to the first of December 1815.

For some days previous to presenting the Memorial, a copy of the following notice was left at all the Committee Rooms.

The Brethren are respectfully informed, that the Memorial to be presented his R. H. the Duke of Sussex, our M. W. Grand Master, will lie for signatures, at the Crown Tavern, St. Martins Lane, Charing Cross, until 8 o'clock next Saturday Evening, and not after that time, as it must be presented to the Grand Master on Sunday 29th Instant.

Appendix J
The Prince Hall Declaration of Independence

On 17 June 1827 brethren of the African Lodge decided 'we are and ought of right to be free and independent of other lodges'. The Master was chosen to write and publish the Declaration of Independence and 'he was given the privilege to make a choice of whom he thought proper to assist him and also to write the independent charter'. The following was adopted without further loss of time as it is dated the following day:

DECLARATION OF INDEPENDENCE Proclaimed by the AFRICAN GRAND LODGE in the City of Boston, Commonwealth of Massachusetts and United States of America through her Officers. Be it known to all whom it may concern, That we the undersigned Past Masters of the A.G.L. being regularly made so under a Charter given to our Worthy Brothers Prince Hall, Boston Smith and Thomas Sanderson (colored brethren) by Lord Howard, Earl of Effingham, acting Grand Master under the authority of his Royal Highness, HENRY FREDERICK, Duke of Cumberland &. &. &. Grand Master of the Most Ancient and Honorable Society of free and accepted Masons, do assume and take upon themselves the responsibility of declaring ourselves free from the government and control of our Mother Grand Lodge of England, by whom our Charter dated the twenty-ninth day of September A.L. 5784 A.D. 1784 bearing the Grand Seal of London was given, or any other Lodge or Lodges whatsoever—Allowing ourselves to be bound however to the most excellent principles and solemn ties of Ancient Freemasonry. We do therefore declare ourselves henceforth free from said Instrument dated above and do Create, under the head and title of the AFRICAN GRAND LODGE No. 1 to have and to exercise the same power of the other Grand Lodges, Granting Warrants and Charters and establishing Lodges among our brethren for the good of Masonry, when they are found worthy. And to prove more fully our sincerity and to establish beyond any doubt our intentions we have caused to be published in a paper called the Columbian Sentinel printed in this city said Declaration.

We do agreeably to the power vested in us present this GRAND CHAPTER to our most Worthy Brethren RICHARD POTTEN, C. D. DeRANDAMIE and Rev. THOMAS PAUL, Royal Arch Masons and their Successors to hold and to keep the same for the benefit of Masonry and the good of our Brethren:—On whom we do solemnly enjoin strict observance to ancient usages and customs that the same may be preserved unsullied and transmitted in its purity to succeeding generations, that they may under its happy influence enjoy peace, prosperity and safety forever.

Done Agreeably to, or in conformity with the Declaration of our Independence of the same date and accepted by the Lodge this eighteenth day of June A.L. 5827 A.D. 1827 whereunto we give our hands and seals.

John T. Hilton
Walker Lewis } —W.M. & Past Masters
Thomas Dalton

Appendix K
Royal Arch Chapter Manifesto (1765)

(Folio 2b)

TRANSCRIPT OF MANIFESTO

WE THE COMPANIONS OF THE E.G. & R.C. commonly called the Royal Arch, being this Twelfth Day of June in full Chapter assembled having duly consider'd and maturely deliberated on the present state of the Chapter, have come to the following resolutions: which we declare our firm purpose to *abide by, stand to,* and *perform.* And no addition shall be made to, or Alteration of, any of these Resolutions, but in full Chapter, and that with the approbation of two thirds of the Members present.

1st. We Resolve to Hold a Chapter at the Turk's Head Tavern in Gerrard Street, Soho,

Friday

on the second ~~Wednesday~~ of every Month at Six Oclock in the Evening.

Two Guineas

2. That every Member shall pay ~~Twenty six shilling~~s Annually towards defraying the current Expenses of the Chapter.

3. Every Brother who desires to pass the Arch, or to become a Member of this Chapter must be regularly proposed in open Chapter: and it is expected that the member proposing such a One, be able to give a satisfactory account of the Brother so proposed. Any Member may without offence demand a Ballot: and if on being had there shall be found more than two negatives against such Brother, he shall not be permitted to pass the Arch in, or become a member of, this Chapter.

(Folio 3a)

Two

4. Every Brother passing the Arch in this Chapter shall pay ~~One~~ Guinea to the publick Stock.

Two

5. Every Brother becoming a Member of this Chapter shall pay ~~One~~ Guinea for such admission to the publick Stock.

6. That none but Members, shall be admitted to sit in the Chapter unless on very particular occasions, and then such Visitors, shall pay half a Guinea each to the current expence.

7. If any Brother so far forgets himself as to behave indecently or disorderly in the Chapter, or to be intoxicated with Liquor therein: Or if by speech or Behaviour in the World, he so demean himself as to reflect dishonour on the Craft, and do detriment to the Chapter, he shall be admonished for such misconduct by the E.G. as becometh a Brother, in open Chapter: but if he remains incorrigible or holds the authority of the Officers and Chapter in contempt, he shall be expelled the Chapter without favour and never after admitted into the same on any condition whatsoever.

8. If any Companion of the Chapter shall neglect to pay or cause to be paid, his annual proportion towards the ordinary expences of the same, longer than the Fourth meeting of the Current Year, his name being duly called over, He shall no longer be deemed a Member, and his name struck out of the List accordingly.

(Folio 3b)

9. That a proper Coffer with two Locks & Keys differing the one from the other, be provided for the preservation of the Robes. Jewells &c. belonging to the Chapter,

Janitor

which shall be reposited therein as soon as the Chapter is closed, by the ~~Tyler~~ with all care, and a Key of Lock No. 1 given to the E: Z.L.: and another alike to the Principal Sojourner. And a Kay of Lock No. 2 to each of the Secretaries. And the Jewell's &c. shall not be lent, or carried out of the House where the Coffer is kept, unless with consent of all the Officers. And if such a thing be done contrary to this Order, the person or persons so offending shall forfeit one Guinea each, to the common Stock, and make good any damage that such Jewells &c. may have received by means of the said offence.

10.   That the Principal Secretary E. shall keep the Cash of the Chapter, but he shall make no disbursement whatsoever but by order of the E: Z.L.: with the approbation of the Chapter. And it will become him to have Minutes of his Accompts Ready Authenticated at every meeting of the Chapter.

11.   And that none may offend thro' Ignorance, or at least that there may be no excuse for Ignorance of these Laws, the E: Z.L.: shall order the Principal Secretary to read them distinctly from time to time at his discretion, in open Chapter.

(Folio 4a)

12.   There shall be an Election of Officers to conduct this Chapter at the first Meeting after the Feast of St. John the Evangelist every year. Which Officers then regularly chosen and invested shall continue in Authority one whole year. And if any Officer is absent on any night of meeting the E: Z.L.: shall appoint any able and experienced Brother to supply his place for that Night. And if the E: Z.L.: shall unavoidably be absent, the next Officer in Authority shall officiate for him, or appoint who he judges proper to do it. And the Brother so officiating shall in all respects have ample Authority for that Night.

And in witness of our *Approbation* of, and *Compliance* with, these Regulations, we join a general assent signing our Names to the same.

Jn° Maclean	Chas Taylor	Robt Blake
David Ant. Keck	John Brooks	Ephr G. Muller
J. Ayanson	Chas Swinden	Edmd Henry Pahen
Fras Flower	Jn° Hamilton	1John Evans
Jn° Hughes	Frans Camm	John James Bourcard
James Galloway P.S	Edwd Price	John Shield
Joh. Jam. Rouby	Rd Williamson	John Beckett
Robert Chambers	1J. B. Rich	J. Richiardi
Thomas Jenkins	Lewis Masquerier	John Coyne
Benjn Strotman	Michael Thackthwaite	W. Wm Manning
Dd Hughes	John Buckley	Thos French
Richd Adams	Geo. Gally	George Keith
1Thos Dunkerley	John Hutchinson	J. M. Allen
	John Sutter	Anthy Deveyer
		John Griffiths
		William Guest

Note: [1] With the exception of Dunckerley and Rich, whose names were interpolated later, the names down to and including Evans exactly correspond with, and with one exception, appear in the same order as, those in the list of the Brethren present on 10th July, 1765. The names of Dunckerley, Rich and the last 12 Brethren are in different inks.

Appendix L

The Charter of Compact (1766)

TRANSCRIPT OF THE CHARTER OF COMPACT

THE MOST ENLIGHTENED EAST
I∴TN∴OTGA∴OTU∴∴∴∴∴

To all the Enlightened, Entered∴Passed∴∴Raised∴∴∴and Exalted∴∴∴∴ And to all others whom it may concern under the Canopy of Heaven, HEALTH, PEACE and UNION.

We, the Right Honourable and Right Worshipful Cadwallader Lord Blayney, Baron Blayney of Monaghan in the Kingdom of Ireland, Lord Lieutenant and Custos Rotulorum of the same County, and Major General in His Majesty's Service (P.) Grand Master of Free and accepted Masons, And also Most Excellent Grand Master of the Royal Arch of Jerusalem send Greeting.

WHEREAS We have it principally at Heart to do all in our Power to promote the Honour, Dignity, Preservation and Welfare of the Royal Craft in general as well as of every worthy Brother in particular; and also to extend the benefits arising therefrom to every created Being, according to the original Design of this Heavenly Institution; first planned and founded in Ethicks, and including in its grand Scheme every Art, Science and Mystery that the Mind of Man in this sublunary State is capable of comprehending AND WHEREAS We having duly passed the Royal Arch have found our dearly beloved and Most Excellent Brethren, James Galloway, John McLean, Thomas Dunckerley, Francis Flower, John Allen, John Brooks, Thomas French and Charles Taylor and the Rest of our Excellent Companions of the respectable Chapter held at the Turk's Head Tavern in Gerrard Street, Soho, in the County of Middlesex, not only to be perfect Masters in every Degree of the Royal Craft in its operative, but likewise, by their Study and labour to have made considerable advances in the SPECULATIVE or truly sublime and most exalted Parts thereof AND WHEREAS Our said Most Excellent Companions have requested Us to enter into Compact with and to grant to them Our Charter of Institution and Protection to which We have readily concurred NOW KNOW YE that in tender Consideration of the Premises, and for the Purposes aforesaid, We HAVE Instituted and Erected And, by and with the advice, Consent, and Concurrence of Our said Most Excellent Companions, in full Chapter Assembled (testified by their severally signing and sealing hereof) DO by these Presents as much as in Us lyes Institute and Erect them Our said Most Excellent Bretheren and Companions, James Galloway, John McLean, Thomas Dunckerley, Francis Flower, John Brooks, Thomas French and Charles Taylor, and their Successors Officers for the Time being of the Grand and Royal Chapter jointly with Ourself and Our Successors Most Excellent Grand Master for the Time being from Time to Time and at all Times hereafter to form and be, The Grand and Royal Chapter of the Royal Arch of Jerusalem Hereby Giving, Granting. Ratifying and Confirming unto them and their Successors All the Rights, Priviledges, Dignities, Ensigns and Prerogatives which from Time immemorial have belonged and do appertain to those exalted to this Most Sublime Degree; With full Power and absolute Authority from Time to Time as Occasion shall require and it shall be found expedient to hold and convene Chapters and other proper Assemblies for the carrying on, improving and promoting the said benevolent and useful Work. And also to admit, pass and exalt in due Form and according to the Rites and Ceremonies Time immemorial used and approved in and by that most exalted and sacred Degree, and as now by them practised, all such experienced and discreet Master Masons as they shall find worthy AND WE DO FURTHERMORE hereby Give, Grant, Ratify and Confirm unto Our said Most Excellent Brethren and Companions and their Successors, Officers of our said Grand and Royal Chapter for the Time being, full and absolute Power and Authority in Conjunction with Us or our Most Excellent Deputy for the Time being to make and confirm Laws, Orders and Ordnances for the better conducting and regulating the said Most Excellent and Sublime Degree throughout the Globe as well as of their said Grand and Royal Chapter and from Time to Time to alter and abrogate the same Laws, Orders and Ordnances as to them and their Successors shall seem meet: And also to constitute, superintend and regulate other Chapters wheresoever it shall be found convenient and as to Us or Our Deputy and the said Grand Officers, Our and their Successors for the Time being, shall seem fit AND it is also declared, concluded and agreed upon by and between Us and Our said Most Excellent Companions, James Galloway, John McLean, Thomas Dunckerley, Francis Flower, John Allen, John Brooks, Thomas French and Charles Taylor, the said Most Excellent Grand Officers, AND THESE PRESENTS FURTHER WITNESS that We and the said Most Excellent Grand Officer Do hereby for Ourselves severally and respectively and for Our several and respective Successors, the Most Excellent Grand Master, and the Most Excellent Grand Officers of the said Grand and Royal Chapter of the Royal Arch of Jerusalem in manner and form following, that is to say FIRST that the Most Excellent Deputy Grand Master shall preside and have full Power and Authority in the Absence of the Most Excellent Grand Master SECONDLY That the Jewels worn or to be worn from Time to Time by the Most Excellent Grand Master, Deputy Grand Master, and Grand Officers shall be of the Form and figure, and bear the same inscription as delineated in the Margin hereof And that the like Jewels, only omitting the Sun, Compass and Globe, shall be worn by the two Scribes and three S:N:R:S; And also that the like Jewels shall be worn by the Rest of the Excellent Companions, except that in them shall be left out the Triangle &c. in the center thereof THIRDLY That every Companion shall wear according to ancient Custom an Apron indented with Crimson, and the Badge ⊞ properly displayed thereon, And also the indented Ribbon or Sash of this Order FOURTHLY That the Common Seal of this Grand and Royal Chapter shall bear the like Impression as the Jewels worn by the Most Excellent Grand Officers FIFTHLY That for every Charter of Constitution to be granted by and from this Grand and Royal Chapter shall be paid into the Common Fund thereof at least the sum of Ten Guineas SIXTHLY That none but discreet and experienced Master Masons shall receive Exaltation to this sublime Degree in this or any other Chapter that may hereafter be duly constituted; Nor until they shall have been duly proposed at least one Chapter Night preceding. Nor unless ballotted for and that on such Ballot there shall not appear one Negative or Black Ball SEVENTHLY That every such person so to be exalted shall pay at least the Sum of Five Guineas into the Common Fund of the Chapter wherein he shall receive Exaltation; towards enabling the Companions to carry on the Business and support the Dignity thereof EIGHTHLY That none calling themselves Royal Arch Masons shall be deemed any other than Masters in Operative Masonry: Nor shall be received into any regular Chapter of the Royal Arch or permitted to reap or enjoy any of the Benefits, Dignities, or Ensigns of that Most Excellent Degree, Save and except those who have received or shall or may hereafter receive Exaltation in this Grand and Royal Chapter, or in some Chapter to be chartered and constituted by Us, or Our Successors, Most Excellent Grand Officers as aforesaid, And Except those coming from beyond the Seas; Or such as shall obtain Certificates of Adoption from this Our Grand and Royal Chapter; For which Certificate shall be paid in to the Common Fund the Sum of One Guinea at the least NINTHLY That there shall be a General Chapter of Communication of the excellent Companions of this Grand and Royal Chapter with all other Chapters that shall or may hereafter come under the Protection of and be chartered by the same as aforesaid on, or as near as conveniently may be to, the Feast of Saint John the Evangelist yearly, or oftener as Occasion shall require and it shall be found convenient, for the Purposes of conducting, promoting and well ordering of this sublime Degree, and the Business and Affairs thereof in such manner as shall from Time to Time be found most expedient TENTHLY That at and upon the said Feast of Saint John the Evangelist, or the General Chapter of Communication held next to such Feast, the Most Excellent Grand Master, Most Excellent Deputy Grand Master and the other Most Excellent Grand Officers of the Grand and Royal Arch of Jerusalem shall be chosen and elected: Which Election shall be by a Majority of the Companions present at such General Chapter by Ballot AND LASTLY That the Grand Officers so chosen and elected shall continue to serve and be in Office for the Year ensuing: unless some or one of them shall happen to decline, in which Case, or in Case of the Death of any of them or otherwise it shall be found necessary, a special General Chapter shall be called for an Election to supply his or their Place or Places IN WITNESS whereof We the said Most Excellent Grand Master, and the

Most Excellent Grand Officers have hereunto severally signed our Names and affixed our Seals in full Chapter assembled for this Purpose at the Turk's Head Tavern in Gerrard Street, Soho, aforesaid this Twenty second Day of July in the Year of the Birth of Virtue 5∴3∴7∴9∴A.L. 5770(1). A.D. 1766(7).

IN TESTIMONY of our ready Acceptance of and perfect Compliance with this Charter of Institution and Protection above written, and the Laws and Ordnances thereby prescribed, We the Rest of the Excellent Companions of this Most Excellent Grand and Royal Chapter, have hereunto severally subscribed our Names the Day and Year above written.

Manchester
Pignatelli

Blayney
James Galloway
John Maclean
Thos. Dunckerley
Fras. Flower E:S
Jn. Allen N.
John Brooks P.S.
Tho. French S.
Chas. Taylor S.

Henry Chittick
G. Borradale
John Turner
W. Ross
Robert Kellie
John Derwas
Samuel Way
R. Berkeley
John Bewley Rich

Anglesey
Thos. Morgan
Jas. Heseltine
William Guest
Ro: Simpkinson
Rowland Holt
J. P. Pryse
Jno. Hatch
Lewis Masquerier
David Hughes

The treatment of dates in the *Charter of Compact* is of some interest. The dating of biblical incidents was completed in 1650 by the Rev Ussher, Archbishop of Armagh. According to the *Bible Concordance* published by the Oxford University Press those dates were added as marginal notes in the bible in 1701 by Bishop Lloyd. Even though Ussher's dating was only one of several arrangements available, his was the system that influenced masonic use. The Creation, and we have to ignore the point that it is biblical legend, was calculated to have occurred 4004 years prior to the Christian era and when that figure is added to the year 1766, when the Charter of Compact was drawn up, we are supplied with 5770 *Anno Lucis* or *Year of Light*, "For God said, Let there be light and there was light". The Christian era is identified by the term *Anno Domini* or *Year of our Lord* and has become known as the *Common Era*. However, the dating for the *Year of the Birth of Virtue*, and an explanation for the use of that term has completely eluded masonic students. By using a similar calculation to that which was employed previously one would arrive at 1375 AD but that year has no significant contribution to offer and so the enigma remains.

Appendix M

William Preston and the Lectureship

William Preston was born in Edinburgh on 20 July 1742, the son of a classical scholar who was 'Writer to the Signet', a lawyer in that city. His father died in 1751 and William Preston was then taken into the care of a friend, a blind man who had similar scholastic attainments and one who was to have great influence on his future. He was apprenticed to the brother of his guardian and was able to continue contact in reading, transcribing and generally assisting in work undertaken by his tutor. After his guardian died Preston was able to give full play to his developed talents.

Furnished with letters of recommendation Preston arrived in London in 1760 and promptly found employment with Wiliam Strahan 'the King's Printer' with whom he remained throughout his life. A number of Scottish brethren in London sought to form their own lodge and applied to the Grand Lodge of Scotland for a Warrant only to be informed that it would be a masonic infringement for that to be done, but recommending them to make a similar application to the Antients Grand Lodge in London with whom they were in fraternal accord. A Dispensation was obtained to enable them to meet together and form a lodge and it is generally accepted that William Preston was their second Initiate on 20 April 1763 at a meeting held at the White Hart Tavern in the Strand. When that lodge was formally Constituted it was given No 111 on their Register. With others Preston became dissatisfied with the status of that lodge, or with its Grand Lodge, and joined a lodge under the Moderns Grand Lodge. They persuaded the members of No 111 to apply to the Moderns for a Warrant and that having been done the lodge was formally Constituted a second time but on this occasion as Caledonian Lodge No 325; it has survived to the present day under that name and appears on the current Register as No 134.

After an extensive study and research of masonic material, and in consultation with experts with whom he associated, Preston published *Illustrations of Masonry* in 1772. It followed the various masonic lectures that he had given, particularly one at a Gala Meeting when influential Grand Officers had been present. In the Preface he wrote:

> ... When I first had the honour to be elected master of a lodge I thought it my duty to inform myself more fully of the general rules of the Society; in order that I might be able to explain to the brethren under my direction, their utility and importance; and officially to enforce a due obedience to them. The various methods I adopted with this view, excited in some of superficial knowledge, an absolute dislike, of what they considered as innovations; and in others of more enlarged faculties, a jealousy of pre-eminence that the principles of Masonry ought to have checked. Notwithstanding these discouragements, I persevered in my intentions, of supporting the dignity of the Society, and of discharging with fidelity the trust reposed in me. ... (2nd Edn 1775)

Further editions of that book included further material and it soon began to be classed as an indispensable possession for each lodge; it went into many editions, and was reprinted in other countries, such was his spread of masonic knowledge.

Preston attended many lodges of Instruction to propagate his system of Lectures and he brought brethren together to form a special Lodge in which they were demonstrated. It is from the Sections and Clauses of those Lectures in the three degrees that explanations and interpretations of so much of the ceremonial construction and symbolical significance has been made available.

In 1813 HRH the Duke of Sussex wrote to the Lodge of Antiquity and expressed his appreciation of William Preston:

> ... Long has the Lodge of Antiquity been remarkable for its zeal in Masonry, and greatly is that Lodge and the Craft indebted to the diligence and example of my worthy Brother your Past Master Preston, whose name must be dear to every admirer and well wisher of our ancient Order. ...

After an illness lasting nearly five years William Preston died in London on 1 April

1818 and was buried in St. Paul's Cathedral. A report in the current *Gentleman's Magazine* stated:

> ... in consequence of the rain the Female Orphans belonging to the Freemasons' Charity in St. George's Fields were not able to follow in procession but mustered at the Church under the care of the Treasurer ... and returned to the house of the deceased where they partook of wine and cake.

In his Will Preston bequeathed Consols to the value of £500 to the Girls Institution, £500 to the General Charity Fund, and £300 the interest from which was 'to be applied for some well-informed mason to deliver annually a Lecture of the First, Second or Third Degree of the Order of Masonry according to the system practised in the Lodge of Antiquity during his Mastership'. It was to ensure perpetuation of his system.

The Lectures were given each year following, with a few exceptions until 1862 and then they lapsed. A revival was effected in 1924 the Lecturer so appointed then being permitted to give a prepared Paper on a subject of his own choice. The Lectures were suspended for the duration of the 2nd World War 1940–1946 but resumed in 1947. Guidelines have been laid down by the Board of General Purposes and two brethren 'of learning and responsibility from whom the Trustees shall appoint the Prestonian Lecturer for the year' is foremost.

The honour of the appointment as Prestonian Lecturer was made clear in December 1984 when seven of the fourteen then surviving Past Prestonian Lecturers were summoned to attend the Quarterly Communication of Grand Lodge to receive a jewel that had been approved by the MW the Grand Master HRH the Duke of Kent. It is a medallion with a bust profile of William Preston in contrasting metal with the surrounding words 'Prestonian Lecturer' and is to be worn as part of Craft regalia during the lifetime of the brother so honoured. It is suspended from a dark blue collarette (see page 86) and a small variation in the jewel occurs in that which is worn during the year of appointment, which transferred to each successor. All the jewels remain the property of Grand Lodge and arrangements have to be made for their eventual return.

The appointment is not a fund-raising exercise but, by tradition, the amount paid to the Lecturer from the William Preston Bequest heads the Charity in which the Lecturer's interest is focussed.

Index

compiled by Frederick Smyth
Member of the Society of Indexers

Lodges and Royal Arch chapters are under the English Constitution unless otherwise designated and, unless a location is given (or is obvious from its title), meet (or met) in London. Masonic bodies still in existence are usually indexed under their modern titles and numbers.

Page numbers in bold type (**60-1**) denote the more important references, those in *italics* (*60-1*) illustrations or their captions; 'q.' stands for 'quoted'.

Abbreviations used include: (A) for the Antients; (IC) and (SC) for the Irish and Scottish Constitutions; others are, it is hoped, self-evident.

* distinguishes members of the Quatuor Coronati Lodge and

† identifies other contributors to that lodge's transactions, *Ars Quatuor Coronatorum* (referred to in the text as *AQC*).